the first mile

Essentials of Entrepreneurship

WHAT IT TAKES TO CREATE SUCCESSFUL ENTERPRISES:

Mentoring experiences at TiE

Perspectives from world-class authorities

Collaborative authorship of over 60 experts

TiE® The Indus Entrepreneurs

TiE: A global, not-for-profit network of entrepreneurs and Professionals, Was founded in Silicon Valley, California, USA in 1992. www.tie.org

Publisher: Joan O'Neil
Editor: David Pugh
Developmental Editor: Kate Shoup Welsh
Managing Editor: Stephanie Corby
Text Design & Composition: Plan-it Publishing

This book is printed on acid-free paper.

Published by Wiley Publishing, Inc., Indianapolis, Indiana

Printed in the United States of America

ISBN: 0-4714-4559-2

10 9 8 7 6 5 4 3 2 1

Dedication

Dedicated to all who believe in volunteerism and learning.

Table of Contents

FOREWORD

The Book

Knowledge constitutes the *"First Mile"* of the journey of entrepreneurship. This is the labor of love of many and a first-of-its-kind compilation of perspectives and expert knowledge, primarily geared toward entrepreneurs in the early stages of their undertakings. Conceived with the backdrop of several years of mentoring experience at TiE, the book addresses many of the common questions and issues faced both by young entrepreneurs as well as by those who are well on their entrepreneurial way. It also augments the core mission and commitment of TiE: that of mentoring and supporting entrepreneurial people and their endeavors everywhere.

The book is a collaborative effort of a four-person editorial board and a team of TiE members and sponsors with knowledge and experience in relevant fields. These individuals brought not only their expertise but also their passion to share it. Thus, the book exemplifies the collaborative volunteer effort that is the hallmark of TiE. It has been written with the entrepreneur in mind, but will also be of considerable value to students and professionals. This introductory edition, primarily intended for distribution in the U.S., may eventually be adapted to other countries with appropriate changes reflecting local regulations and practices. We also hope that this will be the first of many publications by TiE as we continue to nurture the entrepreneurial ecosystem by bringing together people with talent, ideas, and experience.

The book starts with a perspective on entrepreneurship discussing the attributes of a region or a nation, which foster the spirit of risk taking and economic value creation, and the characteristics of successful entrepreneurs. In Chapter 1, Prof. C.K. Prahalad and Kanwal Rekhi elaborate on these aspects. Their ruminations are followed by interviews of three well-known personalities, Eugene Kleiner, Narayana Murthy, and Peter Senge. They share their years of experiences touching on both the business and human aspects of the entrepreneurial process. Subsequent chapters topically cover expert views of the various aspects of entrepreneurship such as business planning, funding, finance, the human equation (including the significance of soft skills), business presentations, legal matters, marketing, and sales.

Readers are advised that this book is only a guide—an honest attempt by committed individuals to educate those embarking on their own entrepreneurial journeys. But as we all know, there is no *one size fits all* when it comes to entrepreneurship. Direct advice from mentors, professional advisors, and peers has no substitute, but we hope this book can serve as a useful supplement.

ABOUT TiE

TiE, a not-for-profit global network of entrepreneurs and professionals, was founded in 1992 in Silicon Valley, California, USA. Although its birth name, The Indus Entrepreneurs, signifies the ethnic South Asian or Indus roots of the founders, TiE stands for *T*alent, *I*deas, and *E*nterprise. It is an open and inclusive organization that has rapidly grown to more than 40 chapters in eight countries. TiE endeavors to cultivate and nurture the ecosystems of entrepreneurship and free-market economies everywhere, as it sees this to be the single most powerful instrument of economic prosperity.

Membership fees, event fees, and contributions from sponsors financially support TiE. These sponsors, some of the biggest names among corporations and service providers (venture capital, law, accounting, and consulting), also participate in designing and conducting various programs for TiE members. Elected officials and other volunteers conduct most of the TiE operations and activities.

The membership structure of TiE includes Charter Members, who are invited based on their accomplishments and willingness to help the next generation of entrepreneurs. The general membership of TiE is open to anyone who pays nominal dues and can thus access the various activities and services, including mentoring by Charter Members.

Further details about TiE can be found at http://www.tie.org and http://www.tiesv.org.

We would like to hear from our readers. Any questions or comments about *The First Mile—Essentials of Entrepreneurship* can be sent to http://www.tie.org/tiebook/feedback.

Kailash C. Joshi, Ph.D.
Chairman, TiE Editorial Board
President, TiE Silicon Valley
Santa Clara, California

Acknowledgments

We would like to extend our sincere thanks to the following individuals, who contributed generously of their time and expertise in preparing this book:

- The TiE Editorial Board Members

  Ken Hausman, Managing Director, Osprey Ventures, and TiE Charter Member
  Mike Hildreth, Senior Partner, Ernst & Young, and TiE Charter Member
  Sridar Iyengar, President-Elect, Tie Silicon Valley, and former KPMG Senior Partner
  Eugene Kleiner, Narayana Murthy, and Peter Senge for their advice, insights, and most importantly their time.

- The authors and contributors, who collectively brought forth the most current and germane information for the book. The combined list follows:

Sanjana Anand	PEOPLE DYNAMICS
Ruby Rekhi Bal	NETLINK CONSULTING SERVICES
Mary Jane Bedegi	GREENOUGH CONSULTING GRP
Jayaram Bhat	BHAT & ASSOCIATES
Vijay Bobba	THE McKENNA GROUP
Ron Bohlin	KNOWLEDGE IMPACT
Samir Bukhari	WILSON SONSINI GOODRICH & ROSATI
Harpreet Chadha	NEW YORK LIFE
Naren Chaganti	CHAGANTI & ASSOCIATES LAW FIRM
Rahul Chandra	WALDEN INTL.
Kalyani Chatterjee	KPMG
KP Chaudhuri	GSI INC.
Alex Chen	BROBECK, PHLEGER & HARRISON LLP
Ravi Chiruvolu	CHARTER VENTURES
Subhash Chowdary	SELF CORP. INC.
Ben Connors	BEN CONNORS & ASSOC.
Mark T. Curtis	SALOMON SMITH BARNEY
Theresa Dadone	PROPEL SOFTWARE CORPORATION
Mark Dempster	SEQUOIA CAPITAL
Gurjot S. Dhaliwal	TiE
Shamini Dhana	SILICON VALLEY BAK
John Fogg	GRAY CARY LLP
Greg Gallo	GRAY CARY LLP

Paresh Ghelani	2020 COMPANY LLC
Firth Griffith	BEACH HEAD CAPITAL
Tim Harris	CLARENT CORPORATION
Rob Hunt	GIRVAN INSTITUTE OF TECHNOLOGY
Nita J. Itchhaporia	ITCHHAPORIA LAW FIRM
BV Jagadeesh	NETSCALER
Lokesh Jindal	THE McKENNA GROUP
Raj Judge	WILSON SONSINI GOODRICH & ROSATI
Prasad Kaipa	SELF CORP INC.
Guy Kawasaki	GARAGE TECHNOLOGY
Kenzo Kimura	AVERY ASSOCIATES
Paul Kimura	AVERY ASSOCIATES
Doug Leone	SEQUOIA CAPITAL
Kumar Mallavalli	Founder, BROCADE COMMUNICATIONS
Tom Milus	SELF CORP. INC.
Curtis Mo	BROBECK, PHLEGER & HARRISON LLP
Ben Nagrani	TiE
Aloka R. Naskar	BROWN VENTURE ASSOCIATES
Rishi Navani	WEST BRIDGE CAPITAL
Gopal Patwardhan	GIRVAN INSTITUTE OF TECHNOLOGY
C.K Prahalad	PRAJA INC., PROFESSOR - UNIVERSITY OF MICHIGAN
Vimu Rajdev	RAJEX, INC.
Sanjeev Rao	ERNST & YOUNG
Kanwal Rekhi	TiE BOARD OF TRUSTEES
Paul Sabharwal	ENTREPRENEUR
Raj Sampath	HEIDRICK & STRUGGLES
Prashant Shah	HUMMER WINBLAD VENTURE PARTNERS
Venktesh Shukla	EVERYPATH INC.
Tina Singh	BAY VENTURE COUNSEL, LLP
Ritu Tariyal	WILSON SONSINI GOODRICH & ROSATI
Roma Trakru	INFOBRIDGE, INC.
Tyzoon Tyebjee	SANTA CLARA UNIVERSITY
Anita Vasudevan	VENTURE LAW
Lisa Waits	BROBECK, PHLEGER & HARRISON LLP
Rod Werner	COMERICA BANK
David Wright	NASDAQ INSURANCE
Kelly Breslin Wright	AT HOC
John De Yonge	ERNEST & YOUNG
Kyung Yoon	HEIDRICK & STRUGGLES
Mark Yowe	HEIDRICK & STRUGGLES
Naeem Zamindar	INTEL CAPITAL

- Kate Shoup Welsh for her editorial revisions of the text for consistency and style
- Anne Beirne for her initial editorial revision and standardization of chapters
- Prasad Kaipa for his interview of Peter Senge
- Arian Dasmalchi for her interviews of Eugene Kleiner and Narayana Murthy
- The TiE staff members:

  Raj Desai, Executive Director, for project and budget management
  Rahima Valji, Project Manager, for management of content
  Ben Nagrani, Special Project Manager, for management of the final print
- Raj Judge and Samir Bukhari of Wilson Sonsini, Goodrich and Rosati for their support of all contractual documents
- Stephanie Corby, Karen Hattan, and David Pugh at John Wiley for their bringing this project to life.
- The editorial work by Ernst & Young.
- Vish Mishra and Pooja Goyal for their assistance with the final review of the manuscript.

Kailash C. Joshi, Ph.D.
Chairman, TiE Editiorial Board
President, TiE Silicon Valley
Santa Clara, California

one 1 CHAPTER

The Entrepreneurial Spirit

Kanwal Rekhi, Chairman - **TiE Board of Trustees**
CK Prahalad, Prof, **University of Michigan** and Chairman - **Praja Inc. & TiE Trustee**
Eugene Kleiner, Founder - **Kleiner, Perkins, Caufield & Byers**
Narayana Murthy, Founder & Chairman - **Infosys Technologies LTD**
Peter Senge, Founder - **Center for Organizational Learning**

Silicon Valley, its current troubles notwithstanding, is an envy of the world. It has been a dynamo that has driven the entire U.S. economy forward. Over the last two decades, myriad entrepreneurs have started new companies that have developed technology innovations that have boosted the productivity in almost every industry, and have made the U.S. economy among the most productive and dynamic in the world—especially astounding considering that in the early 1980s, the U.S. economy appeared to be losing out to those of Germany and Japan.

At the same time, in the southern city of Banglore in India, entrepreneurs, starting from scratch, have built a world-class software industry. This industry has grown at the compounded annual growth rate of 60% to almost $10 billion in size, employs half a million people, and is expected to grow ten-fold in next decade. This has completely changed the outlook for the Indian economy from one of hopelessness to a bright prospect of a knowledge-based productive economy serving the world markets in the modern fields of information technology and biotechnology.

It is clear that entrepreneurs can transform societies by adding economic dynamism, setting them on their way to increasing prosperities. It is also very clear that entrepreneurs are the only source of new wealth and productive jobs in society. It takes only a small part of the population—no more than 1–2%—to become successful entrepreneurs to pull the whole society along. It makes sense, then, that through the course of history, those countries that have nurtured entrepreneurial culture have been the most prosperous and dynamic.

What, then, are the traits that differentiate entrepreneurs from the rest of the population? Are entrepreneurs made or born? Why are some societies more entrepreneurial than others? What is the enabling environment that encourages entrepreneurial behavior and makes entrepreneurs thrive?

Entrepreneurial Traits

No single trait defines entrepreneurs. Rather, it is a combination of traits that gives them an edge. One trait that seems to be necessary (but not sufficient), however, is leadership. Entrepreneurs must, at minimum, be skilled enough to assemble teams, provide vision, and inspire confidence. In addition, entrepreneurs are, by necessity, intelligent, hard-working, and street smart. They also are fast learners. Some other traits, in no particular order, are

- **Intellectually honest.** Intellectual honesty is a hallmark of entrepreneurs. They are constantly reassessing their assumptions and discarding the ones that can no longer be defended. Entrepreneurs also have a very realistic awareness of their own strengths and weaknesses. They are their own harshest critics.
- **Confident.** Entrepreneurs are very confident—but not arrogant—people. They bring a winning attitude to everything they take on.
- **Results oriented.** Entrepreneurs are obsessed with producing results. They have no use for mindless processes.
- **Value oriented.** Entrepreneurs are instinctively value oriented. They are financial thinkers and are natural with numbers. Notions of costs, expenses, value-added, margins, prices, and profits are ingrained in them!
- **Innovative.** Entrepreneurs are "out of the box" thinkers. They question the conventional wisdom and think of newer and better ways of doing things. Entrepreneurs thrive when they are out of their element!
- **Generalist.** Entrepreneurs are by and large generalists rather than specialists. Entrepreneurs must understand and manage every aspect of the business, and not favor their own area of expertise.
- **Risk taking.** Entrepreneurs are action oriented and risk takers, but are smart and calculating in their approach and don't take foolish risks. They are also constantly looking for ways to eliminate the risks they may have assumed.
- **Persistent.** Entrepreneurs are very persistent. They are not easily discouraged. They typically outlast the competition.

- **Efficient.** Efficient use of resources is at the heart of entrepreneurship.
- **Knowledgeable.** Entrepreneurs are very knowledgeable about their environment. They make it their business to know all they can about their markets, competition, and technologies.
- **Fair.** Entrepreneurs bring a strong sense of fair play to the table. They are very aware of the contributions of others. They also have a win-win mindset with respect to fellow workers and customers.
- **Competitive.** Entrepreneurs are very competitive and constantly benchmark themselves against the best in the industry.
- **Opportunistic.** Entrepreneurs are very opportunistic in their approach. They become very tactical when it suits them while maintaining their overarching strategic vision.
- **Inward looking.** Entrepreneurs internalize problems rather than externalize them. They do not blame others for their failures. They also do not need outside validation to feel confident.
- **Rebellious.** Entrepreneurs have no respect for established order. Indeed, they typically benefit when the established order is upset.
- **Self motivated.** Entrepreneurs draw their strength from deep inside them. They by and large do not need much help from others. A simple spark or inspiration is normally enough to get them started.

Not all these traits are necessarily present in every successful entrepreneur. A healthy combination of these traits, however, is present in most successful entrepreneurs.

Enabling Environment

Hardy entrepreneurs can function in almost any environment, but for them to do well, conducive environments become necessary. Governments can help provide the enabling environment. This environment at minimum has functioning free markets with rule of law and strong property rights at their core. Governments can also provide favorable tax regime to encourage the formation of risk capital pools. For entrepreneurs to really thrive, many other factors, including soft cultural factors, also play a role. These include

- **Role models.** Role models are very important, giving budding entrepreneurs inspiration and confidence to take the initial risk. For example, the success of a handful of Indian entrepreneurs in Silicon Valley during the 1980s inspired hundreds more to try in the 1990s, both in Silicon Valley and in Banglore.

- **Support networks.** Support networks play a crucial role in educating entrepreneurs, helping them find partners, and providing mentoring if needed. The formation of TiE and NASSCOM put a strong focus on entrepreneurship, thereby turbo-charging the entrepreneurial activity among Indians in Silicon valley and Banglore.
- **Acceptance of failures.** Failures must be viewed culturally as learning experiences and not looked down upon.
- **Respect for entrepreneurs.** Societies that hold entrepreneurs in high esteem encourage the entrepreneurial behavior in the broadest section of the society. Large numbers must try so that enough will emerge as winners to help society at large.
- **Entrepreneurial experience.** The presence of entrepreneurial companies in the environment provides a supply of potential entrepreneurs.
- **Access to capital.** Access to seed and venture capital plays an important role in encouraging entrepreneurial capital. Venture capitalists also provide crucial advice and connections in early days of start-ups.
- **Availability of talent.** Availability of talent is a major contributor to the formation of entrepreneurial companies. Most entrepreneurs come from the ranks of experienced professionals.

Hard government-supported infrastructure has been found not to be as effective as the supportive policy regime in the development of entrepreneurial clusters. For example, the Multi-Media Super Corridor in Malaysia and the ultra-modern IT Park in Tokyo Bay have produced no bursts of entrepreneurial activity, while the emergences of Silicon Valley and Banglore have been almost spontaneous and have developed a strong self-sustaining culture of entrepreneurship.

Conclusions

Entrepreneurs are at the heart of the success of modern societies. Societies must pursue policies that encourage entrepreneurial behavior, but do not necessarily need to support entrepreneurs directly. Cultural factors play a crucial role. A free-wheeling market economy is most conducive to entrepreneurial behavior. It is not very clear what traits or combination of traits foretells entrepreneurial success. Society must encourage the broadest possible participation in entrepreneurial activities and honor and reward the winners.

Profiles of Success

Interview with Gene Kleiner

Eugene Kleiner was a founder of Fairchild Semiconductor, where he played a key role in the growth of the company and of the semiconductor industry as a whole. Eugene received a Bachelor of Science Degree in Mechanical Engineering from the Polytechnic University of New York and a Master of Science Degree in Industrial Engineering from New York University. In 1989, he was awarded an Honorary Doctorate of Engineering Degree from the Polytechnic University of New York. He is a founder and consulting partner of one of the country's leading venture-capital firms, Kleiner Perkins Caufield & Byers, and is also active in venture capital on his own behalf. He serves on the advisory boards of Paine Webber R&D Partners, Intersouth Partners, and Capital Resource Partners. In recent years, Mr. Kleiner has been associated with a number of technology-oriented companies as a director or founder, including Tandem Computers, Genentech, and Resound. Mr. Kleiner also serves as a director of several private high-technology companies. He and his late wife, Rose, have two children.

Q: What are the top factors that have contributed to your success as an entrepreneur?

Gene Kleiner (GK): To have sufficient technical knowledge and to be a risk taker.

Q: Can you describe some of the risks you took early on?

GK: I left a very secure job in New Jersey to move to California and do something different. If you do something high risk and it doesn't work out, then you have to turn the risk into some virtue. That's what we did. We decided to form our own company and we did that.

Q: Tell me a bit more about the early days, when you started Fairchild. What were some of the biggest challenges you faced?

GK: One critical challenge was asking IBM to tell us what kind of solutions they would like to have that they couldn't get anywhere else. They gave us specs on something we had never done before and asked us if we could do it. And we said "Yes, of course." We thought we could do it, but had never done it before. This was a risk to our reputation. If we hadn't been able to deliver it that would have set us back a year or two. But we were able to deliver it.

Q: What were some lessons that you learned during the initial startup time? Are there any things you would have changed or done differently given the chance to go back in time?

GK: Looking back, I'm amazed at how well we did. If we had to plan it today, I'm not sure we would have been so successful as we were. We were under pressure to do something no one had ever done before. I was recently thinking about some of the equipment, such as the furnaces we built, that had never been built before. We built them, and they worked. You have to have confidence in what you're doing—and you have to be desperate enough!

Q: Can you talk in more detail about a specific technical challenge you had?

GK: I mentioned we had to build furnaces with a very high temperature. The temperature couldn't vary by more than half a degree or so. There wasn't this kind of furnace anywhere else in the world. But we did find heating elements we thought would do the job and we sent for the heating elements in Sweden and built the furnace—and it worked. Another thing was the photo-engraving process. We used some basic photo-resist. It had been used before for making circuit boards, but we used it on very small geometries—and it worked.

Q: One objective of the TiE book is to provide some mentor tips to aspiring entrepreneurs. Are there any questions you would have asked a mentor when you started out?

GK: We had questions, but had no one to ask. We had specific technical questions. We didn't ask anyone the general business questions. In hindsight I'm glad we didn't. Having confidence in yourself is important. We eventually asked someone questions about the marketing of the products. We did get someone from the outside to take care of the marketing.

Q: Is there a certain personality type that makes a better entrepreneur?

GK: Yes. Again, it goes back to confidence. There are so many unknowns and so many risks that you take every day. If you don't have the confidence, you'll never get it done. Confidence is great, but it should be based on advanced education and hopefully some experience. Out of the eight of us founders, we had six PhDs.

Q: Describe the past, present, and future challenges facing entrepreneurs.

GK: Since I'm a hero of the past, I would say that was the way to do it. We relied on educational background and some experience and confidence. We weren't lazy. But this has changed. People thought they could delegate some of these things. Too many people with incomplete knowledge got involved and thought they could buy the knowledge, but they couldn't offer the same quality.

Q: Are you talking about the Internet bubble?

GK: Yes.

Q: How has the startup environment changed since then?

GK: It has gone back to how it was in the beginning. You can't talk yourself out of things. You can't cook the books. I think it's a healthy environment now.

Q: Other than what we've talked about, do you have additional advice for someone who would want to start a business at this time?

GK: You should have enough financial reserves for a couple of years so you're not pressured into doing something you don't want to do. You should know the whole business, and not just a part of it. That doesn't mean you have to be involved in every detail, but you need to understand the whole business.

Q: For those lucky enough to have more than one potential investor, how would you decide which one to go with?

GK: Normally you can have more than one investor. But if you have to choose one, it's whoever writes the check fastest. Of course, that's if everything else is more or less equal.

Q: How do you decide how much money to take? A lot of entrepreneurs tend to take too little, right?

GK: Most of the time, you need more money than you think you do. If you have a tight budget and that's the money you raise, chances are you will have to raise more money before you finish the project. It will be very difficult to get that second round of funding. You'll have an incomplete project, and trying to get more money is more challenging. If you're very successful, the initial money you take isn't that critical. If you fail, that's it. Ask for the money you need. It may take you longer to spend it, but it gives you a better assurance of success.

Q: What are the top three things VCs look for when they look at a business proposal?

GK: I look at the market and ask if anyone wants or needs this thing they are selling. That's the big thing I look at. If that isn't there, you really don't have anything. Of course then I ask myself if it can be made, and if this group is the one to make it.

Q: How about technical expertise and a seasoned management team?

GK: Yes, that's important. I certainly don't want them learning on the job—or at least not too much.

Interview with Narayana Murthy

Mr. Murthy (NRN) has served as Chairman of the Board and Chief Executive Officer of Infosys since 1981, when he founded the company with six software professionals. He also served as Managing Director of Infosys until February 1999. While at Infosys, from 1992 to 1994, he served as the President of NASSCOM. He has also been a member of the National Information Technology Task Force of India and a member of the Prime Minister's Council on Trade and Industry. He is a Director of the Board of the Reserve Bank of India (RBI). He has received several honors and awards, including Businessman of the Year 1999 by *Business India*, and has been featured in *Asiaweek*'s Power 50, a list of Asia's most powerful people. He is a Fellow of the All India Management Association (AIMA) and the Computer Society of India (CSI). He received a Bachelors Degree in Electrical Engineering from the University of Mysore and a Masters Degree in Technology from IIT Kanpur.

Q: What are the top three factors that have contributed to your success as an entrepreneur?

Narayana Murthy (NM): The first thing is a relentless focus on an idea that makes a difference in the marketplace. We knew that we could reduce the poverty in India by developing software. When we started Infosys in 1981, there were so many factors against us. There was no venture-capital funding available in India. It was almost impossible to get funding, but we captured it.

The second thing was that I assembled a team with a mutually exclusive and collectively exhaustive set of skills and experience. We had people who understood technology, strategy, and human resources. Of all the companies founded in India, we're the only company that has come this far. In other instances, companies had all their expertise in one area, such as finance or HR.

The third success factor is a strong value system. To last, an organization must have a strong value system. This is the behavior in a community that makes everyone feel committed. In the end, the organization benefits. The value system includes putting the community interests ahead of your own. It means not using corporate benefits for your own benefit. A value system is like the rudder on a ship. If you have a value system that helps you through difficult times, you come out ahead.

Q: Can you describe some of the risks you took early on, when you launched Infosys?

NM: It wasn't that big of a risk, really, although I did leave a good job. I was the head of a software division for a software company. I was the number-two person in that company and had put in about 12 years in the industry. Five of the Infosys startup group were young fellows who were just out of college for a couple years. Then there was another colleague who was my assistant at the software company. As a whole, we didn't have too much to lose. We would conduct the experiment and work hard. If it didn't work, we would get up and dust off our knees. We didn't have venture-capital money, so the only thing we put on the line were our own careers.

Q: Tell me a bit more about the early days, when you started out. What were some of the biggest challenges you faced?

NM: We had no office, so we started out in the bedroom of my small, 700-square-foot apartment. It was a challenge to attract all the smart people we were eventually able to recruit with no name, no money, no brand recognition, and no physical or financial assets. The most important success factor is the ability to recruit and retain the best and brightest talent. We had almost nothing to offer them. When we recruited some people in 1982, I managed to borrow some table space from the company of a friend of mine. Then I had to go and talk to another friend who had access to a large computer center. He gave us computer time during the night for an attractive rate. At the time, we had only one customer. My wife pawned her jewelry and silver to help pay our employees' salaries. The best part about it was that we did not have to compromise our value system.

Q: What were some lessons that you learned during the initial startup time? Are there any things you would have changed or done differently given the chance to go back in time?

NM: I think one key lesson we learned is that people are the most important asset of any knowledge organization. You must attract and retain the best and brightest. To do this, you need to create an environment of respect. We wanted to create a company for and by the professional. This meant creating an open environment where the best idea is revered and accepted.

Another thing I learned is the importance of speed, imagination, and execution with excellence. Each day you should ask yourself these questions: Are we doing things faster than yesterday? Are we bringing in more creativity today? Are we executing these ideas with excellence?

Third, we learned that in a knowledge organization, people are analyzing and acting on conclusions. You have to walk the talk. We learned that the investors understand that in any business there will be ups and downs. They want you to deliver the bad news proactively, as well as the good news. Then they might say, "They may not be that smart, but at least they're honest!" And like I said, a strong value system is very important.

Q: What questions would you have asked a mentor when you started out?

NM: The key question I would have asked would have been, "How do I validate a good idea?" The biggest source of failure is that entrepreneurs don't understand whether an idea will be successful or not.

Q: How do you validate the worthiness of an idea?

NM: You must ask the fundamental questions about whether the idea brings about a clear value proposition. Will it reduce costs, increase productivity, or grow your customer base? If it's an existing idea, you have to ask how much improvement it will bring. If it's about improving comfort level, that may work—but it's not as good as lowering cost and increasing productivity and customer base. Then, you have to speak about the value proposition in simple sentences, not complex terms. That's the first and foremost thing.

The second question is, how do we balance the short-term and long-term needs? This includes determining how to make sure the choices you make don't compromise your value system. When you're an entrepreneur sacrificing time and energy, the thing that delivers you is that you're sacrificing these things for a worthwhile cause. If you don't see the benefits you expect in the timeframe you've set, you start to have self-doubts about the success of the idea. At this time, you need someone with experience to say, "These things happen and it may take more time—but it will be worth it in the end."

Q: How does the current economic climate affect entrepreneurial efforts? What does an entrepreneur have to do to survive in this downturn?

NM: The important thing to remember is that in a downturn, the focus on the value proposition is even more than in normal times. People are ready to put money on many ideas in an upturn. In a downturn, people want the best bang for their buck. They are much more focused on evaluating the market-worthiness and benefits the idea brings to the market. Second, you have to be much more focused on controlling costs and retaining people. You have to do it with much greater seriousness and better productivity.

Q: Describe the past, present, and future challenges facing entrepreneurs.

NM: In the past, and in the future, the challenges will be more or less the same. It's all about converting mental energy and creativity and intelligence into wealth. To do that, you need a great idea, a market that's ready for it, a good team that will make sure the idea goes to market quickly, and a strong value system. Then of course you need financing.

The biggest challenge is simply this: How do I make sure that I bring together a set of people who believe in an idea with tremendous conviction and are ready to sacrifice for the sake of the idea? How do I raise the aspirations of my people and make them feel more confident about the company? It can be very easy to lose hope and faith in what you're doing. This is where leadership is very important. There has to be a leader to raise aspirations, make people confident, make sure they see the dream, and make sure people don't get tired running the marathon. These are the attributes that will always be mandatory in the past, present, and future.

Thanks to globalization, ideas now come from all over the world. In the past, most business ideas came primarily from the United States, and some from Japan and Europe. Today, entrepreneurs can come from China, India, and Singapore. Globalization in entrepreneurism is the shift that is taking place. Venture capital will flow to anywhere in the world. You will have more entrepreneurs and much more competition.

Q: What are the top three things VCs look for when they look at a business proposal?

NM: If I were to evaluate a plan, I would look for quantifiable measures of how the idea would improve the marketplace. For example, you must be able to say "My idea will reduce the cost by 8 percent in this market segment." I want a simple sentence—a value that is tangible. I'm not so much into ideas that improve the comfort of people. I want ideas that make companies more profitable, control costs, and bring in more customers.

The second thing is that I want to look at the team. I want to see a mutually exclusive but exhaustive set of skills. Third, I want to see the value system. I ask myself, "Can these people run the marathon? Do I see commitment? Is there one person who can lead them and say the buck stops here? Do these people truly believe in the idea?" And, of course, the market must be ready.

Interview with Peter Senge

Peter M. Senge was named the "Strategist of the Century" by the *Journal of Business Strategy*, one of 24 men and women who have "had the greatest impact on the way we conduct business today" (September/October 1999). While he has studied how firms and organizations develop adaptive capabilities for many years at the Massachusetts Institute of Technology (MIT), it was Peter Senge's 1990 book *The Fifth Discipline* that brought him firmly into the limelight and popularized the concept of the "learning organization." Since its publication, more than 750,000 copies have been sold and in 1997, *Harvard Business Review* identified it as one of the seminal management books of the past 75 years.

Q: What are some of the key soft skills for entrepreneurs who are building enterprises of the future?

Peter Senge (PS): By definition, an entrepreneurial venture is a sense of shared vision, people who share common passion. It [entrepreneurial venture] is the art of creating balance between convergence and divergence. People have a clear idea and common focus about a particular product, particular results, or particular customer or market. They can work together with common values when all they have to work *with* in the beginning is creativity. The convergence and focus on product or customer or market should not kill the creativity.

It is a sophisticated field. Classical OL [organizational learning] skills would be very useful here. Conversational skills would need to be good for building good entrepreneurial teams in the beginning. Very few people are good in dealing with conflict. Conflict, when dealt with appropriately, could be very generative but many people end up just having fights in the name of conflict management. They don't really harness the creative potential.

Q: What are the critical soft skills and learning skills for building an executive team?

PS: It takes off from where we began a minute ago. Very few executives are good in dealing with conflict in teams. I really do think that basic inquiry skills, the ability to distinguish interpretations from data, the ability to pose questions that really help people learn more from the situations in which they find themselves. I really don't know how else to say it. It is developing shared appreciation of the reality in which they are working; and it is pretty hard work. The Appreciative Inquiry (AI) work of David Cooperrider et. al. would be very useful here. It is about dealing with differences and potential conflicts appreciatively. That seems to be quite crucial.

Q: I have outlined my critical top-ten list of soft skills for you (presented later in the chapter). These are the top-ten soft skills that I have come up with for entrepreneurs to build sustainable and profitable enterprises that stay long after they are gone. Do you feel these cover what you would consider as key skills?

PS: I think they are great. The only thing at this point that I detect missing is something about developing a theory of business. Peter Drucker keeps saying that people make implicit decisions and barely make the theory explicit. Without an explicit and coherent theory, a company does not sustain for long. Mental-model tools help to make that explicit, but how you interrelate different images and mental models the executive team has into a coherent picture—what is our theory, where are we at, how do we generate value, key sources of distinctiveness? Are we sophisticated in building shared understanding? How do we look for disconfirming evidence that identifies what is wrong with our theory?

Q: Many entrepreneurial companies that were built in the new economy model were missing the theory of business. I once invested in a company that became pretty big very quickly and it looked like they created a very successful company. The founders moved out and started other stuff, and suddenly the company collapsed and disappeared. It has happened so many times recently that you wonder what the value proposition was and what its distinctive source was.

PS: I also think you can integrate what is implicit in *doing* in an entrepreneurial venture into your *knowing-doing* gap. You should look seriously at your *doings* like how you make decisions and what you spend your money on. If I were to be an outsider looking at this, what would be the theory of business that I think you have? Compare that to what you say your theory of business actually is. You will find very interesting gaps between what you do and what you know about what you do—a slightly different way of looking at knowing-doing gap. People always beat themselves up because they don't always do what they say they will do and what they should do. The key is in finding out how to work with them. Why are we doing what we are doing? How come we are not following what we know?

Q: I think that is a very good point you are raising, Peter. I also say that knowing-doing gap cannot be bridged directly. We have to understand why we do what we do and why we say what we say. We have to get into what are we feeling when we do what we do? What is the spirit behind our actions and who are we being? These are important questions that throw light on the knowing-doing gap. I appreciate what you say.

From a global perspective, do you see things that entrepreneurs should pay attention to? Are there things that they traditionally ignore but that they should pay more attention to?

PS: Well, the obvious part of that is diversity. When you are an entrepreneur, you network and connect with people who have a fair amount of commonness with you. I think you get to be homogenous. I always think of companies like Shell. It is Dutch and English. The core of the company is bicultural. There are not too many companies like that. That type of multi-cultural, diverse team from the beginning would add a lot of value. It prepares you as you grow. You deal with more and more different kinds of people, markets, customers, technologies. Having different points of view at the core helps you significantly. It increases your net worth.

Q: That is a critical point, Peter, and in Silicon Valley, the potential exists for such collaborations but does not happen very often.

PS: Unilever is the same way. They are also Dutch and English. It is very interesting to watch how they make decisions.

Q: Great. With TiE, we are getting exposed to many others. Otherwise, we create companies with others whom we are very comfortable with. There are many Indian startups, Chinese startups, et cetera, but rarely do Chinese and Indians create an entrepreneurial venture together. It happens with Americans and Asians, but still the feeling is that Asians are good technical people and we need Americans for management. We have to really look at our mental models because if we just keep doing what we are doing, we keep getting what we are getting—a mixed success.

Do you see any Asian contribution or Indian contribution—their uniqueness—that we should pay attention to in building the companies that we build?

PS: Over the last ten years, I have found tremendous alignment between the basic ideas of organizational learning and Asian cultures. I think *The Fifth Discipline* has sold more copies in China than any other country other than the U.S. I think it is very popular in India as well.

I think people appreciate the fact that you don't have to follow the model of Western capitalism. It is very important for two reasons. One, if you are helping the country, you will develop your own style. Number two, a new model is needed in the world because Western capitalism is a dead-end. You cannot grow the world economy based on Western capitalism because of its extreme levels of waste and its disregard for human capital. I think there is enormous potential for the Asian economies. They will pioneer the kind of capitalism that respects natural capital, social capital, and human capital, I think. It could be a discontinuous big contribution of the 21st century. I really believe that.

Q: That is a great point, Peter. If I might follow up on that, you said Western capitalism disregards the human capital and Asian approaches enhance it. Can you say how we can enhance human capital from either Western or Eastern perspectives?

PS: Of course. There are lots of things we can say about messages and practices, and we have already talked a bit about that. Lying behind all these tools and messages is a matter of point of view. The reason I say that about Asian cultures is they have a different degree of integration about the spiritual perspective. In Western cultures, by and large, we have almost externalized spirituality. What I mean by that is that we have to go to church to experience spirituality. In the extreme form, we do whatever we do during the week and go to church to repent on Sunday. There is a lot of spirituality in the Western world, don't get me wrong. But it is more on the periphery than central to everyday life. Especially Christianity which is not based on everyday development. It is based on repentance and redemption.

Asian cultures have more integral concept of spirituality. It is a more practice-oriented approach. That means it is not about what you believe, but it is what you practice and it is a matter of discipline. What practices do you commit to on a day-by-day or hour-by-hour basis? It gives a very different orientation. If you really experience and you are continually cultivating your ability to experience spiritual orientation moment by moment, you naturally relate to people. You naturally relate to all natural systems in a very different way than if you are trying to add on the top of your everyday way of doing things a spiritual orientation. There is a possibility of contributing something very different like that to the business world.

That affects the ability to naturally gravitate to the primacy of human capital. That really is the key. Are the living systems primary or secondary? If they are the beginning to the orientation, if you naturally respect all life, and that is your starting point, then everything is secondary. That would be very different approach.

Q: Can you suggest some simple guidelines that entrepreneurs can take on and keep in mind in developing human capital?

PS: Let us start with something simple. What practice are you taking on to guide your day-to-day life? It is not enough to say, "I run, I go to gym," because they are physical exercises (that are important by themselves) but not sufficient in my opinion. Start out with some spiritual exercises. Each individual has to choose his or her own personal practice whether it is meditation, or tai chi, or yoga; I don't care. It is a discipline that they have to cultivate. Secondly, there are team practices, simple dialogue practices like check-in. I think any of the mental-model practices like acknowledging their left-hand columns or where they are on the ladders of inference. Also, you can explore different scenarios and spiritual development. You pick some and then maintain some practice.

Q: Any cultural practices that you recommend?

PS: Culture is a bit of a problematic word. What I would focus on is very particular settings like meetings. Develop skills that will help you run very productive and focused meetings. It does not mean that they are always focused, but that there is good balance between focus and divergence as well as between inquiry and task. Most people hate going to meetings. They think meetings are a waste of time. If they can learn how to run productive meetings, that would be good.

Let us take a couple more examples. Performance reviews: How do we go about reviewing performance? Do we do it in a way that leads to learning? Are there particular practices that allow performance to be reviewed in an appreciative way? Similarly, budgets: How do you deal with them productively? My main point is, don't spend so much time thinking about your culture. Take particular practices that are relevant to a particular kind of work, so that they can impact the meetings, performance reviews, and budgets. Take routine things that you have to do and make them *learningful*. Particular practices for developing particular skills.

Q: Any last comments that you want to make?

PS: We need to recognize the importance of entrepreneurs to national economies. So far, dealing with social and environmental problems has been centrally government issues, particularly in developed economies. These developed economies are trying to work with developing economies. There is no hope for developing economies without strong vital entrepreneurs. The problem of working with big multi-nationals is that you develop the skills but you do not develop the infrastructure. I think there needs to be a balance. There is nothing wrong with multinationals in the developed countries, but they tend to squeeze out the entrepreneurial sector, and that has been the pattern. I was talking with a banker from Nigeria. He pointed out to me that Shell is 60 percent—*six-zero percent*—of the Nigerian economy. He founded a very successful bank in Nigeria. He was very clear that there is no hope for Nigeria without an entrepreneurial sector. It is very difficult. In all kinds of ways, big companies make it very difficult for the entrepreneurs. We have to learn to work with each other. That is the key. Entrepreneurs and big businesses have to learn to work together.

Q: Can you comment on entrepreneurs and their role in building sustainable enterprises of the future.

PS: Now, I am assuming you are talking about natural capital and environment when you use the word *sustainability*. Nobody has really looked at building sustainable enterprises so far, at least thoroughly. Somebody in SFO is looking at criteria for investors—very specific things in terms of social and environmental impact. Social investment has been growing a lot. Long-term financial performance is not compromised. It is about setting standards. Big businesses have to do that just like quality standards have been set by them before. It is still a mystery why we drive these cars instead of cars that give 200-miles a gallon. Only companies that are financially stable are doing hybrid vehicles—Honda and Toyota. Many other companies cannot venture into working on risky propositions.

My recommendations to entrepreneurs: Form associations and develop various kinds of networks. There is so much to learn here and the biggest problem for entrepreneurs is isolation. This is the area where there is so much to learn and it seems like a natural place to share best practices. Don't do it alone.

It is best if we learn together. It is something that you have to do together as coalitions.

two 2

CHAPTER

Business Planning

Chair: Gopal Patwardhan, COO - **Girvan Institute of Technology**

Co-Chair: Robert Hunt - **Girvan Institute of Technology**

Rahul Chandra - **Walden International**

Paresh Ghelani - **2020 Company LLC**

Ben Nagrani - **TiE**

Rishi Navani - **West Bridge Capital Partners**

Introduction

There's no doubt about it, entrepreneurs are a special breed. They're passionate about their ideas and their business goals, and they're willing to work hard over extended periods of time to make their dreams a reality. The entrepreneurial spirit transcends geography, race, language, and economic conditions.

Over time, lots of studies have been done about the entrepreneurial mindset. It's a fascinating subject for academics and researchers, who probe the social, political, and economic factors involved. Governments, hoping to attract or retain bright business people whose ideas and success may help local economies, are equally interested in what makes entrepreneurs tick. In fact, there is a whole body of research that tries to identify what makes an entrepreneur an entrepreneur, and, even more important, what makes an entrepreneur successful.

Our experience leads us to a simple conclusion. We believe that entrepreneurs are particularly attuned to a universal and inherent human trait: the desire for freedom.

The goal of this chapter is not to try to help you evaluate whether you are one of those individuals who has the "statistically proven" characteristics of a successful entrepreneur, nor is it to tell you what issues you should think through before deciding to become an entrepreneur yourself. We suspect that if you're reading this book, you've already made your decision. We do think, however, that you'll benefit from understanding some of the typical obstacles you will face upon becoming an entrepreneur, and how, given your particular personality, you can best confront those challenges.

In short, our goals for this chapter are to

- Provide you with an opportunity to evaluate your abilities and goals and help you judge their compatibility.
- Allow you to develop a framework for evaluating the opportunities you see before you.
- Help you understand some of the special operating problems of emerging businesses, focusing on how they differ from going concerns.
- Provide you with some useful concepts and techniques, which will help you to navigate the start-up ramp.
- Get you started on an effective business plan.

The New Venture Ramp

Bringing order to start-up efforts is key to your success; this chapter provides a step-by-step roadmap of what needs to be done at each phase of the start-up process. The various phases include

- Planning
- Prototyping
- Market development
- Launch

tip Building a venture requires a lot of groundwork. Skipping steps in the early stages will inevitably cause problems further down the line. So, take the time to think deeply, put proper structures in place, to build a broad and firm foundation that will give you a better chance to succeed.

PHASE 1: Planning

The planning phase of the start-up effort involves three main stages, all of which are discussed in detail in the sections that follow:

- Stage 1: Ideation and exploration
- Stage 2: Concept development and architecture (Needs Assessment)
- Stage 3: Feasibility study

Some Things to Consider Before You Begin

Be warned: Your life is about to change. As you build your company, everything about you will be tested, from your personality, to your work habits, to your self esteem. It's a good idea to begin by taking stock of who you are, what you want, and why. Consider this an exercise in self awareness, with the goal of recognizing where your foibles might interfere with your entrepreneurial goals.

To begin, consider looking at some of the personality tests developed by management professors and psychoanalysts, many of which are available on Web sites and in books about personality development, leadership, and the like. When you do, ask yourself some of the questions that are posed. If you already have a team in mind, you may find that going through these questions together helps you build a better awareness of each other's strengths and weaknesses.

Here are the some key questions to ask yourself:

- Am I the type?
- Am I so keen on doing something that I am willing and able to learn the 90 percent that I don't already know about a business?
- Am I ready to work for 12 to 18 months (or more) without clear visibility into the future?
- Am I willing to go out and solicit my family, friends, and their friends for support, and risk being ridiculed by them for my foolishness, listen to and evaluate the advice everyone gives me, but only blame myself when things go wrong because I've chosen to take or not take that advice?

In addition, here are a few key points you'll want to remember:

- You will never be without a boss. In fact, you will have to answer to many more people than you probably ever have.
- Entrepreneurs are risk-takers, but successful entrepreneurs are those who minimize as much risk as possible. They try to build companies with the most likely chance of success for themselves, their families, their investors, their suppliers, their customers, and their employees.
- Almost all successful entrepreneurs succeed because they are persistent.

Stage 1: Ideation and Exploration

Typically, the ideation process begins without any premeditated intent. Whenever you have an idea, however, you should capture it. Explore each idea thoroughly, in a structured way, even if you are exploring several at the same time.

You might develop the idea for your business as a result of seeing a window of opportunity in an area in which you have long held a strong interest. Indeed, you may have already spent some time exploring the opportunity by looking at websites, speaking to potential customers, visiting tradeshows, and so on. Exploring the environment and surveying the minds of creative individuals are key to developing a great idea. As you do, it is good practice to maintain a log of your thoughts and observations for future reference. Use a simple notebook or a voice recorder to capture discussions you have.

Once you have clearly identified and examined your idea, write it down in plain language. Forget the hyperbole. Try to come up with one clear sentence that describes what you propose to do, making it understandable for any reader. Then ask yourself these questions:

- Why do I want to do it?
- How do I know that customers want the product?
- Can I make the product?
- Can I sell/distribute the product?
- How much time and emotional energy am I willing to give?
- How much capital can I invest?
- What profit do I want and what other benefits do I expect from this business?

Stage 2: Concept Development and Architecture (Needs Assessment)

Once you have identified your idea, you need to develop a description of the system, features, and processes that will allow you to discuss the idea with others. It is a good idea to develop diagrams that visually describe your idea and a system flow chart showing how it works. This is particularly crucial if you are planning to develop complex or hi-tech products.

Next, make detailed notes and a survey of competitive product offerings. Gather as much information as you can about similar products, such as how they work, what customers say about them, and how they are different from yours. Create a table to summarize this information for future reference, and prepare a set of arguments explaining why your product will be better than any competitive offerings.

Finally, you'll want to assess exactly what you need to get the business up and running. Here's what you need to do:

- List the assets that are essential to the development of the product, including the people, equipment, expertise, and raw materials.
- Make a rough estimate of what it will cost to make the product (including fixed-asset and working capital-requirements).

Stage 3: Feasibility Study

A *feasibility study* is a "back of the napkin" projection that provides a framework for a more formal business plan. Once you have clearly defined your idea and listed the resources that you need to launch it, it is critical to determine, in a quick and dirty manner, whether your idea is viable as a business. Simply put: Will it make money? A feasibility study for a new venture typically should involve a bottom-up estimation of the revenue, an analysis of cost factors, and risk definitions.

Performing a feasibility study will help you decide whether the business is a go by answering the following questions early in the game, before you have formally solicited other stakeholders:

- Is this the only venture I should consider?
- With my profit expectations in mind, what sales revenue would I need to produce my desired profit?
- What are the risks? Does the return justify the risks?
- Is there a disaster sequence? How will I know if I am on that cliff?
- What are the contingency plans?

Estimating Revenue

When estimating revenue, you'll need to perform a bottom-up analysis by looking at the market in terms of your product and substitutes. Here's how:

1. Estimate the total number of units that will be sold in the first three or five years after launch. This is the total available market (TAM).
2. Determine the average price now being commanded for products like yours ($Y).
3. Estimate the market penetration you expect to accomplish in three to five years (X%).

Once you've assessed these figures, you can estimate revenue by applying the following formula:

Projected Revenue = (TAM) ($Y) (X%)

Calculating Costs

Production costs include the following:

- **Fixed costs (FC).** Fixed costs are those that do not vary based on the number of units you produce or the number of customers you serve. These costs include general administration, product development, research, and so on.
- **Marginal costs (MC/Unit).** Marginal costs are those costs that are directly linked to the production of an additional unit or the satisfaction of an additional customer. These costs include those associated with sales, production, customer service, delivery, and so on.

note Although it is difficult to clearly break down each factor of production into fixed or marginal costs, it is important in order to determine a business's feasibility to be able to assess these at least in a rough manner.

To assess net cost, then, use the following formula:

Net Cost = FC + (MC/Unit)(Number of Units Produced)

Once you've established your net cost, you can determine your net margin by applying the following formula:

Net Margin = Projected Revenue–Net Cost

Assessing Risk

As you complete your feasibility study, you must consider the three types of risk involved in starting a business:

- **Technology/product risk.** Will your product provide your customers with benefits that justify its cost?
- **Market/adoption risk.** Is your target customer ready to accept your offering? Factors that determine this include access to the target customer (channel access), whether adoption is predicated on a change in user behavior, and your ability to communicate the value proposition to your target customer.

note You'll learn more about value propositions later in this chapter.

- **Execution/team risk.** How are you going to make it happen? This covers your strategy to capture market share and how you will efficiently operate (procure, manufacture, develop products, sales, and customer service) your business.

Moving ahead on the new-venture ramp means constantly trying to minimize risks. In the next section, you'll learn how you can minimize product and technology risk by instituting a systematic prototyping and testing cycle.

Other Planning Issues

In addition to the planning issues already discussed, it is useful to consider whether your business is primarily a service provider, a seller of goods, or both. Understanding the mix of goods and services that your particular business provides to its customers is vital when considering the key areas of your business. Issues that might be extremely important to a product-based business, such as inventory, can have much less significance for a service provider.

- The customers of a service business expect that something will be done for them. A Web-hosting business is an example of a predominantly service business. Customers who pay $19.95 per month for a full service expect to have their website hosted with agreed terms. A consulting service is also predominantly service-oriented.
- The customers of a product-based business, in contrast, expect that they will acquire something. A customer who calls a mail-order house and orders a PDA expects to acquire a particular PDA. The customer isn't really looking for the firm to perform any services, beyond shipping the goods and billing.
- The customers of a business that provides both products and services expect a lot. For example, a homeowner who negotiates with a heating contractor for the installation of a new furnace expects to acquire property and to have services performed as well. The contractor is expected to dismantle and remove the old furnace and deliver and install the new one. The entire transaction is based on the provision of a package of goods and services.

Service Businesses

The starting point of a service business is the fact that there are certain things that people will pay to have done for them. Maybe they don't know how to do these things themselves. Maybe they don't have the time. Maybe they don't have the special tools. Whatever the reason, your business exists because other people are unwilling or unable to do what you do. The focus of a service business is on results. So, from a planning perspective, what's of particular importance to a service business?

Your appearance and demeanor can be critical if you are engaged in personally performing services. The same holds true if you have employees. You are, in some sense, selling yourself to prospective customers. You are asking them to trust you to do something for them, and there is at least some commitment to an ongoing relationship with the customer. The impact on your plan may be something as simple as planning for the expense of a uniform service and for regular cleaning of service vehicles.

Another issue service providers face relates to billing and collections. When goods are sold, there is a clear event that triggers the need for payment. For a service provider, however, the event that should trigger payment might not be so clear. For example, a contractor may feel that he should be paid when he informs the homeowner that the job is complete. The homeowner, however, may feel that he has a right to have the work inspected before tendering payment. One way to reduce the possibility of this type of problem is to seek progress payments as a job proceeds. Another is to plan cash-flow requirements realistically, providing for the chance that a certain portion of what you are owed might not be immediately forthcoming.

If you personally are responsible for getting new customers and also for providing services to them, it is critical to manage your own time well. Many personal service businesses require the owner to spend substantial time doing presentations, preparing bids or estimates, or doing other sales-related activities to acquire future business. To the extent that your time is spent on these activities, you aren't *currently* working on your present business.

Product-Based Businesses

A business primarily engaged in the sale of products has a focus that is different from that of a service-based business. In a product-based business, customers don't, for the most part, expect extensive personal services to be performed as part of the deal. They want a black box router, or semiconductors, or new flight-simulator software.

In some cases, your business may be the only source for the product. Some software, for example, is available only by mail from the manufacturers. If you want their product, you buy it from them. But even with such unique products, there are generally similar competitors. At the other extreme are businesses that carry goods that are widely and readily available. The bottle of pop purchased at the convenience store could just as easily have been purchased at the gas station, a vending machine at work, or a deli.

This suggests that businesses based on a unique product face a somewhat different environment from that faced by businesses carrying products that are widely available. In the case of a unique product, the competitive advantage your business should enjoy is based on the *product* itself. In the case of fungible products, your ability to sell turns on factors *other* than the identity of your product. This distinction should be kept in mind when formulating a business plan. Of particular significance is how long you can expect a unique product to remain unchallenged in the market place. If you're having some success, you can bet others will rush to break your temporary monopoly.

Another factor to be considered is the identity of your customers. Retailers sell to the general public at large; wholesalers sell primarily to retailers; and manufacturers can sell to wholesalers, to retailers, or to the public directly. Where does your business stand in that hierarchy? Who are your customers? For example, consider a manufacturer expecting to use established wholesale channels to distribute a new product. Not only must the wholesalers and retailers be convinced to carry the product, the retailers must generate sales sufficient to make the product profitable. Successfully selling to the distributors doesn't ensure successful marketing of the product to the ultimate consumer.

Mixed Goods and Services

A business that provides its customers with both goods and services will probably have a somewhat more complicated business plan than a business that primarily provides either goods or services. There are many logistical considerations relating to managing the interaction between the delivery of goods and the performance of services. The financial aspects of a mixed-goods-and-services business require careful scrutiny. The relative mix between goods and services must be managed to maintain a reasonable return on the entire enterprise. Pricing is more of an issue because you are trying to cover the wide variety of components that make up the entire package. How do you associate your labor costs with the cost of goods sold? The business-planning process affords you with an opportunity to examine this and other relationships that can impact on the profitability of your business.

PHASE 2: Prototyping

When you decide to go ahead with your idea, it's time for the building and testing phase. This phase of the start-up effort involves three main stages, all of which are discussed in detail in the sections that follow:

- Stage 1: Prototype development
- Stage 2: Alpha testing for technical demonstration of capabilities
- Stage 3: Product specification and technical-compatibility report

note For some kinds of businesses, it may or may not be viable to build a full-scale prototype. Once you've decided to proceed, however, it is useful to go through a set of trials or tests in a lab or controlled environment before rolling the product out to customers.

note If your offering is a service rather than a product, the prototyping phase will involve similar activities except that the output will be a refined and well-oiled process flow outlining how the service offering will be provisioned to the end customer.

Stage 1: Prototype Development

Your first task is to build a demonstration (*demo*) version of your product or service offering that conveys to some extent the value proposition you plan to offer in the commercial version.

In building your prototype, you will get a better idea of what costs and resources will be associated with the full-scale version. Although it is safe to assume that building the prototype will be significantly more costly than building the commercial product, it is a good idea to use the real costs associated with prototype development as a base for calculating the costs of producing (or provisioning) the commercial offering.

tip Your customers should be involved throughout the entire prototyping phase; listen to their feedback, and incorporate it wherever possible. (Be sure to include a friendly customer or technical tester—your alpha customer.) Most importantly, don't ignore the naysayers! They will be as important to you as your cheerleaders. Actively seek out negative opinions. The feedback may be useful in helping you improve your product. Besides, if you can convince a skeptic, you will be better equipped to convince venture capitalists to part with their money.

Stage 2: Alpha Testing for Technical Demonstration of Capabilities

The alpha test is the first real proof of the technical viability of your product—and hence your business. In alpha-testing stage, you get your prototype into your alpha customer's hands. Let him play with it, and see if it works and whether he likes it. The role of the alpha customer is to give you feedback on usage problems, technical difficulties, integration with other products or systems, and so on. You should keep in close contact with your alpha testers and monitor the way they use your product or service; it's also a good idea to document what happens with a case study.

Stage 3: Product Specification and Technical-Compatibility Report

At the end of the alpha phase, compile a report for yourself on how the field trial went. In it, list the following:

- Problems and difficulties encountered by the customer and how you will solve them as you modify the prototype for beta launch
- The features the prototype lacks and what you think the costs (based on your experience with this "build") with the full-scale version will be
- All technical failures of the system and plans on how to avoid them in v2

PHASE 3: Market Development

Once you've built your prototype, tested it, and taken your alpha customer's feedback to heart (either addressing his concerns or fixing the problems he found), it's time to begin the market-development phase. This phase involves four main stages:

- Stage 1: Beta testing and customer-value determination
- Stage 2: Detailed market study
- Stage 3: Channel identification, alliances, and partnerships
- Stage 4: Pre-launch (market-entry planning)

Stage 1: Beta Testing and Customer-Value Determination

Many entrepreneurs make the mistake of calling version 1 of their offering their beta. The key difference between the alpha (version 1) and the beta is that while the former is merely a technical validation of the functionality and applicability of the product, the beta is in fact a key market risk-minimization milestone.

As such, during the beta-testing phase, you should try to

- Estimate the customer's *cost of ownership*—that is, what your customer will have to spend, in terms of time and money, before your product is able to deliver the value you profess it will.
- Estimate the cost of delivering the product to and supporting a customer (that is, channel/delivery costs, customer-service costs, and so on).
- Learn how the customer values the product (and, as a result, how much he is willing to pay for it!).

Stage 2: Detailed Market Study

Many first-time entrepreneurs spend endless hours and effort designing the product or service they intend to offer, and little or no time assessing whether a market exists or can be created for their offering. *Market research* is a way of collecting information that you can use to solve or avoid these (and other) types of marketing problems. It provides you with data you need to develop a marketing plan that works, enables you to identify the specific segments within a market that you want to target, and helps you to create an identity for your product or service that differentiates it from your competitors' offerings.

note There are thousands of computer programmers with skills to write programs effectively, but relatively few have the skills to identify the need for a product, let alone successfully sell it. Don't get so caught up in your passion for what you are doing that you overlook the business realities.

Almost in parallel with the beta test, it is advisable to undertake a thorough market study. Although you will have already surveyed the market, a more detailed analysis of the size and scope of the market is necessary after, or as you get feedback from, your beta tests. This is important because by now you have a much firmer handle on what your product is like—how it works, and possibly to which market segments it most applies.

As you conduct your market study, you'll want to

- Identify market opportunities.
- Evaluate customer needs.
- Consider niche markets.

note This section briefly reviews the salient points related to market studies. For more detailed information, see Chapter 8, "Marketing and Sales."

Identifying Market Opportunities

Preliminary research is one of the best and most effective ways to identify market opportunities or potential. There are two ways to approach market research: One way is to hire outside consultants, which, needless to say, can be quite costly. The other way is to do your own research using the Web and your local library as resources to gather data. Whichever route you choose, you'll want to investigate factors such as competition, the area economy, the demographic breakdown of your client base, and the availability of potential customers. After considering the size of the market as well as the potential market for new customers, you must determine the following:

- Is the market flat, growing, booming or declining?
- What are technological developments or other elements affecting the market/industry?

- Are there distinct market segments?
- Is the market local, regional or national?

note Too often, entrepreneurs neglect this stage because it is an expensive and time-consuming process, or because they don't want to hear any negative feedback (be wary of your natural tendency to believe that your offering is perfect). Be warned, however, that you can't succeed unless you do your homework!

Evaluating Customer Needs

In evaluating customer needs, you want to pay close attention not only to what products and services are out there, but what *could be* out there. If you can satisfy a customer need that exists but is not currently being met by a competing product or service, your business will be off to a good start. Hence, the best way to find out is to talk directly with future or potential customers who need your product or service. Take time to visit potential clients and talk to people in the business. When you can look at the world from your prospective customers' perspective, you can identify their needs or wants.

Your market research in this area should begin with a market survey. Before you start your research, however, you might want to meet with a consultant, talk to a business or marketing professor at a local college or university, and contact your local business-administration (SBA) district office. They can offer guidance with the first steps in market research. Done right, your market research will give you a full view of the following critical information:

- **Industry information.** Identify all the latest trends and compare the statistics and growth in that industry. What areas seem to be expanding and what areas are declining? Is this industry creating a new type of consumer? What technological developments are affecting the industry?

  note Make sure that you're getting into a thriving, stable industry. It's not advisable to start a new business in a field that is on the decline.

- **The customer or consumer.** A thorough market survey should help you make reasonable sales forecasts for your new venture. To do this survey, you need to determine the market limits or physical boundaries of the area in which your business sells. You will also need to identify and study the spending characteristics of the local population. Estimate the area's purchasing power based on competitive analysis in order to estimate how much of the total sales volume you can reasonably obtain.

- **The competition.** Based on your collective industry and consumer research, a clearer picture of your competitors will emerge. Do not underestimate the number of competitors in your field. At all times, keep an eye out for potential future competitors as well as current ones. Study their strategies and operations, which should provide you with potential threats and opportunities, weaknesses and strengths.

Considering Niche Markets

No product or service can be all things to all people. The more narrowly you can define your target market, the better. This process is known as *creating a niche*. Offering a narrow line of products or services that, by its nature, is directed at fairly narrow niche markets is a better strategy for the new firm than trying to get too big too fast. In this way, a start-up company can often eliminate the need for extensive distribution or sales organization and simplify their marketing process.

Stage 3: Channel Identification, Alliances, and Partnerships

Clearly, unless you can sell your products or services, your company will have no future. Channel identification is the road to early positive cash flow. Getting orders and selling to paying customers is the name of the game. You do this by communicating information about your offering to as many potential customers as possible and then selling it.

When you first start out, it's unlikely that you'll have a large direct sales force. That means you need to use external channels to help get your products or services into the hands of paying customers. One of the most effective ways to leverage the advantages of a channel is to enter into licensing and private-label resale agreements with appropriate organizations. Other means of partnering include joint marketing and promotion, developing relationships with value-added resellers (VARs), and so on. The high-tech industry, in particular, abounds with representatives, distributors, agents, wholesalers, and VARs with well-established customer bases. These organizations actively seek to represent new products/services.

note For a more detailed discussion, see Chapter 8.

Stage 4: Pre-Launch (Market Entry Planning)

By now, you should have a good understanding of what product your customers want, where your customers are, what they're willing to pay, and what you need to do to get them to make the purchase. (Make sure you document all these factors in a marketing plan, discussed in Chapter 8.) Your next step is to launch your product. (The post launch phase of your venture covers the entire time period between the time you cease to be in "start-up mode" and the time you exit the market. That's when you're running your business as a "going concern.")

Before you do, however, you'll want to think long and hard about your pricing strategy. Our best advice is, never price your offering too low. If you take a good look at the top 10 companies in your space, you'll probably find that they are profitable but they're not offering the lowest prices. That's because they have established *value*, a benefits-to-price ratio. This suggests that buyers, when making a purchase decision, select what they consider to be the best value. It further suggests that value is equal to the benefits they perceive divided by the price. Remember, price is only one aspect of the overall purchase-decision process.

There are two ways to increase your customer's perceived value of your offering: by increasing the benefits or decreasing the price. Because you don't want to price your offering too low, however, it's typically prudent to beef up the benefits in your offering. Ultimately, you want to surround your offer with so many benefits of great value that you can command a higher price. Indeed, for a start-up, the only way to high prices is to have an offering that provides both tangible and intangible benefits for which users are willing to pay a premium. It is also a means of gaining market share and becoming profitable at the same time. You can do this by adding new and innovative features to your product to outdo your nearest competitor.

Top Reasons Why Businesses Fail

The majority of small businesses fail within the first few years. Most of these failures, however, resemble one another in important ways. Once you identify this comprehensive nature of failure, you can increase your own chance of success; that's why we've included here the top reasons why businesses fail:

- **Procrastination.** When you are your own boss, you will find that tasks and paperwork pile up on your desk. Putting them off is like piling up debt; eventually, they could overwhelm you.
- **Ignoring the competition.** Consumer loyalty has declined sharply in recent years. Today, customers go where they can find the best products and services, and the best value—even if that means breaking off long-term business relationships. Monitor your competitors, and don't be ashamed to copy their best ideas (without violating the law, of course). Better yet, devote some time to formulating a new business model, products, or services that can give you the edge.
- **Ineffective marketing plan.** Contrary to the popular cliché, few products or services sell themselves. If you don't have time to market your product effectively, hire an experienced person to do it for you. Marketing keeps your products selling and money flowing into your business, which makes your business run. It's crucial that you do it effectively.
- **Ineffective customer service.** Once you attract customers, you'll have to work hard to keep them. Customer service should be a key aspect of your business. If you don't follow through with your customers, they'll find someone who will.

- **The wrong team**: You may be great at making routers or selling computers or programming, but that's not enough to make a business successful. Successful business owners tend to be adept at a number of tasks, from accounting to marketing to hiring. If you lack the versatility, partner with someone who can complement you with his or her expertise.
- **Failing to validate your customers:** This may sound obvious, but too many entrepreneurs assume they know exactly what their customers need without bothering to ask. Take the time to learn about your customers, and build your business plan around their needs and desires.
- **Cash-flow problem.** This is probably the most common problem in businesses, and could turn serious enough to shut you down. You need to know how to track the money coming into and out of your business; even a profitable venture will flounder if it runs short of cash. In addition, you must learn to make cash-flow projections that will help you decide how much money you can afford to spend and warn you of imminent trouble.
- **Closed-mindedness.** Everyone goes into business with some preconceptions, but don't be surprised to find that many of yours are wrong. Look for mentors who can give you advice and will let you run your ideas by them before you make important financial commitments. In addition, you should read books and magazines about small business, visit business-related Web sites, and network with your peers in the business community.
- **Poor planning.** Start with realistic but precise goals for your firm, including deadlines. Create a "check and gate" system by creating a set of milestones. Every time you reach a milestone and before you enter next gate, reevaluate how and what you are doing, and whether you are in tune with your business plan (discussed in the next section). Certain things you have planned for or market conditions may have changed; be ready with an alternate plan or resolution for a new challenge. Don't just say that you want to increase sales; instead, decide that you want sales to reach *x* amount by next year. Then write down the steps you can take to meet those goals on time, and set deadlines for completing those steps. Consult your goal list every day, and make sure you are doing what you need to do to meet your objectives.
- **Mixing personal and professional issues.** Failing to keep personal and professional issues separate can really take a toll on your business, and can cause a great amount of confusion in day-to-day operations (thereby affecting the growth of your business).

The Business Plan

The business plan is the ultimate tool for communication and marketing to all stakeholders, including strategic partners and investors, in a new venture. In fact, a well-written, detailed business plan that answers many questions up-front can go a long way in convincing investors to back you. The business plan must be a well-thought-out, universal document, and should describe the business you are undertaking and how you plan to execute it. The business plan must articulate the strengths of the business, as well as your long-term goals for the business. It also must, however, clearly outline the risks associated with the venture, while painting a picture of the pot of gold at the end. The business plan should stress business and financial aspects versus technical details, and should address the information needs of all stakeholders. There must be a smooth transition from the big-picture vision to the steps that are necessary in starting and growing the business.

note A key success factor in all new ventures is the management team. With a clearly outlined business plan, which outlines your approach to solving a problem in the marketplace, you will be able to attract a good management team whose skills meet the needs of your business; in turn, that will improve your odds of successfully executing your plan. In addition, the process of creating a business plan allows the key members of the management team to reach consensus, allowing you to define a common agenda that everyone can agree on and then be fully committed to.

For you, the entrepreneur, however, the business plan is much more than a communications and marketing tool. It should help you evaluate the complexity of your undertaking and build your commitment to the venture. By diligently putting together a business plan, you will have a clear sense of the challenges that lie ahead and the resources you will need to meet them. A business plan also provides clear evidence of the viability of your venture. Indeed, for entrepreneurs, the greatest value derived from a business plan is in its development. This is an excellent example of a situation in which the journey is more critical than the end result.

The key parameter for judging the viability and quality of a business plan is your ability to use this document to hire employees (co-founders), gain buy-in from your alpha customers, and most importantly, negotiate an investment in your company from a potential investor who is not a friend or family member (who tend to invest in you rather than your business).

This section discusses the use of the business plan as an important tool to define concepts, recruit stakeholders, refine ideas, and develop strategy—in other words, from value creation to value extraction. You'll also find some easy-to-use tools to help clarify your ideas and begin the development of your business plan.

The Key Ingredients of a Good Business Plan

Business plans are dynamic in nature. They are living documents that will need constant modification as you develop a clearer focus and continuously reevaluate your strategy. They are also living documents in the sense that they communicate your enthusiasm. The business plan must tell a story that compels action and one that the audience can clearly understand and get excited about. It must paint a picture that can be easily visualized. At the same time, it must be crisply written, from cover to cover, so that it is easy to read. Avoid flash. Write in a professional manner. Make your business plan a forthright account of your thoughts. Your enthusiasm as conveyed by the plan, the quality and depth of your thinking, and its professional presentation will ensure that your business plan stands out from the pack.

More specifically, your business plan should contain the following components:

- The business definition
- The mission statement
- Market and environment information
- Strategy information
- An overview of the technology/product
- Financial information

First, however, you should include an executive summary, discussed next.

The Executive Summary

The executive summary, the first part of your business plan, is a key element of the document. Think of it as the carrot that will keep potential stakeholders reading. It must be crisp and concise, must summarize all the key sections of the business plan, and must convey a clear, powerful message. Specifically, the executive summary should include the following:

- Business description
- Information about the management team
- Information about your market and your sales strategy
- An assessment of your competition
- Financials and funding information

Business Description

This is the first and most important section in the executive summary. The goal here is to clearly portray the company's business objectives. Precisely describe the product you intend to build or the service you intend to offer. Explain the differentiators between your offering and those of your competitors, and highlight what important customer need you are satisfying. Provide additional details about the customer pain point you intend to address. The most basic arguments in your executive summary are your value proposition, and how your offering is different from what's currently on the market.

Management Team

The focus in this section should be on the background of the key members of the management team. It's critical to emphasize three main points here:

- Describe what past experience (i.e. domain expertise) do particular members of the team have that makes them the right fit for this venture.
- Explain how the team as a whole forms a well-rounded unit with complementary skills to handle the various challenges.
- Describe the team's past successes in new ventures, and how those experiences have prepared them for this venture. This information is often the most convincing argument you can make. Nothing inspires more confidence than a team that has a track record of building successful companies.

Market and Sales Strategy

The first step in defining your market in your business plan is to clearly define who your customer is. Be as specific as possible! For example, an enterprise software company might be focused on large financial-services companies. After you've clearly identified your customer, it is significantly easier to correctly estimate your market size. Make sure, however, that the estimated size of the market is based on the customer that is identified. For example, the market size for a wireless LAN service provider focusing on the consumer market is not the entire wireless LAN market; using that market would lead to an artificially large figure. The relevant market in this case is the *consumer* wireless LAN service market.

After you have clearly described the customer and the market size, shift your focus to outlining specifics such as the sales strategy, economic arguments for the sale, and why the decision maker would find the product attractive. The sales strategy should include elements such as the necessary sales channels and partnerships, and the number of people you will need to execute the strategy. The more specific this strategy, the better; that way, your audience will be able to visualize the process. In today's tougher economic times, the ROI or other economic rationale is critical because customers have significantly restricted budgets.

note This argument must be believable. If you have to stretch to make the argument, then you have a weak case.

Competition

If you claim in your business plan that you have no competitors, then you are signaling one of two things: that you are going after a market that is not attractive, or that you haven't done your homework. Don't think that having competitors is a bad thing; it can indicate a thriving industry. Once you have identified your competitors, describe in your business plan your company's strengths and weaknesses relative to those of your competitors. Outline how you intend to address the weaknesses, and why you believe you will be successful. The critical point is to articulate your sustainable competitive advantage. Additionally, specify any industry or regulatory issues that could change the competitive dynamics.

Financials and Funding

The financial section of your business plan should outline how much capital you need to raise, how you will use the proceeds, when you expect to be profitable, and how you intend to finance your business. The amount you need to raise should be based on your sales strategy, hiring plans, capital expenditures, and expected timing of customer traction. Make realistic assumptions; most often, entrepreneurs develop financial projections that have, for example, no connection to the sales strategy, and that have grossly exaggerated revenues and profitability. This leads the person reading the plan to believe you don't understand the business or simply aren't credible.

Once you've hammered down the executive summary, you can focus on the other aspects of your business plan, discussed next.

The Business Definition

As an entrepreneur, one of the things you should be prepared for is how to respond to the one question that you will be asked several times a day. Whether a potential hire or a prospective investor, your janitor, or your recruitment agency, everyone wants to know "What is it you do exactly?" You may have anywhere from 30 seconds (when answering your investor) to several minutes (when answering your janitor) to get the idea across without limiting the scope of your business. And, of course, the response you're looking for when you complete your monologue is "OK, I get it!" rather than some distant, confused look. Think of this as your 10-second spot during the Super Bowl, with millions of viewers dying to get back to the game and several other advertisers behind you waiting to make their pitch.

If blowing millions of dollars by not getting your message across during the Super Bowl doesn't scare you, try imagining yourself in an elevator with your dream venture capitalist. These are busy people, who are eager to shut off their receptors as soon as they conclude that the pitch doesn't interest them. In those crucial 10 seconds, before that elevator reaches its destination, your only means of sparking their interest in you and your organization is your elevator pitch.

Although its importance seems obvious, many entrepreneurs do not spend enough time properly defining their business or developing that crucial elevator pitch. Too often, entrepreneurs are vaguely certain that they will carry it off whenever they are posed with the inevitable question. They don't encapsulate a message that is

- Easily understood and not grandiose or flowery. Describe your business in here-and-now terms.
- Helpful in providing the right cues to the listener's thought process.
- Simple and consistent.

By honing your elevator pitch, you stand to reap many benefits, including the following:

- It's easier for your partners to bring you value if they understand what you do. For example, getting the right message across to your recruitment company can cut down your hiring cycles by enabling your recruiters to deliver only the 100 percent–fit candidates.
- Your story will stay longer in people's minds if they understand it better, and therefore will have a better chance of reaching potential investors, customers, and partners through circuitous means.
- In advertising, the first five seconds determine whether the viewer hits the remote. Likewise, a well-defined business description helps ensure your listener stays tuned in.

Classifying Your Company

The natural tendency of your listener is to classify your company in a familiar slot, and that slot depends on your message. That's why you should keep the following two points in mind:

- **Who are your customers?** Defining your customers up front is a great reference point to describe what service or product you'll provide to them. Be specific.
- **What are you planning to sell?** Is it a service or a product? Is it a component, a system, appliance, sub-system, platform, device, or tool?

Communicating the Value Proposition

- If your business delivers cheaper products to the market faster, you should quantify the degree of difference you achieve against your competition.
- If your product or service is for the brave new world, the value proposition needn't focus on the degree of improvement but rather on how it empowers your customers and what problems it solves for them.

Here's an example of an effective value proposition:

> Acme Software is a solution for the industrial and occupational training industry. Our software provides trainers with capabilities to integrate digital content into an interactive diagram-based system to accelerate understanding of complex information.

The Mission Statement

The *mission statement*, also called a *vision statement*, reflects the long-term aspirations of your organization. As its founder, you are putting down on paper what you would like to see this venture achieve in its ability to serve customers, attract and retain employees, and reward investors. An effective mission statement must resonate with all stakeholders as well as customers. It must express the organization's purpose in a way that inspires commitment, motivation, and confidence.

The mission statement of an organization, as formulated by the founder or founding team, allows succeeding managements to develop strategic plans to realize the vision you establish. It is important to realize, however, that unlike business strategies that may change over time due to the vagaries of the environment or because of competitive forces, mission statements should be written so they remain relevant over a much longer timeframe. For example, a company's mission statement may read "Acme will be the leader in developing and marketing communications solutions." A *strategy*, on the other hand, might state "Acme will develop the fastest and most efficient communications router for the WAN market."

A good mission statement must answer the following:

- **What needs does the organization address?** In other words, what is its "raison d'être"?
- **Where would you like to see the organization go?** Is it the organization's aim to become the largest, the best, or the most respected in a particular sector? What are the major organizational goals in the next three-to-five years?
- **What principles guide the organization?** What value system will the organization follow to reach its goal? Is there a singular guiding principle that will drive the growth of the organization?
- **Who does the organization value most?** Its customers, employees, or the shareholders?

In addition, the writing style for your mission statement should be

- Convincing, and should convey honesty
- Succinct and in the active voice
- Free of jargon
- Concise, so that anyone connected to the organization can readily repeat it

The Market and the Environment

note Developing a marketing plan is discussed in detail in Chapter 8. Here we simply list a few key points that relate to the creation of a business plan.

Market Definition

When defining your market in your business plan, keep these key points in mind:

- Define the market you are addressing very clearly. Not being sufficiently focused in a small but definable market segment is better than being able to make a case for a small slice of a larger but loosely defined market.
- Say how big a need there is for what you want to sell or do. Be clear that you are not a solution looking for a problem.
- Explain how and why the prospective customer's pain is not eased by products or services already available.
- Establish why there will be a continuing and growing need for your product or service, and explain how this growth will occur (i.e. growth rate and time horizon).
- Say how you plan to be a leader (20–40 percent) in a well-defined segment rather than settling for a small share (e.g. 1 percent) of a big market that is loosely defined. (Avoid market definitions used in the popular press.)

The Environment

To describe in your business plan the macroeconomic environment in which your business will operate, use Porter's 5-Forces Model. This model attempts to assess how the suppliers, customers, competitors, and substitute products in a given industry are likely to interact. The main reason for this kind of analysis is to paint a picture for yourself about sources of potential and existing competitive advantages and barriers to entry that you will need to be overcome, as well as potential threats. You should

- Describe suppliers to your industry and how they operate.
- Describe the competition in terms of current competition and potential threats.
- Describe the developers of products or solutions that could substitute for your offering, even if not directly competing with yours.
- Describe the market (customers and channels) with respect to their power vis-à-vis your industry.

In addition to the Porter analysis, try to describe the stages of the Industry Life Cycle (in your industry), and describe where you are in it.

Market Analysis

Complete the following exercise to aid in analyzing the market for your offering

Scope Analysis: Who Is Your Target Market?

Provide a detailed description of your idea for your product or service

- What will this idea be used for? ______________________________
  ____
- Where are similar products/services utilized? __________________
  ____
- Where do your prospects go to acquire this product or service? ________
  ____
- What do your prospects spend on this type of offering? ____________
  ____
- What demographics do your prospects belong to? ______________
  ____

This exercise will help you put yourself in your customer's shoes, better understand their habits, and identify emerging trends and patterns. It will eventually help you create your business vision and mission, and assess who your customer is.

- Develop a market-segmentation matrix based on identifiable customer characteristics: demographic, size, type of needs with relation to the product/service offered, location, culture, and so on.
- Discuss your rationale for your view of the market.
- Talk about other market characteristics including attrition rate, dislocation rate, and sales-cycle time.

Competitive Analysis

When performing a competitive analysis for inclusion in your business plan, answer the following:

- Who are the competitors in the marketplace?
- How are they doing?
- What are their strengths and weaknesses?
- How will you position your offering against competition?
- Why will customers buy your offering rather than that of your competitors?

Chances are, any business you start will have competition. Therefore, you must take into consideration what you will be able to offer your customer that provides a significant advantage over your competitors' offerings. Whether it's faster service, better selection, lower prices, better quality, or anything else that potential customers really care about, you should stress this advantage in your sales and marketing communications strategies at the onset.

Market Risk Summary

It's imperative that you include market-risk information in your business plan, including the answers to the following questions:

- Will your company be a leader in its space?
- Is there a high barrier to entry/strong competitive advantage?

In addition, you should discuss issues such as the inertia of the installed base and changes in consumer behavior in this section of your business plan.

Strategy

To identify your strategy in the context of your business report, you'll want to include information about the following:

- Value proposition
- Value creation
- Value spread
- Value capture and extraction (the "go to market" strategy)

Value Proposition

Developing a strong value proposition requires a step-by-step approach that identifies who your constituents, users, or customers are and from where the dominant money is coming. Start with a broad stroke and then narrow it down until you have a clear picture and sharp market-focus:

- Identify the burning problem, the pain: Find the predominant emotion associated with the big problem.
- Write down the company's tag line.
- Put the market definition together: What do you really do? What is your offering and what are its benefits?

Value Creation

- Describe how your offering creates value for the customer. ("Will the dogs eat the dog food?")
- Will the technology/innovation be adopted?
- How does the technology map to current customer behavior?
- Will the product/technology be able to displace current players and new competitive offerings, offering alternative approaches to solving "the problem"?

- What are your company's sources or potential sources of competitive advantage?

Value Spread

- Based on the market segmentation, which customer cluster receives the greatest benefits?
- How can each customer cluster be accessed?
- What is the marginal cost associated with new-customer acquisition?

Value Capture and Extraction: The "Go to Market" Strategy

- How do I plan to enter and penetrate the market?
- What techniques will I employ to access customers and reduce customer-acquisition costs?
- How will I build barriers to entry or raise the bar for new entrants?
- How do I plan to promote my product and increase the customer base?
- How do I plan to price to different customer clusters?

Technology/Product Overview

It is extremely important to be able to communicate the value created by developing or assembling a new product or service offering in the marketplace. This section of your business plan should describe in elegant simplicity how, through an innovative method of assembly or a groundbreaking new invention, this value has been created. Technologists turned entrepreneurs love to write this section in a business plan; the challenge is being able to link this section clearly with the rest of the plan. To do so, consider these points:

- The objective of describing the product and technology is to explain to the uninitiated how what you propose helps make things better.
- Using block diagrams and schemas or flow charts in this section is a good idea, because very often a pictorial frame can map out visually the cleverness of your invention or innovation.
- It is important to use this section to demonstrate how you plan to further develop the idea or invention to create products or services for which, at this point, you have only a vision.

This section of the business plan should be restricted to about two or three pages of text with no more than two or three paragraphs covering the following points:

- **Product architecture.** Describe the product or system in detail, including diagrams, schemas, and block illustrations as needed to explain concepts, and a summary of patents and key intellectual properties.

- **Product-development road map.** Describe the roll-out of future products including how the learning curve will enable you to build the next product better than the competition, and briefly design the rationale for the next phase of product roll outs (include risks).
- **Technology/competency review.** Describe key patents, copyrights, trademarks, and so on, as well as unique know-how and team competencies, and discuss you IP strategy to protect key assets.

Financials

The final part of your business planning should focus on financial planning. This section touches on the three financial statements no business can do without:

- **The income statement.** The company's performance during a period.
- **The cash-flow statement.** Reports the company's cash movement during the period, categorized by operating, investing, and financing activities.
- **The balance sheet.** Portrays what the company owns and what it owes at the report date.

Familiarity with these statements is critical to any entrepreneur, and gaining this familiarity early rather than later is strongly advised.

The Income Statement

A sample income statement for a start-up in a planning stage should broadly look as shown here. This format is ideally suited to a planning stage, and serves as a common language for the entrepreneur and potential investors.

Sample Income Statement [$ Million]

	Q1	*Q2*	*Q3*	*Q4*	*Year 2*	*Year 3*	*Year 4*	*Year 5*
Units Shipped '00/ Market Share	0	0	0	0	3	9	21	47
Income	0	0	0	0	5	12	35	70
Gross Profit/Loss	0	0	0	0	1.25	3	8	15
Gross Margin	0	0	0	0	3.75	9	27	45
Operating Expense								
R&D	5	6	7	10	15	17	15	15
SG&A	2	2	3	5	10	15	17	18
Net Profit/Loss	(7)	(8)	(10)	(15)	(21.25)	(23)	5	12
Head Count								
Engineering	15	20	25	35	35	35	35	35
SG&A	2	2	4	8	12	15	15	15

When drawing up your income statement, keep the following in mind:

- Investors want to understand the business potential over a three-to-five-year period. There are two approaches you can follow when forecasting revenues: a bottom-up approach, which takes into account any visible sales contract or a customer-wise revenue potential; or a top-down approach, which forecasts a total available market and predicts a market share, an average selling price (ASP), and revenue.

note Generally, it is acceptable to provide a detailed first-year quarterly projection, and use a top-down revenue number from the second year onward. Similarly, the income statement provides a detailed cost breakdown for the first year or until a milestone is reached. For subsequent periods, a less-detailed approach is acceptable. The details (without getting lost in them) are also a good indicator of the depth you have gone into in thinking up the business.

- The business will be attractive to investors only if there is a potential for extraordinary growth. The quantifiable opportunity to capitalize on this growth must be captured by the projections made in the income statement. A careful definition of the addressable market is required because the revenue growth rates usually follow the market growth rates. It is common to find growth rates in the 100–200-percent range in the initial years, as depicted by the well-known hockey-stick growth chart. Acceptance of these growth rates is determined by various factors, such as the viewer's level of optimism and general market conditions. The entrepreneur, however, must back these numbers up, who must have convincing arguments, especially during economically downward cycles. Conservative estimates are always easier to back, and typically reflect the entrepreneur's maturity, but have the downside of perhaps not being found attractive enough by investors.
- The income and cost projections lead to the gross margins, which is of utmost strategic importance from a business-feasibility angle. *Gross margin* is the excess of sales over cost of sales, and represents the value add of any business; indeed, without a strong gross margin, you don't have a compelling business offering. Indicative gross margin for a software company is in the range of 98 percent, and about 40–50 percent for any other start-up.
- By including average head count in this statement, a complete picture can be presented; people cost is a critical element in the early years of a start-up.

- Multiple years of operational loss are no longer in fashion. Conventional business sense of financially sound operations generating cash within a reasonable time frame stands the vagaries of business cycles.

The Cash-Flow Statement

The second-most important statement for an entrepreneur is the cash-flow statement. A well-written cash-flow plan can efficiently indicate the vital signs of your business. Your business can survive without cash for a short while, but it will need to be liquid to pay the bills. A cash-flow statement, usually constructed quarterly or even monthly for the initial years and annually for subsequent years, compares your cash position at the end of the time period to the position at the start, and the constant flow of money into and out of the business over the course of that period. Simply put, this statement establishes whether your business is eating up cash or generating cash.

A cash-flow statement deals only with the money circulating in the business. Expenditures such as stock, raw materials, machinery, tax and salaries, and repayments on overdrafts and bank loans eats up cash.

A start-up requires high doses of cash inflows through investment activities to counter the high "gross cash burn" during initial periods of zero or minimal sales. During this period, most start-ups do not have significant working capital considerations, and it is generally acceptable to ignore working capital changes until the first commercial shipment takes place.

When planning cash flow, keep the following in mind:

- **Plan well for your cash needs.** You don't get many chances to go out and raise cash. It is equally harmful to plan to raise significantly higher cash than your actual needs as it is to plan too tightly. That said, it is near impossible to get the cash requirements absolutely right; it is always safer to raise a few months' worth of extra cash—especially in an uncertain fundraising environment.
- **Cash is king.** Push out any unnecessary items and budget for them only when they are absolutely necessary. For example, don't budget for a VP in sales if you are still 12 months away from lab trials.
- **Timing is everything.** Every investor in a start-up is keen to know when the cash burn will stop—i.e., when the business turns cash-flow positive. Make sure that the cash flow ties in with next financing events as well as the cash flow–positive position.

The Balance Sheet

A balance sheet is useful because it provides information about how much capital is used in the business, how liquid the assets are, and a breakdown of how the business is financed. Not all your financing needs will be met by equity, so the quality of your balance sheet will also likely affect your banker's decision.

The important aspects of a balance sheet are as follows:

- Preparing an opening-day balance sheet
- Undertaking a close study of the asset needs of the business
- Discussing lease versus buy options and the implications of such decisions on your cash-flow position

tip Use notes to explain any assumptions underlying your financial projections. If the projections are based on market estimates made by an independent research group, mention the source. Discuss assumptions related to costs, and mention any third-party data being used. For example, mask costs provided by a fab partner over the next five years affecting the cost of per chip. Also explain some of the risk factors associated with the assumptions such as market uptake slower than expected can lead to projections not being met.

Top Business-Planning Slip-Ups

As you develop your business plan, it's easy to make mistakes or leave out important elements. Here are a few of the most common business-planning pitfalls, and some tips on how to avoid them:

- **Lacking a vision.** You are very excited and it's tempting to roll up your sleeves and jump right into the details of your business: evaluating products, studying market segments, and sizing up your competition. Yet it's possible to get so caught up in the process of planning a business that you lose sight of what you're planning for. Before you get lost in the details, take a step back. Outline a clear vision and articulate your thoughts. Develop a mission statement and use it to define short-term goals. Once you have a clear road map for your business, your journey will be smoother and it will give you more confidence.
- **Failing to solicit opinions.** The most experienced entrepreneur can still benefit from a different point of view and have a fresh look. Even if you're the only person involved in your business, ask someone who can study your plan objectively and point out possible weaknesses you might have overlooked.
- **Bypassing the business plan.** The biggest mistake of all is failing to create a business plan in the first place. Planning is hard work, and there's no guarantee it will make your business succeed. But a good business plan is still the best way to transfer your vision into a realistic, tangible business.
- **Creating an unrealistic budget.** You can't create a solid business plan without a budget and a financial forecast, but a budget should be the product of all the other elements in your plan. If you don't have a clear picture of your industry, customers, competitors, and market conditions *before* you develop a budget, your numbers aren't likely to reflect reality.
- **Failing to get market validation.** Validating the company and product position in priority target markets is one of the most important activities a company can do. It

saves time and valuable development and marketing resources by testing a product concept, an idea, a position, and customer-buying drivers before a product is launched or engineered. Market validation can be done by large companies exploring a new market or product line as well as by start-up companies that may be looking for funding or introducing their first product. This is an in depth and intense process that involves determining a position and priority market/buyer segments to test, creating a database of target customers, and contacting high-level decision makers for one-on-one interviews. The results provide valuable insights that enable a company to better define a unique position and test buyer requirements and reaction *before* a product is built and introduced. Market validation is usually done along with a marketing strategy, to take the client through market and position development.

- **Failing to validate your customers.** This may sound obvious, but too many entrepreneurs assume they know exactly what their customers need without bothering to ask. Take the time to learn about your customers, and build your business plan around their needs and desires.
- **Failing to identify what makes you different.** A cookie-cutter business plan might help you get started, but it won't help you succeed. And although it's helpful to look at your competitors, you shouldn't model your business after theirs. After all, you're in business to beat the competition. Learn from your competitors' strengths, but also learn how to spot their weaknesses and use them to improve your own business plan. You can have the same product as your competitors' but having a different business model can give you the edge in the marketplace.
- **Underestimating the competition.** You're asking for trouble if you assume your firm will be the only game in town, or if you fail to take existing competitors seriously. Instead, use your competitors as a great source of information about what works and what doesn't.
- **Overlooking the risks.** Creating a business plan isn't about avoiding risk; it's about minimizing and managing risk. That's why a good business plan anticipates possible challenges and includes a variety of scenarios for meeting those challenges. There's a difference between a calculated risk and recklessness, and your business plan can help you make that distinction.
- **Not expecting the unexpected.** Every business plan must have room to allow for unexpected changes. Part of this involves creating budgets and marketing plans with some built-in flexibility; but adapting to change also requires you to accept that you might have to modify or even abandon business practices that worked well in the past.
- **Not identifying your reward.** Be clear on what it is that you want to get out of this venture. Building a business involves hard work and struggle, but it should also include a clear set of rewards, both for you and your employees. When you set goals in your business plan, include some concrete motivation that goes beyond the satisfaction of a job well done.

three 3

CHAPTER

Legal Matters

Co-Chair: Raj Judge - **Wilson Sonsini Goodrich & Rosati**
Co-Chair: Anita Vasudevan - **Venture Law Group**
Co-Chair: Curtis Mo - **Brobeck, Phleger & Harrison LLP**
Lisa Waits - **Brobeck, Phleger & Harrison LLP**
Samir Bukhari -**Wilson Sonsini Goodrich & Rosati**
Naren Chaganti - **Chaganti & Associates Law Firm**
Alex Chen - **Brobeck, Phleger & Harrison LLP**
John Fogg - **Gray Cary Ware & Freidenrich, LLP**
Greg Gallo - **Gray Cary Ware & Freidenrich, LLP**
Nita J. Itchhaporia - **Itchhaporia Law Firm**
Tina M. Singh - **Bay Venture Counsel, LLP**
Craig W. Johnson - **Venture Law Group**
Ritu Tariyal- **Wilson Sonsini Goodrich & Rosati**

We've all heard lawyer jokes, and everybody laughs at punch lines that lampoon stuffy corporate attorneys, ambulance-chasers, and "do anything for a buck" stereotypes. But the real last laugh comes when you, the entrepreneur, team up with a trusted attorney who will help you structure your company on a firm legal foundation, which is an important ingredient to your ongoing success. Playing a critical role throughout a company's life cycle, attorneys can make the first vital contributions in the early stages, when they work closely with the entrepreneur to prepare for funding as well as for life *after* funding.

Indeed, seasoned attorneys representing early-stage companies provide more than just legal advice. They often also review business plans, introduce companies to venture capitalists and other strategic partners, and provide referrals to other service professionals. Attorneys are your insurance: Without their expert advice in how to properly structure your company and operate it as it grows rapidly, you risk losing everything.

The most obvious safeguard attorneys provide is against illegalities. Equally important to the entrepreneur, however, is that attorneys can make sure that all the necessary procedures and structures are in place to help make your company more attractive to investors. Put simply, they help ensure your company will be fundable down the line. Don't cut corners here; if you don't properly structure your company, and if you aren't in a position to properly operate it as it grows rapidly, you risk everything. Early-stage errors often profoundly affect later events in a company's life cycle, such as an IPO or acquisition. Entrepreneurs and the early management team must work closely with an attorney-advisor from the outset. That makes this chapter critical reading!

Focusing on providing guidance for early-stage companies, from establishing the structure through the first round of venture financing, this chapter looks at the most fundamental legal issues entrepreneurs face when starting a company. We'll discuss formation and governance, developing and protecting intellectual property, employment and equity compensation issues, compliance with immigration rules, and planning and documenting angel and venture-capital financings.

note Each of these topics is linked closely to the other, and as such they must all work in synch. Failure to execute properly in one area may well result in adverse consequences in other areas. For example, if you set up an LLC rather than a C-corporation, you may find it more difficult to attract the best employees because of the inability to issue incentive stock options in that form of entity.

Once your company is formed, you must build value by developing and protecting the intellectual property (IP). Because nothing scares away potential investors faster than doubts about a company's IP ownership, you must consult a knowledgeable intellectual-property attorney to develop an IP strategy and deal with IP issues at various stages in your company's life cycle. In this chapter, we'll discuss the various forms of intellectual-property protection and the major intellectual-property issues your company will face.

Then, this chapter gets to your most important assets: your employees. Entrepreneurs must worry about both attracting new employees and retaining existing ones. Think "stock options;" that's the currency high-tech employees use to evaluate jobs. We'll explain them and get into the immigration and employment laws that also affect your business. Finally, with the appropriate structures in place, we get you to the money—specifically, venture-capital funding. Attorneys play a critical role in advising companies on financing options and terms. In this section, we'll tell you about the different type of investors and how to judge investment terms.

Formation and Governance of Start-Ups

What Legal Entity Should I Choose?

A first step in setting the stage for funding is choosing an entity that will facilitate the business, tax, and capital-raising objectives of the company. The entrepreneur is faced with a daunting array of entities when determining how to structure the company; C-corporations, S-corporations, and limited-liability companies represent a few common choices.

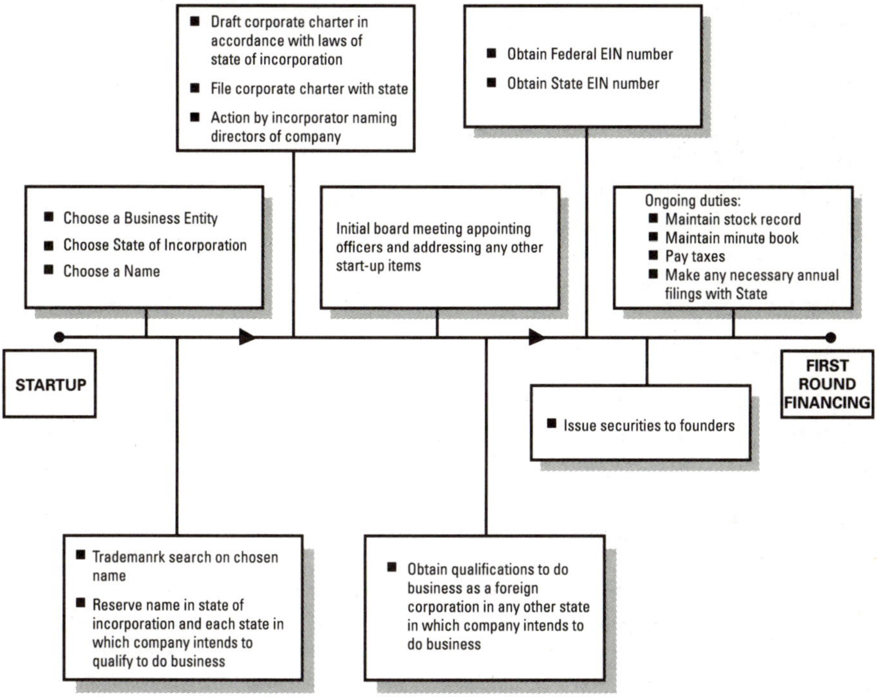

C-Corporations

For most companies seeking a traditional first round of venture capital, the list of relevant types of corporations quickly narrows to one: the C-corporation. Indeed, a *C-corporation* is the most common form of corporate structure for venture-funded companies. This type of corporation is favored by venture investors because the owners of C-corporations—that is, the stockholders—have limited liability for the debts and liabilities of the corporation, and are not subject to the numerous eligibility restrictions applicable to other business structures.

Pros and Cons of C-Corporations

Pros	Cons
The C-corporation allows for various classes of stock, such as common stock and preferred stock. In addition, investors in a C-corporation can purchase *convertible preferred stock*, which is the most common form of venture investment.	Corporate formalities (such as having regular board meetings) are required and are relatively expensive compared to other business forms.
The law relating to C-corporations is comparatively stable and well developed. Because venture investors often take a seat on the company's board after they've invested, they like to be in a familiar environment—one in which they understand the scope of their legal duties to the corporation and its shareholders and the indemnification protections available to them under applicable law.	Stockholders in C-corporations endure double taxation, because profits are taxed first at the corporate level and then again when distributed to stockholders.
C-corporations have centralized management.	
C-corporations are legal entities; they exist, and continue to exist, separate from the individuals or groups that formed the corporation.	

S-Corporations

An *S-corporation* is a form of corporation that has the distinguishing attribute of a partnership—namely, a corporation in which profits and losses pass through to the corporation's shareholders without first being taxed at the corporate level.

Pros and Cons of S-Corporations

Pros	Cons
"Flow-through" taxation addresses the major disadvantage of the double taxation that occurs with C-corporations.	S-corporations are unable to issue separate classes of stock, which is a key element of venture financings.
	The shareholders of S-corporations may only consist of individuals, undercutting the possibility of investment by institutional venture funds.

Limited-Liability Companies

A *limited-liability company*, or *LLC*, is a form of business organization that combines some of the beneficial attributes of partnerships and corporations, but that also has significant drawbacks in the context of venture financings.

Pros and Cons of LLCs

Pros	Cons
Like partnerships, LLCs are only taxed once, as profits flow through the organization to the members.	LLCs as a form of business organization are relatively new, and the law surrounding LLCs is not as developed as the law of C-corporations. Investors may be, therefore, less comfortable with investing in LLCs.
Like a C-corporation, an LLC is characterized by limited liability, so that individual members will not be personally liable for the entity's debts.	

note It's important to note that both LLCs and S-corporations may be appropriate choices for some companies. That's why you need to seek the counsel of tax and legal experts first. It's easier (and cheaper in the long run) to do things right from the beginning, rather than try to correct a situation later.

What's in a Name?

Entrepreneurs are so intensely focused on the complexities of building a business that important issues surrounding what appear to be simple tasks—such as choosing and reserving a name—are often taken for granted. Investing a small amount of time to carefully choose and reserve a name will yield returns in the form of mitigated business and legal risks. From a business perspective, the company's name or brand can be central to business strategy and product marketing and, accordingly, must be secure from the beginning. From a legal standpoint, a poorly selected name can expose the corporation to a range of legal liability.

Two equally important elements go into choosing and reserving your company's name. First, you must ensure that the name is available, and second, that you're not infringing on any trademarks.

Choose and Reserve a Name with the Secretary of State

The first step involves determining whether the name is being used by or has been reserved by another company. A corporate-services firm such as CT Corporation can inquire with the Secretary of State in the state where the corporation will be formed as to whether the name is available in that state and in any other state where you plan to do business. The cost for the search and reservation is approximately $150.

Pay Attention to Trademark Issues

Reserving a name does not grant trademark rights or authorize a company to use a particular business name in commercial activities. The risk for a newly formed corporation is that its name will infringe upon the trademark rights of another entity and expose the corporation to a lawsuit alleging trademark or trade-name infringement. Before reserving the name, make sure that the name is clear through a series of basic trademark searches, with which a law firm can assist you for a small fee.

Secure the Domain Name

In addition to ensuring that the name is available and does not infringe on any trademarks, you'll also want to secure a domain name—preferably the same as your company's name or trademark—for your company's website. Check into the availability of a domain name early, because doing so often eliminates certain choices for company names and trademarks.

Where Should I Incorporate?

The majority of venture-backed companies are incorporated in a handful of states such as California or Delaware. That's because relative to other states, California and Delaware have corporate laws that are well developed, stable, and transparent, all characteristics that ultimately reduce the risk to investors. Moreover, because venture capitalists and their counsel are familiar with conducting financings under such laws, the speed and efficiency with which a transaction moves will likely be accelerated.

In deciding where to incorporate your company, you must weigh these considerations:

- First equity financing
- Daily operations thereafter
- Long-term goals

Delaware is the state of choice for most companies, because of the relative stability of its corporate law. Over the years, the Delaware court system has provided a large body of legal decisions that clarify and interpret the Delaware corporate statutes. Moreover, the Delaware court system and administrative infrastructure is highly advanced and is capable of rapidly responding to the demands of businesses incorporated in that state. Court systems in other jurisdictions may not be organized to deal as efficiently with corporate matters. From an investor's perspective, this amounts to an additional investment risk. Rest assured, investors are already wary enough. There's no point in handing them another argument as to why they shouldn't invest in your company.

The following table highlights certain differences that should be considered when choosing between Delaware and other jurisdictions.

Delaware Versus Other Jurisdictions

	Delaware	*Other Jurisdictions*
Signatures	Permits faxed and electronic signature by any authorized officer for filings.	May require receipt by the state of original signature by the incorporator or, in the case of amendment or restatement of the Articles, by certain specific officers.
Review of filings	Filings are reviewed and accepted upon submission.	Filings may be reviewed before acceptance.
Names	The name of a business may not be *exactly* the same as the name of another corporation existing in Delaware.	May have a stricter requirement that the name of a business cannot be *similar* to the name of another corporation existing in the state without the consent of the other corporation.
Number of directors	Permits a statement in the bylaws that the board of directors shall determine the number of directors.	May require the number of directors, or a minimum and maximum, to be set forth in the bylaws.
Anti-takeover measures	Permits a corporation to adopt measures to protect a corporation from a takeover attempt.	May permit some measures, though there is probably less judicial guidance as to legality of various defensive measures than in Delaware.
Size of the board of directors	Permits the board alone to change the authorized number of directors.	May require majority shareholder approval of changes regarding number of directors.
Loans to officers and employees	A corporation may make loans to, guaranty the obligations of, or otherwise assist its officers or other employees when such action, in the judgment of the directors, may reasonably be expected to benefit the corporation.	A corporation may make loans to, x ability of a corporation to make a loan or guaranty to or for the benefit of a director or officer without shareholder approval.
Indemnification and limitation of liability	The law of indemnification is generally favorable to directors and is well understood.	Other jurisdictions may have similar indemnification provisions, but in all probability, these provisions will not have been as thoroughly adjudicated, and therefore will not be as well understood, as Delaware indemnification provisions.

note Regardless of where you choose to incorporate, the states in which you conduct significant business and operations may have jurisdiction over some of your activities. Your attorney can explain to you in greater detail the impact of statutes such as Section 2115 of the California Corporations Code, which governs certain activities of companies that conduct business in California but are incorporated elsewhere.

What Is the Corporate Charter For?

A company's charter document lays out basic information about the corporation. It is filed with the Secretary of State of the company's state of incorporation, and contains basic corporate information for the entity such as its name, address, and business purpose. There are only minimal legal requirements as to what must be included in the corporate charter.

Function and Content of the Corporate Charter

The corporate charter (referred to in some states as the *certificate of incorporation* and in others as *articles of incorporation*) is a public document that amounts to a contract between the incorporators and the state. It's not usually a very big document. The initial charter may be only a page or two long and cover the few basic items required by the corporate code, such as the corporation's name, its address, the nature of its business (all you really need to state is that the purpose of the business is to engage in any lawful activity), and a description of the type of stock the corporation is permitted to issue.

Filing the Certificate

Once the certificate of incorporation has been drafted to the satisfaction of the founders and the signature of the incorporator has been obtained, the document is ready to be filed with the relevant Secretary of State.

Amendment to Certificate of Incorporation

As your company matures, your certificate will grow too. With each new financing or other corporate transaction, you will need to file amendments. For example, the certificate of incorporation gives a snapshot of the company's capital structure. In order to change any detail of the snapshot—say, to change the authorized number or shares of common stock—the company must file an amendment showing the changed provision or file an entire amended and restated certificate with the Secretary of State. Remember that the certificate of incorporation may not be changed without the approval of the board and stockholders.

Why Does My Company Need Bylaws?

While a company's certificate of incorporation is a public document filed with the state upon incorporation or amendment, the *bylaws* of the corporation are for internal use only and set forth most of the details regarding governance rules of the corporation. Simply put, bylaws set forth the company's internal rules of the road.

Function and Content of Bylaws

In many jurisdictions, the rules with respect to what may be covered in the bylaws are flexible. They may contain any provision that is consistent with the law or with the certificate of incorporation. Typically, the bylaws will provide detailed guidelines for basic corporate activities, such as the mechanics of shareholder and director meetings, procedures for providing notice, and the required contents of records and reports. The bylaws also describe indemnification of directors and officers and duties, rights and powers of officers and directors.

Adoption and Amendment

The initial bylaws may be adopted by the incorporator or by the initial directors if the directors are named in the certificate. The board of directors may adopt, amend, or repeal the bylaws until the company has issued stock for consideration. Once the corporation sells stock, the bylaws may be adopted, amended, or repealed by the stockholders or by the board of directors if the board is delegated this power in the certificate of incorporation.

What Are the Roles of the Directors, Stockholders, and Officers of a Corporation?

From a legal standpoint, there are three prominent bodies that comprise the elements of a corporation:

- Directors
- Officers
- Stockholders

Under corporate statutes and case law, each entity has been granted certain rights and powers, which can at times overlap or even conflict. You should be aware of the different functions of each body.

The Board of Directors

The board of directors is the centralized supervisory body that directs the business and affairs of a corporation. The board of directors does not wield its rights or powers in its own self-interest, but instead acts in what's called a *fiduciary* capacity. This means that the board is under a legal duty to act in the best interests of the corporation and its stockholders. Directors, when acting for a corporation, must act as a board; individual directors, acting as such, cannot bind the board. The board may act by attending a meeting, either in person or telephonically (noticed in accordance with the corporation's bylaws), or by unanimous written consent. If the board opts for a meeting, it is necessary that a sufficient number of board members be present to constitute *quorum*, (in Delaware that's a majority of the total number of authorized directors) unless the corporation's bylaws or certificate of incorporation provide otherwise. If no quorum exists, the decision, or resolution, of the board will not be valid.

The Role of the Officers

Managerial power rests in the officers, who run the day-to-day affairs of the corporation and carry out the directives of the board of directors. Although the credibility of the business plan is of obvious importance to venture capitalist and angel investors, equally important to such investors is the ability of a team of officers to execute upon that plan. The titles and duties of the officers are set in the bylaws or in a resolution of the board of directors. Typically, a corporation's board would include the following:

- Chief Executive Officer
- Chief Financial Officer
- President
- Vice President
- Treasurer
- Secretary

The Role of Stockholders

Stockholders have little direct voice in the day-to-day management of the company. Indeed, stockholders are given power only to influence certain extraordinary corporate actions, such as a merger, a consolidation, a reorganization, or a dissolution of the corporation; a sale or a transfer of all or substantially all of the corporation's assets; or an amendment of the certificate of incorporation or bylaws. Stockholders who disagree with the actions of the board or officers, can sell their stake in the company. Like directors, stockholders may act by either a properly noticed meeting (annual or special) or by written consent.

How Do I Begin Hiring Employees?

In order to get a newly formed business to a minimally operational stage, it is necessary to obtain an Employer Indemnification Number and complete an Employer Registration form. These forms identify the corporation to the relevant tax authorities and lay the groundwork for the hiring of employees; they are the equivalent of your company's social security number.

Obtaining an Employee Identification Number

To the extent a corporation will be hiring employees and thereby subjecting itself to income-tax withholding requirements or the unemployment insurance rules, it is required to submit a Form SS-4 to the Internal Revenue Service. That gets the company an identification, or an Employer Identification Number, often called an *EIN*. (You can get an EIN over the phone by calling a local IRS office.) A company's EIN is just like an individual's social security number, in that it identifies the company for the purposes of state and federal tax filings.

Employer Registration Form

The company must also file an Employer Registration Form in any state in which it has employees in order for the company to be registered with that state. For example, in California, you would file a Form DE-1 with the Employment Development Department in order to obtain an account number.

Issuing Stock in a Corporation

What Are the Different Types of Stock?

Stock refers to a security that represents ownership in a corporation. Different classes of stock with different rights and preferences may be authorized and issued by the company. For a private company, a preferred class of stock is usually issued to investors in the company, while employees receive common stock. The capital structure should be laid out in great detail in the company's certificate of incorporation.

note Most venture-backed companies have common and preferred stock.

Common Stock Versus Preferred Stock

The simplest form of equity security is common stock. Within a company's ownership structure, common stockholders have the least priority. Senior to common stock, with superior rights to the assets of the company, is preferred stock. It is likely that a corporation's first financing, if venture backed, will consist of selling Series A preferred stock to investors. Typically, a preferred security is one that

- In a liquidation event, entitles its holder to receive some multiple of his/her investment out of the corporation's assets prior to any junior security holder.
- Grants the holder a preferred call on earnings of a corporation in the form of a regular, cumulative dividend.

- Has some form of anti-dilution protection and rights of conversion to common stock.

In certain jurisdictions, particular rights and preferences of stock will necessarily deem the security "preferred" as a matter of statutory law.

The Effect of Preferred Stock on Founders' Common Stock Holdings

Founders typically own the bulk of their company holdings in form of common stock (which they have received either by way of stock-option grants or through founders' stock issuances). There's a fine balance here because the more generous the rights and preferences granted to the preferred holders, the less likely it is that common-stock holders will see as much of a return on their stock. So care must be taken in negotiating all these terms.

How Do I Issue Stock to the Founders?

The issuance of stock is one of the first major decisions faced by a new corporation, and there are many issues that must be considered. Like decisions with respect to vesting and restriction of shares, this is a decision that may be revisited by potential investors, who may demand a modification of the capital structure of the company before investing. In deciding how much stock to issue to the founders and the terms of the stock take into account the contribution to the venture by the founders to date, such as the assignment of intellectual property, though a more important consideration may be the expected contributions of the founders going forward, especially if the company is early stage.

note This is a tricky area. Now is the time—if you haven't already done so—to consult a corporate and securities lawyer.

How to Characterize the Sale or Transfer of Founders' Stock

Now we're beginning to talk about money. The way founders' stock is transferred to a founder may affect the founder's taxes, so you need to be aware of a number of factors:

- To ensure proper characterization of the issuance, the company may require the founder to pay the fair market value of the company's stock in cash. Such a transaction will not trigger any tax. Because of the risks involved in a venture, however, and the likely scarcity of capital, some founders find themselves unwilling to actually put cash into the company.
- Another way to ensure proper characterization of the issuance is to have founders receive equity in the company in consideration of *sweat*—that is, both past and future services to the company.

note With either of these alternatives, you need to be able to justify the low price of the stock issued to the founders. This is particularly true if a financing is imminent. The IRS may well show great interest if, for example, a company issues shares to founders at $0.01 in consideration for past and future services and shortly thereafter conducts a financing and issues shares for $1.00. The IRS may determine that the founder received stock at a price below actual value, and it may choose to characterize the spread as a taxable gain to the stockholder. Here are a couple of ways you can minimize that risk:

- Start your corporation at least long enough in advance of a financing so that there exists a period of time and a series of events that might be used to account for the rise in value of the stock.
- Once the preferred stock is issued, the founder can argue that the difference in share price is due to the superior rights and preferences of the preferred relative to the common stock.

What Are the Required Elements of a Founders' Restricted Stock-Purchase Agreement?

There are common elements found in all founders' stock purchase agreements; some are necessitated by law, and others are implemented in order to protect the company's interests. The founders are usually the key asset of a start-up and they routinely receive huge chunks of stock in the corporation. For this reason, in order to adequately protect the company's future interests, most investors will require certain standard provisions to be included in a founder's stock-purchase agreement prior to financing the corporation if they are not included in the founder's stock-purchase agreement at the outset.

tip Anticipating what investors will demand will save hassle later.

Restrictions Based on Federal and State Securities Laws

Founders must agree to subject their stock holdings to certain restrictions, some of which are required as a matter of federal and state securities laws. Because founders' stock is usually not registered with any federal or state agency, the stock may not be sold or otherwise transferred except in accordance with federal and state laws and regulations. A reminder of these rules and regulations is usually stamped right on the founders' stock certificate.

Contractual Restrictions

The restricted stock-purchase agreement will also require an additional legend on the stock certificate that states that the shares represented by the certificate are subject to certain restrictions on transfer as contained in the restricted stock-purchase agreement. These additional restrictions might include

- **A market standoff provision.** This is a way of ensuring that if the company goes public, there won't be a sudden rush to sell the shares and destabilize the market price. Under a market standoff provision, a stockholder agrees not to sell or otherwise transfer any shares or other securities of the company for a certain period (usually 180 days) following the effective date of a registration statement of the company—that is, once it goes public.
- **A right of repurchase.** This allows the company to buy back for a nominal amount whatever shares are still subject to repurchase (not vested or earned), upon the termination of the stockholder as an employee of the company.
- **A right of first refusal.** This gives the company the right to purchase some or all of the shares offered for sale by the stockholder. It's a way for the company to minimize the distribution of shares in the company to outsiders.

Vesting

Companies issue inexpensive common stock to founders and employees, but the stock *vests* (is earned) only through providing services to the company over time. This works as an incentive for founders and employees to commit their time and efforts to the company. What is customary with respect to restricted stock depends both upon norms in the venture-capital industry as well as norms in the particular industry in which the corporation operates. That said, vesting over a period of four years with initial vesting only after six months or one year of service (this is sometimes referred to as the *cliff* period) and monthly vesting thereafter has become something of a default. From the company's perspective, it only makes sense to grant this inexpensive equity in the company if the company can properly align the interests of the company and the stockholder. A critical misstep an unwary company might make, however, is to sell common stock to founders without subjecting such stock to customary vesting and transfer restrictions in order to properly bind (by *golden handcuffs*) the founder to the company.

Potential Tax Liabilities of Restricted Stock

Although restricted stock makes sense from the perspective of investors and the corporation, it does bring with it a significant tax risk for holders of such stock under Section 83 of the Internal Revenue Code. Under normal circumstances, you will be taxed on the difference between the original issue price of the shares and the fair market value of the shares at each incremental vesting event. Because there will likely be no market for your shares (assuming you have not yet gone public), this means that you may owe taxes upon stock that you cannot sell.

The 83(b) Election

To avoid potential tax liabilities, talk to your lawyer about filing an 83(b) election. Section 83(b) of the Code provides a solution to the tax liabilities associated with restricted stock, because it allows a taxpayer to file a notice with the IRS of the taxpayer's choice to pay tax at ordinary income-tax rates on the difference between the value of the stock received and the price of the stock at the time of purchase. If the stock was purchased at its fair market value, this difference will be zero. Thereafter, the stock will be treated as a capital asset, and any gain thereon will be taxed (at appropriate capital rates) upon the sale of stock. To take advantage of Section 83(b), you must file an 83(b) election form with the IRS within thirty days of purchasing the stock.

Governing a Corporation: Proper Corporate Conduct, Duties of Directors and Officers, and Indemnification

Are Stockholders Liable for the Debts and Liabilities of the Corporation?

Generally speaking, stockholders are not liable for the debts and liabilities of a corporation, but if the corporate form is being abused, this protection could be lost. As long as the company abides by certain corporate formalities and ethical guidelines, the stockholders will be protected from claims against the corporation.

tip	Follow corporate formalities, and the risk of stockholder liability is low.

The Corporate Veil and Limited Liability for Stockholders

One of the great advantages of a corporation is that it provides limited liability for stockholders. The corporate structure can be used to shield stockholders from responsibility for the corporation's liabilities and is commonly referred to as the *corporate veil.* A corporation and its stockholders are distinct bodies under corporate law. All things being equal, stockholders are not responsible for the acts of the corporation. This is especially important with respect to debts or obligations that a corporation might accrue. Generally, stockholders bear only the economic risk of loss of the money they paid for their stock.

Piercing the Corporate Veil for Improper Conduct

The *corporate veil* has limits and, if abused, it may be "pierced." That means that a stockholder will lose the protection of the corporate veil and become liable for claims against the corporation. One way in which the corporate veil is pierced is by demonstrating that the stockholder and corporation are not in fact separate persons, but rather the corporation is the stockholder's alter ego.

In order to make sure that the corporate veil remains intact, the corporation must

- Keep the corporation adequately capitalized.
- Avoid commingling of assets.
- Avoid self-dealing or interested transactions, unless all interests are disclosed.
- Observe corporate formalities and keep accurate corporate books.

The observation of corporate formalities indicates to the court that the legal fiction of the corporation as a separate person is being acknowledged and maintained, which will undercut any "alter ego" cause of action. Corporate formalities include

- Holding regular board meetings and annual stockholder meetings
- Obtaining appropriate board and stockholder approval for the corporation's activities
- Keeping accurate and up to date corporate minute books, which accurately track the decisions of both the board of directors and stockholders

Are Officers and Directors Liable for Actions by the Corporation? If So, Can They Be Indemnified?

Directors and officers of the corporation are bound by certain fiduciary duties of loyalty and care toward the corporation and its stockholders, established by corporate statutes as well as by state case law. The breach of these duties can result in the personal liability of directors and officers. The company may limit their liability by providing for indemnification, but these indemnification provisions are also subject to applicable state law limitations.

Duty of Care and Business Judgment Rule: Was the Corporate Action Reasonable?

In simple terms, the duty of care requires that a director or officer exercise a degree of skill, diligence, and care that a reasonably prudent person would use under similar circumstances. The duty of care might be violated by inactivity, grossly negligent behavior, or simple negligence. Directors often defend claims of liability by asserting the *business judgment rule*, which is a presumption adopted by many courts that in making a business decision, the directors of a corporation acted on an informed basis in good faith and with an honest belief that the action was taken in the best interest of the company.

Duty of Loyalty: Was the Corporate Action Fair?

The duty of loyalty demands that directors and officers act in good faith in the best interests of the corporation and its shareholders. The question that directors and officers must ask is whether the action might be characterized as a conflict of interest, or more specifically, self-dealing (transactions between the corporation and its director) that results in unfairness to the corporation and stockholders.

Other Sources of Liability

In addition to liability for breach of fiduciary duties, directors are also subject to certain other liabilities under state statutes regarding, among other things, the distribution of dividends and redemption of stock. Likewise, certain officers may face liability under state statutes for failing to pay withholding taxes.

Indemnification

Liability of directors and officers may be limited by indemnification—or reimbursement—by the corporation. Indemnification statutes offer protection for acts or omissions of the director or officer acting in his or her official capacity. Such reimbursement might consist of litigation costs, settlements, and attorneys' fees.

Complying with Federal and State Securities Laws

How Do Securities Laws Affect My Company?

Founders, especially those not represented in the early stages by counsel, must remain aware of the fact that sale and issuances of securities—such as stock, options, warrants, or notes—are regulated by a complex, interlocking regime of federal and state securities law.

CAUTION: Always consult legal counsel when contemplating a transaction that could trigger consequences under applicable securities laws.

Federal and Blue Sky Securities Law

Federal securities law is comprised essentially of six statutes, the most important of which, for private companies, is the Securities Act of 1933, as amended. This statute regulates the offering of securities and further prohibits fraudulent or deceptive practices in any offer or sale of securities. State securities law varies from state to state and is known as *Blue Sky Law*. In order to comply with these laws, the securities to be sold must either be registered—a costly and time-intensive process—or exempted from registration at both the state and federal level.

Risks of Noncompliance

As the time for initial stock issuances approaches, founders would be well advised to seek advice of legal counsel to navigate this complex area of corporate securities law. Failing to comply with securities law requirements can pose a host of difficulties for start-ups down the line:

- The company and founders may bear liability for certain material misstatements or omissions that are not disclosed to investors.
- Remedying a securities violation can be a costly and time-consuming endeavor.
- The illegal sale of securities may trigger a rescission right for those who bought the unregistered or un-exempted securities.
- As a part of a financing, the company's counsel is usually required to provide a legal opinion that the company is not and has not been in violation of securities laws. Counsel's inability to provide such an opinion may affect the company's ability to close the financing.

General Corporate Matters

What Kind of Records Must the Company Keep?

A corporation is required to keep a careful record of organization material, its corporate activities, and a stockholder ledger. This is not only for its own organizational purposes, but also because such records provide historical evidence of the company's compliance with proper corporate procedure; investors will almost always want accurate current information on the company before investing, and certain shareholders have a right to inspect the company's records.

Organizational Binder, Minute Book, Stockholder Ledger

Organizational materials such as the certificate of incorporation and bylaws are collected into an organizational binder. This binder should be kept current, and amended copies of either the certificate or bylaws should be added to the binder as adopted. Minutes of board and stockholder meetings (along with notices thereof) and board and stockholder consents are collected in a minute book. Similarly, a record of all company stockholders—as well as a record of the sales, issuances, and other dispositions of stock in the corporation—are recorded in the company's stock ledger. Financial records should also be kept.

Importance of Complying with Corporate Formalities

Corporate formalities might appear to be a simple clerical task—especially in comparison to the many daunting tasks required to build a business—but they are essential to success. A corporation's books, records, and minutes should be kept accessible and in working order for many important reasons:

- Corporate formalities must be followed in order to ensure the protection of the corporate form, such as limited liability.
- Before making an investment, potential investors will engage in due diligence (an investigation of the company), which will include an examination of the company's finances, its activities to date, and whether such activities had the requisite board and stockholder authorization and approval, as evidenced by the minute book and other records.
- In most jurisdictions, stockholders, usually upon written demand, are entitled to inspect the stock ledger, list of stockholders, and the books and records of the corporation for any proper purpose.
- In some states, directors are protected when relying in good faith on records of the corporation.

What Is Required to Do Business in States Other Than My State of Incorporation?

As they grow, most companies will start conducting business in states other than the one in which they are incorporated. The threshold level of activity required before a company must qualify to do business in a state depends on the particular state, but once that threshold is crossed, the company must take certain actions in order to remain in compliance with state law. Before conducting business in a given state, you must be aware of state qualification requirements.

Foreign Qualifications

Often, corporations will be incorporated in one state but will do business in another. For instance, many companies in the Silicon Valley are in fact Delaware corporations. Because these companies do business in California, each is required to file a Statement and Designation by Foreign Corporation with California. Other states have different requirements; it is possible that each state where the company intends to do business requires a foreign qualification.

The definition of "doing business" in a given state may include something as slight as having a salesperson working from his home. You will need to investigate whether the scope and nature of your company's activities in each state will trigger a qualification requirement, or whether your company's presence in the state is sufficient to subject it to other laws and regulations of the state.

Failure to Properly Qualify

Failing to properly qualify to do business has two main consequences. First, the state may take action inhibiting (or indeed prohibiting) the corporation from conducting business activity in the state. The failure to properly qualify to do business will also slow down a financing. Investors will view the failure of the company to qualify as a risk, because such failure puts the company in violation of a law or regulation. (And as we've pointed out before, investors are risk averse.)

Other State and Local Regulations

Depending on the nature of the business, the corporation may be subject to other laws and regulations that are industry or trade specific, or that are imposed by the local governments, such as local business licenses. Often, the local business-development office will have comprehensive pamphlets or manuals that list the various laws and regulations of the locality to which a corporation will be subject.

What Tax Issues Should I Be Aware Of?

Corporations are subject to taxes at the federal level, the state level (in its state of incorporation and in each state in which it is qualified to do business), and possibly the local level. Corporate taxation involves many complicated issues; be sure to consult a tax advisor.

Sales Tax

Most states also impose a sales tax. For example, California has a complementary sales and use tax regime. Corporations that expect to make any sales of tangible personal property must obtain a seller's permit from the California State Board of Equalization.

Local Tax

Along with the IRS and state agencies, local government authorities may also impose taxes on the business. These authorities should be contacted to determine what real property, personal property, gross receipts or payroll-based taxes, or other taxes and fees may be expected.

Developing, Protecting, and Leveraging Intellectual Property

Intellectual property (IP) equals competitive advantage. Each type of IP confers on the owner a different set of exclusive rights that can be leveraged to give a company competitive advantage in the marketplace and/or a meaningful source of revenue. Similarly, a well-protected and leveraged IP portfolio can significantly increase the value of a company to its shareholders.

So, where to begin? It is important to understand the basic characteristics of the various types of IP, each of which will be discussed in turn in this section. It is equally important to consider how a little careful planning and effort at each stage of your company's growth can enable you to significantly increase shareholder value. Your legal team should include experienced business lawyers who are well versed in practical strategies to help you win the IP game at every stage of your company's life cycle.

The Basic Forms of Intellectual Property and How They Fit into Your IP Strategy

The following basic forms of intellectual property protection are discussed in this section:

- Patents
- Trade Secrets
- Copyrights
- Trademarks and domain names
- Unfair competition
- Privacy rights

Patents

Patents are very powerful tools in a company's IP portfolio. A *patent* entitles the owner to absolutely exclude others for 20 years from using, making, selling, and importing the invention. Patents are issued for

- New and useful mechanical or electronic machines, including software
- Manufacturing methods such as supply-chain processes
- Methods of doing business
- Chemical compositions such as pharmaceuticals and genetic sequences
- Designs
- Asexually produced plants

note Patents are not issued for creative expression (such as music or audio-visual displays). That falls under the jurisdiction of copyright law.

A patented thing need not be actually made or used in order to obtain or keep a patent right. Because this is such a powerful right, the claimed invention must be a significant improvement over what was previously known in the relevant field (that is, over the *prior art*). Patent law expresses this concept through the requirement that a patentable invention must be useful, novel, and non-obvious (to someone skilled in the relevant technical area). A significant amount of law exists to help determine whether a specific invention meets this standard.

The main disadvantages of a patent are

- It can be fairly expensive and time consuming to obtain a patent. The public disclosure and/or sale of the patentable invention limit the time period to file an application. Entrepreneurs should consult with a patent attorney well in advance of either of these events.

- A patent is valid for only a limited period of time (20 years).
- In order to be granted a patent, the inventor must publicly disclose the details of how to use the invention in the patent specifications. These conditions allow all interested parties to practice the invention once the patent expires.
- Patents protect a company only in the country where the patent was issued. Consult your patent attorney for guidance on when and where to file additional applications to obtain patent protection in additional countries.

Trade Secrets

A *trade secret* is any information that derives independent economic value from not being generally known to others and is the subject of efforts that are reasonable under the circumstances to maintain its secrecy. Trade secrets can be some of the most important assets of any company because, unlike patents, their protection never runs out—unless of course you let the cat out of the bag.

Typical items protected as trade secrets include financial and marketing information, customer lists, industrial designs, new product plans, software source code, personal information of customers, know-how, and so on. Trade-secret protection requires that the trade secrets be subject to "reasonable efforts to maintain their secrecy." Companies don't have to take all conceivable measures to protect the secrecy, but what amounts to reasonable efforts will vary depending on the specific information that is being protected.

The main disadvantages of trade secret protection are

- A single public disclosure can cause the loss of trade-secret status. When considering whether trade secret is an appropriate form of IP protection for specific information, you will need to decide whether the operation of your business is compatible with the affirmative requirements to maintain secrecy.
- Unlike patents, trade secrets do not protect against a third party's independent discovery of the trade secret, only against the misappropriation (or stealing) of the information.
- Trade-secret protection is of no use if the information is easily discovered—through, for example, the examination of a product.

Copyright

Copyright protects the creative expression of an idea, not the idea itself. In other words, the idea of a romantic novel set in the South after the Civil War is not protectible by copyright. The actual text of the novel "Gone with the Wind," on the other hand, *is* protectible by copyright. Factual information is not subject to copyright protection.

As with trade-secret law, copyright protection does not protect against independent creation, only copying. Any creative expression that can be reasonably fixed in a tangible medium is copyrightable (for example, writings, graphics, art, software code, audio visual–display, film, photographs, video, and maps). Copyright gives the author of a work the exclusive right to control the reproduction, distribution, modification, public display, and public performance of the work.

The duration of copyright protection varies depending on when a work was created and whether the work was created as a work for hire by the author (that is, in the course of the author's employment or as an independent contractor pursuant to a qualifying contract). There is no longer any requirement to put a copyright notice on a work to preserve copyright protection (although it is still a good idea). This makes it harder to tell whether a work is protected by copyright.

Trademarks and Domain Names

A trademark or service mark (*mark*) is used to identify the goods and/or services of a company and distinguish them from others. Trademarks can be words, graphics, sounds, symbols, logos, or slogans in a manner that serves or even smells. A mark functions to distinguish the origin of goods and services in the mind of the consumer. This association is known as *good will.* Good will can be a very valuable business asset.

In the United States, it is possible to obtain common-law rights in a mark simply by using it in commerce. State or federal registration is not required to get protection for a mark in the U.S. because of the existence of the common-law rights. Federal registration with the U.S. Patent and Trademark Office (PTO), however, can afford certain advantages such as establishing nationwide priority of use prior to the first actual use of the trademark in commerce and priority over the expansion of pre-existing common-law uses. State trademark registration is available in cases where nationwide registration is not available (such as for businesses that operate only in a local area).

A search of whether a company has a right to use a particular mark in a particular category of goods should be done before using the mark in commerce. This prevents a company from spending a significant amount of money in promoting a logo or brand name, only to find out that someone else owns the rights to that mark in that industry. Due to the existence of common-law trademark rights in the U.S., it is not enough to search the PTO database (which only catches federal registrations and applications); it is important to have a search done by a trademark search firm and to have that search reviewed by a qualified trademark attorney. Otherwise, you may miss a relevant common-law use of your proposed mark, which could cause problems later for your company. For example, Amazon.com became embroiled in litigation with a local Minnesota bookstore that used the name Amazon.

In the Internet era, most companies want to have a domain name that is the same as their company name or mark. Merely having a mark that includes a particular word or phrase or unique name, however, is no guarantee that an equivalent domain name will be available.

Trademark rights are theoretically perpetual; there is no expiration on the length of time a trademark belongs to a company. Two main restrictions on the use of a mark, however, are

- It must be continuously used in commerce and not abandoned.
- It should not become a generic noun used to describe a type of product or service. Many nouns, such as *aspirin* and *calculator*, were originally a product mark, but its owner lost its rights in the mark once it fell into general use. To avoid this fate, a company should develop and use a set of trademark guidelines and trademark license terms to ensure that its mark(s) are used correctly.

Unfair Competition

Unfair-competition law seeks to prohibit types of behavior that give an unfair competitive advantage in the marketplace:

- Representing your products and/or services as the products or services of others
- Behaviors that seek to confuse, mislead, and/or deceive the public as to the price, quality, source, and/ or identity of products offered by you or your competitors
- Anti-competitive behaviors, such as false advertising and bait-and-switch selling tactics, unauthorized substitution of one brand of goods for another, and theft of trade secrets (such as breach of a restrictive covenant, trade libel, and false representation of products or services)

Trademark infringement (such as using a mark that is confusingly similar to a trademark of another in order to confuse consumers into purchasing your product or service) and misappropriation (such as the unauthorized use of the name or image of a famous person in the promotion of your product or service) are subject to unfair-competition law. The state and federal laws and regulations that regulate unfair competition are focused on protecting the competitive environment of the marketplace. Because of the possible severe penalties and the accompanying bad publicity, it is important to have an ongoing program to ensure that your company's product and marketing strategy and materials will not run afoul of unfair-competition law.

Privacy and Related Issues

Privacy is the control of personal autonomy and personal information, the assurance of secrecy in one's personal communications, the protection of one's identity and image, and the freedom to speak and associate anonymously. The right to privacy is not absolute, and is balanced against others' legitimate needs to receive and access personal information. For example, the disclosure of personal information may be necessary in order to transact business; to work or become employed; to receive health care; to maintain security; to redress civil wrongs; and to prevent, investigate, and/or prosecute criminal acts.

Privacy protection is a broad and diverse area of law that is continually evolving to meet changing concerns and expectations of society. Privacy laws vary considerably by geographical location. For example, the privacy laws of the member states of the European Union are generally much more restrictive than the privacy laws in the United States. Applicable privacy law for a given individual may be determined by the location(s) of the individual(s) whose data is being collected and/or used by your company. Therefore, even if your company is located in the U.S., if you are collecting or using personally identifiable data of residents of other countries, additional privacy restrictions may apply.

Handling IP Issues at Formation

During the formation phase of a company and the initial development of the company's key technology, there are three critical areas in which companies often fail to adequately take IP into account:

- Performing adequate IP due diligence on the company business model
- Ensuring that critical IP is really owned by the company
- Establishing a basic trade secret protection program

IP Due Diligence on Business Model

It's never too early to consider IP issues! Many innovative business models present IP issues, which, if not resolved, can doom the success of a business. Peer-to-peer networks, electronic book distribution, content indexing, reuse of magazine and newspaper articles and photographs, and the storage of MP3 files are all recent examples that have spawned high profile litigation.

It is important to address and resolve IP issues raised by a business model from the very beginning. This will help you avoid becoming sidetracked with litigation that could determine the viability of the company and will actually increase your chances of securing funding. More and more venture capitalists are sensitive to IP issues and will want to see them addressed up front before committing to funding a company. In addition, VCs, strategic partners, and potential acquirers will look to see if a company has built, or is positioned to build, a portfolio of defensible IP rights that will increase the value of the company and provide it with an important competitive edge.

For these reasons, entrepreneurs who spend some time thinking through any IP issues created by their business model (including whether they can develop defensible IP), and who present their IP solutions in their business plans and elevator pitches, will have an easier time attracting investors and business partners.

Depositing IP in the Company

Make sure the company owns the IP rights! This may sound simple, but countless technology start-up companies make this classic and costly mistake when they fail to ensure that the corporation created by the founders actually owns all the IP rights in the technology that forms the basis of the company's products and services.

This mistake customarily occurs in one of two ways. First, a founder who was in on the early development of the concept and/or technology that forms the basis of the company (and thus automatically has an ownership interest in the company's IP) does not transfer his or her ownership rights in the IP to the corporation when it is formed. Typically, a founder will transfer all such IP rights to the corporation in exchange for stock in the company. If, however, a founder is no longer involved in the company when the official corporation is formed, or the IP transfer is not properly handled at formation, the applicable founder(s), and not the company, will own some or all of the IP rights

Second, often in the early days of a company, individuals who are not employees work on the development of the technology. A key—and often misunderstood—rule of IP rights is that in the absence of the execution of the right type of written contract between a company and an independent contractor, the independent contractor—not the company—will own the IP rights in any deliverables developed by the independent contractor. It does not matter if the company pays the independent contractor for the work. In the absence of a proper written agreement the company will, at most, only get an implied license in the IP. The independent contractor owns the IP and may continue to exploit it or even give the it away, including to the company's competitors.

Trade Secret-Protection Program

Too often, start-up companies ignore this critical component of IP protection until it is too late. This is especially disturbing because a basic trade-secret program is not that difficult or expensive to design and implement. The basics of a trade secret–protection program include the implementation of a set of non-disclosure agreements (NDAs) for execution by the company and everyone who may potentially receive the company's trade-secret information, including employees, contractors, visitors, and consultants.

It is important to remember that there is no "one-size fits all" NDA. Most companies need to employ a number of NDAs, with terms that vary depending on the relationship between the parties and the sensitivity of the information that is being disclosed. With a little effort early on, a company can both increase the value of its trade secrets and avoid being accused of misappropriating third-party trade secrets.

In addition, a basic trade-secret protection program requires that your company establish

- Proper entrance and exit procedures for employees
- An on-going program for identifying for employees the level of sensitivity of the company's trade secrets
- Physical procedures for ensuring the security of the trade secrets
- Adequate procedures for handling trade secrets received from business partners and customers (to limit damaging contamination from being exposed to the valuable secrets of third parties)

Handling IP Issues During Development and Upon Commercialization

Once a company is formed and receives its first funding, it typically enters into an intense period of product development. This period poses challenges to the successful development of a protectible IP portfolio. In addition, when a company finally has a product ready for market, IP-rights issues commonly arise. At this point, however, we hope your company has done a good job developing and protecting a strong IP portfolio—although this portfolio will do you little good if you fail to intelligently leverage this IP as you commercialize your company's products and technology.

What follows is but a sampling of issues that technology companies face on a regular basis as they develop and then move to commercialize their products. During both stages—development and commercialization—companies often face the kinds of situations described next. Each requires careful attention to safeguard the company's IP interests and avoid contamination by third-party IP.

Licenses In

As an alternative to developing technology (and the resulting IP) in-house, a technology start-up often decides to save time and R&D resources by licensing third-party technology to use in its products. The terms of the license grant contained in the contract with the third-party technology owner will establish what rights your company has to use, distribute, modify, and sublicense the licensed technology. Remember that any rights not expressly granted in the license are retained by the licensor. In other words, if the license agreement doesn't say you get the right to use the technology in a certain way, you probably can't do it.

The types of license rights that you will need for any specific technology depend on where and how you will use it, as well as on the scope of the different IP rights held in the technology by the licensor. For example, you need different license grants to cover copyrights and patents. This is because the exclusive rights under copyright law cover the right to reproduce, distribute, modify, publicly perform, and publicly display the copyrighted work, and the rights under patent law cover the right to make, use, sell, repair, and import the patented invention. It is not unusual to find that a particular technology (especially software) is covered by both copyright and patent protection. Too often, even experienced IP attorneys fail to adequately take this into account when they draft or negotiate license provisions.

Licenses Out

Another common and potentially lucrative business strategy is to capitalize on your company's IP portfolio by licensing out rights in your IP to others separate and apart from the sale or license of your company's products. Even if you are distributing products developed from your technology, licensing certain IP rights in your technology to others can be a good source of additional revenue from third parties who can exploit the technology in a difference product channel or geographic area.

When deciding how to license out your IP, and how much, it is critical to retain access to the rights that your company intends to use in the future. Also, consider your competitors, actual and potential, when deciding the terms of the license grant. Well-drafted license agreements can produce a lucrative revenue stream; poorly envisioned licenses could result in narrowed options for future growth, or worse, provide your competitors with the competitive advantage of access to your technology.

Going International

Most technology companies cannot be successful unless they can distribute their products and services globally. This is a difficult transition for many companies. Going international will require that the company learn to adapt to different cultural norms in the negotiation and drafting of business agreements. In addition, laws are by their very nature territorial. Each country may have slightly different rules for IP rights, privacy laws, taxation of royalties, and limits on warranties and damages, among others. It is important to consult with your lawyer regarding adjustments to your format contracts before using them with third parties in other countries. Moreover, the fact that your customers are located in other countries may raise thorny issues regarding whose law will govern a given transaction. This should also be discussed with your lawyer where appropriate.

Finally, before exporting your technology out of the U.S., or importing technology that your company developed overseas (through the use of a subsidiary) into the U.S., make sure to check that you have complied with all applicable export laws and regulations.

Critical Employment Issues for the Early-Stage Start-up

So you have put together a business plan, set up your company, perhaps even received a little angel funding, and now you want to start full-speed ahead on executing your business plan. The next logical step is to go out and recruit employees. This should be the easy part, right? Wrong. Unfortunately, this is an area where a number of laws and regulations dictate what a company can and can't do. At this point, a basic understanding of the legal issues that commonly arise in hiring and compensation of employees and engaging experienced legal counsel is necessary to avoid mistakes or omissions that can be very costly at a later stage.

Who Is an Employee?

This sounds like a simple question; the answer, however, is not always simple. If you answer this question incorrectly, your company may find itself with a large bill for unpaid taxes, wages, and benefits. In distinguishing between an employee and a consultant, it is the nature of the working relationship that matters. One important consideration is the extent to which the individual has control over the work process: If the individual is given wide latitude to determine how to do the work, he or she is more likely to be viewed as a consultant. The specific factors that are taken into consideration vary by state and by purpose (such as for federal income tax or state workers' compensation or wage and benefits regulations). If there is any doubt about the status, all applicable rules must be reviewed carefully. If an employee is incorrectly classified as a consultant or independent contractor, your company may incur significant liabilities for unpaid taxes, wages, and benefits.

At-Will Employment

In start-ups, employment is generally *at-will*, meaning that either the company or the employee may terminate the employment relationship at any time for any reason. This gives the company's board of directors and management the flexibility to adjust the workforce as the company's changing needs demand.

Indeed, one of the items that investors check during a financing is that all employment relationships are at-will and that there are no long-term employment contracts restricting the company from terminating employees. Therefore, it is advisable for a company to clearly indicate in all its standard employment documents that employment at the company is at-will. In addition, you should be careful to not imply through conduct or oral statements that employment is anything but at-will.

A company may choose to pay severance or accelerate the vesting of options on termination of employment (discussed later in this chapter in the section titled "Termination of Employment") for certain employees (usually executives), but the agreements with such employees generally indicate that employment is at-will. In other words, the company may terminate the employee's employment with the company at any time, but it may have a contractual obligation to pay the severance due under the agreement.

Confidentiality and Ownership of Inventions

For a high-tech start-up, intellectual property is the most valuable asset. One way you can make sure that your company's critical IP stays within the company is to have all employees and consultants sign a confidentiality agreement. These agreements contain two basic components:

- The employee must agree not to disclose to any third party any confidential information of the company. *Confidential information* is usually broadly defined to include all information the company does not wish to disclose to any third party. This could be, for example, information regarding inventions and discoveries, product information, and customer lists.
- The employee must agree to disclose to the company any inventions made as an employee and agree that all these inventions belong to the company.

Since it is quite common for employees in high-tech start-ups to move from company to company in the same field, protecting trade secrets and ensuring that employees don't use technology owned by their prior employer are issues that every company must consider carefully. In a venture financing, during due diligence, there will be a close study of the company's ownership of technology. Investors and their legal counsel will review the company's agreements to make sure that the company's IP ownership is clean; that means that the company has rights to use all IP owned or used by it.

Sometimes you will find that you want to hire a person who has signed a non-competition agreement with a prior employer. You should have your legal counsel carefully review that agreement with the previous employer to determine whether the proposed employment with your company will conflict with obligations to the prior employer.

Employment Laws and Regulations

Start-ups are sometimes unaware that a number of federal and state employment laws apply to a company with as few as one employee, and that failure to comply with these laws can not only result in substantial liability but can be very distracting to management. It helps to have a basic understanding of the applicable rules, and to establish standard procedures even in the early stages of a start-up. A full discussion of the various employment laws that are applicable to a start-up is not possible here, and state laws vary, but we can highlight areas of major concern.

Discrimination

United States federal law and the laws of most states prohibit discrimination against employees in matters such as hiring, promotion, compensation, disciplinary actions, or termination based on race, gender, age, national origin, religion, or disability. In addition, some states and certain local governments have laws that prohibit discrimination on other grounds, such as marital status or sexual orientation. In addition, federal and state laws prohibit discrimination in employment on a variety of public-policy grounds such as engaging in union activities or collective bargaining, testifying against the employer, and filing state or federal charges or claims (such as workers' compensation claims).

Discrimination claims can result in substantial liability to a company and can be highly distracting to management. Steps that can be taken to avoid such liability include making sure that all employment decisions are based on job-related reasons and adopting and applying consistent policies. Local Chambers of Commerce and small business organizations have hiring checklists and sample employment forms and handbooks that can be a good resource for small businesses.

Wage Regulations

United States federal and state laws require that certain minimum hourly and monthly wages be paid to employees; with respect to this, the first question to be answered is whether the employee is exempt or non-exempt. An *exempt* employee is normally an executive, administrative professional, or outside sales employee who customarily and regularly exercises discretion and independent judgment on significant matters.

Companies in the high-tech industry often incorrectly assume that all engineers fit into the category of an exempt employee, but this may not always be the case. Whether or not an employee is an exempt employee can be a highly complicated question that requires analysis of the duties of the employee and specific rules that are applicable in that situation. The answer is critical because non-exempt employees are due overtime pay to the extent that they work more than eight hours a day or forty hours a week, depending on the applicable rule. Overtime and penalties due as a result of misclassification of employees can be quite large, so a careful evaluation of the specific situation must be done prior to the employee's start date.

Americans with Disabilities Act

The Americans with Disabilities Act (ADA) prohibits discrimination against individuals with a disability who meet the requirements for a position and who can perform the essential functions for a position. The company must provide reasonable accommodations (such as physical modifications of the workspace, special equipment, or flexible hours) unless doing so would cause the employer undue hardship. The ADA rules apply to any company that has five or more employees.

Workers' Compensation

State laws generally require all employers to provide workers'-compensation insurance for employees who sustain injuries arising from employment.

Record Keeping and Posting of Notices

There are a number of state and federal laws that contain specific requirements for retention of employee data and records, such as payroll records, health and safety records, and employment applications; and for posting of certain notices in the workplace, such as notices regarding minimum wage and nondiscrimination laws. Local Chambers of Commerce and federal and state agencies can provide copies of notices that meet the applicable federal and state requirements.

Termination of Employment

Upon an employee's termination of employment the company must address a number of issues. These include confidentiality agreements, non-compete and non-solicit agreements, and payment of wages and severance.

Confidentiality Agreements

An employee's obligation to not disclose or use confidential information obtained as an employee usually continues after termination of employment. It is advisable, however, to remind employees on termination of their continuing obligations under the confidentiality agreement they signed on joining the company, as well as to have them sign a written acknowledgement of their continuing obligations under the confidentiality agreement. It is also important to make sure that employees return all company documents upon termination of the employment relationship and acknowledge in writing that they have done so.

Non-Compete and Non-Solicit Agreements

Companies often want employees to agree that they will not work for competitors of the company after termination of employment, and many states will enforce an agreement not to compete if it is narrow in scope (that is, only restricts the employee from working for specific companies and still allows the employee to work in his or her field) and is for a limited period of time.

note In general, non-competition agreements are not enforceable in California, except for agreements with shareholders of a company in connection with a sale of the company.

High-tech start-ups often find that former employees are recruiting current employees to a new company. A non-solicitation provision, which restricts a former employee from recruiting employees, is often contained in a company's confidentiality agreement and is generally enforceable if it is for a limited time period.

Payment of Wages and Severance

Upon termination, the employee is entitled to all wages for work performed, including pay for unused vacation or PTO time. The company is not required to pay severance by law, but often will have agreements with management employees for a certain amount of cash severance and stock-option vesting acceleration upon a termination without cause ("termination with cause" is often narrowly defined to mean actions such as violation of the company's confidentiality agreement, willful misconduct causing harm to the company, or commission of fraud or felony). The amount of cash severance and stock-option acceleration varies depending on the employee's position, market conditions, and individual factors. The company should make sure that any severance is contingent on the employee signing a full release of claims against the company.

Stock and Stock Options: The Basics

Stock and stock options are an essential and standard part of compensation for employees of high-tech start-ups. There are, however, misconceptions and confusion about how they work. This section addresses the basic terminology and frequently asked questions regarding stock and option grants.

Stock Versus Stock Options

There is a basic distinction between stock and stock options. In a company's early stages, employees are often issued common stock, which the company retains the right to repurchase (usually at the employee's original purchase price) until the employee has vested in or has earned the shares. As the company grows, however, employees are generally issued common stock options or rights to purchase common stock at a specific price and on the terms set forth in the option agreement. Stock options are attractive because employees do not have to pay for the stock up-front. In addition, if certain requirements are met, tax on the option can be deferred until sale of the shares. (See the discussion of incentive stock options later in this chapter.)

Can an Employee Be Paid Solely in Stock?

Entrepreneurs wanting and needing to save cash often want to pay employees only in stock. There are two problems with this approach: Employees are taxed when they receive the stock at ordinary income-tax rates (and the company will have an obligation to withhold for such tax obligations); and the employee will not have any liquid stock with which to pay the tax. There's also the vexing question of whether the company is still in compliance with minimum-wage laws; paying an employee illiquid private company stock will generally not be viewed as enough to meet the requirements of minimum-wage laws.

How Many Shares Should I Set Aside for Employees?

The answer to this question varies depending on the stage of the company and the number of unfilled positions, especially in the management team. Venture capitalists often insist that a sizable pool of shares sufficient for planned hires over the next one to two years be included in the company's fully diluted capitalization prior to a financing.

What Is the Appropriate Size of Option Grants to Employees?

The answer to this question varies depending on the stage of the company, the company's business outlook, market conditions, and the background and experience of the employee. Option grants to employees in a company's early stages tend to be larger in size because the employee is taking a greater risk and will likely undergo substantial dilution by the addition of later investors and employees to the company. Cash compensation to employees in the early stages of the company also tends to be lower than industry levels.

What Should the Option Exercise Price Be?

Employees are generally issued options to purchase common stock with an exercise price equal to the fair market value of the company's common stock on the date of grant. The board of directors of a private company determines the fair market value of the company's common stock. The traditional rule of thumb for early-stage companies is to set the price of common stock at a fraction ($^1/_{10}{}^{th}$ or $^1/_8{}^{th}$) of the price of the company's last round (or upcoming round) of preferred stock financing.

The differential between the preferred stock and common stock price is due to the preferential rights that holders of preferred stock have with respect to matters such as payments on a sale or liquidation of the company, dividends, and voting rights. However, as the company approaches a liquidity event, such as a merger or public offering, the price differential between common stock and preferred stock is reduced substantially, because the company's future performance becomes more certain and the preferential rights of the preferred stock are no longer significant.

What Are the Differences Between an Incentive Stock Option and a Nonstatutory Stock Option?

Most stock plans adopted by high-tech start-ups permit the issuance of both incentive stock options (ISOs) and nonstatutory stock options (NSOs) under the plan. If an option meets the requirements for an ISO under the Internal Revenue Code (the "Code"), the option will be eligible for special tax treatment. As a general rule, to qualify as an ISO, the following requirements must be met:

- The option must be granted to an employee of the company or its parent or subsidiary.
- The value of the shares that may be exercised under an ISO grant in any one calendar year by any employee can't exceed $100,000.

- The exercise price of an ISO can be no less than the fair market value of the stock on the date of grant (if the person being granted the ISO is a 10% shareholder of the company, the exercise price must be no less than 110% of fair market value).

The detailed requirements that must be met for an option to qualify as an ISO can be complicated, and experienced legal counsel must be consulted to prepare a form of plan and agreement that complies with the applicable rules.

An employee will not incur any federal income tax on grant of an ISO. Upon exercise, the employee incurs no tax liability unless he or she is subject to the alternative minimum tax (AMT) under Section 55 of the Code. An employee will be subject to AMT during any tax year if the tax calculated using the formula in Section 55 of the Code exceeds the regular tax of the taxpayer for the year. Upon sale of the shares (assuming that the sale does not occur within one year of the date of exercise nor within two years of the date of grant), any gain is taxed to the employee as long-term capital gain. If the shares *are* disposed of within one year after the date of exercise or within two years from the date of grant, the employee will recognize ordinary income to the extent of the lesser of the excess, if any, of (i) the fair market value of the shares on the date of exercise or (ii) the sales proceeds, over the exercise price. Nonstatutory stock options (NSOs) are stock options that do not satisfy the requirements of Section 422 of the Code and are not eligible for special tax treatment. NSOs are often issued to non-employees such as consultants, who are not eligible to receive ISOs, and to key employees to whom the company wishes to grant options containing terms not permitted by Sections 422 and 423 of the Code or for whom a grant exceeds the $100,000 annual limitation.

There are generally no tax consequences for the option holder at the time of grant. Upon exercise of the NSO, the option holder will recognize ordinary income in the amount of the excess, if any, of the fair market value of the shares at the time of exercise over the exercise price. This ordinary income will be subject to withholding by the company if the option holder is an employee. Upon sale of the shares, the employee will recognize capital gain or loss in an amount equal to the difference between the sale price and the fair market value of the shares on the date of exercise. If the shares have been held for more than one year prior to the sale, the gain or loss will be treated as long-term capital gain or loss to the option holder.

What Is Vesting?

Stock options generally *vest*, or are earned, over time. Options commonly vest over a four year period with $^{1}/_{4}$ of the shares vesting one year after grant or employee hire date (or $^1/_6$ of the shares vesting six months after the date of grant or service commencement) and $^1/_{48}$ of the shares vesting each month thereafter as long as the employee continues to provide services to the company.

What Happens to the Option on an Employee's Termination?

Generally, to the extent that an employee is vested in any shares, the employee must exercise the option 60 to 90 days after termination of employment. Companies often enter into agreements with members of the management team providing for acceleration or immediate vesting of a certain amount of shares held by the employee in the event of termination by the company without cause. (Refer to the section earlier in this chapter titled "Termination of Employment" for an explanation of "cause.") The amount of acceleration varies depending on the employee's position, market conditions, and individual factors.

What Happens to the Option on a Merger or Sale of the Company?

Generally, options are either assumed by the acquiring company, in which case the option becomes an option to purchase stock of the acquiring company; or a new option to purchase acquiring company stock is issued. Alternatively, the option is cancelled and the holders of options are paid what they would have been paid if they had exercised their vested options prior to the merger.

The company's option plan or option agreement will usually discuss the treatment of the option in the event of a merger transaction. Sometimes employees (although usually only management employees) are provided some acceleration of vesting in connection with a merger or acquisition. There are two approaches with respect to acceleration:

- **Single-trigger acceleration.** With *single-trigger acceleration*, some additional shares or all of the shares vest on the closing of the merger.
- **Double-trigger acceleration.** With *double-trigger acceleration*, if the company (or the acquiring company) terminates the employee without cause after a merger, some additional shares or all of the shares accelerate.

note Venture-capital investors often prefer the double-trigger approach because a company's employees are often one of the key reasons behind a particular acquisition. Acceleration of vesting can eliminate the main incentive keeping an employee at the acquiring company after the merger.

Are there Restrictions on the Issuance of Stock to Employees and Resale of Stock?

It is important to realize that when a company issues stock and stock options to employees, it must do so in compliance with federal and state securities regulations. A company may not issue stock or stock options to an employee without registering the stock (such as in connection with the company's IPO) or qualifying under an exemption. Stock-option plans for private companies are generally structured to meet the requirements of federal and state securities exemptions from registration.

Before a company issues stock or stock options to employees, it must consult with experienced legal counsel to make sure that appropriate filings are made and that a securities exemption is available to issue the stock in all applicable states. In addition, employees need to be made aware that stock obtained as an employee through a stock-option plan, like all other private company stock, is restricted stock. As a general matter, it can't be resold and must be held by the employee indefinitely until there is a company liquidity event, such as an IPO or sale of the company to a public company.

Critical U.S. Immigration Issues for Start-Ups

Scenario 1: Sid, Parthiv, Murthy, and Sanjiv want to start a new business. They have the technology and funding, but Sanjiv is on a student visa, which will expire in six months; Murthy is on an H-1B with another company; Parthiv is on a B1/B2 visitor's visa; and Sid is a U.S. citizen. They want to know whether they can start a business, and how doing so will affect their immigration status. Will they be able to work and remain in the U.S.?

Scenario 2: Olga has been working for Company X for the past year. Olga is on Optional Practical Training that expires in six months. Mark, Olga's boss, believes that Olga is an important asset to the company and he will not be able to find another worker with half the skills as Olga. Mark wants to know how he can keep her, and how she can continue to work for the company.

Scenario 3: Ali has invented a new software product idea. He needs 15 software engineers to bring this product to market before his other competitors. He wants to know how he can get the necessary skilled software engineers he needs.

These real-life scenarios are but a few illustrations of how immigration issues affect business. Today, an entrepreneur must consider the immigration consequences, plan for the company's human-resource needs, and work with competent immigration counsel to evaluate and process the necessary documentation to get the temporary specialty workers the company needs in a timely and efficient manner.

In the past, an entrepreneur would not find U.S. immigration law on the short list of important things to consider when establishing a new start up company, but in this growing global economy, immigration law is an essential part of any new business. Immigration is a key factor that must be considered and evaluated prior to establishment of a new entity, particularly if one of the co-founders is on non-immigrant status; it is an important operating tool for growing new businesses; and it is an essential in getting highly skilled workers from the global marketplace

What do you need to know about immigration law to get started? First of all, U.S. immigration is a complex, constantly changing area of law with three major agencies—Immigration and Naturalization Service (INS), Department of State (DOS), and Department of Labor (DOL)—administering the system, and many other agencies playing a role. Second, global and economic events affect U.S immigration law. Immigration no longer consists of solely filling out forms. It involves proper planning, prompt processing and execution, continual tracking and follow up, consistent record keeping, and periodic audits.

note Compliance with U.S. immigration law requires advance planning, prompt processing, effective execution, continuous tracking, consistent record-keeping, and periodic audits.

Navigating U.S. immigration law can be made simpler by working with a well qualified, knowledgeable, and thorough business-immigration attorney. A reliable business-immigration attorney can help you through the perils of immigration and leave you free to focus on your core business. Such an attorney can provide current information on any changes in immigration law or procedure; provide guidance to keep a company in compliance; process and assist to execute the necessary documentation and information required by the various agencies; and provide counsel regarding multiple immigration options, between various candidates, or in case of a merger, acquisition, or dissolution of a company or termination of any candidate.

When selecting a business-immigration attorney, consider whether candidates are members of the American Immigration Lawyers Association (AILA), as well as their reputation, client references, fees, focus of practice, years in practice, use of technology, communication, educational background, publications, industry focus, personality compatibility, language skills, follow through, ethics, and diligence. And of course, you should find out whether any disciplinary actions have been taken against them in the past.

Employment Verification

As an employer, you will have duties and obligations related to the Immigration Reform and Control Act of 1986 (IRCA). IRCA makes employers partners in efforts to reduce the number of illegal immigrants employed in the U.S. You are obligated not to hire an unauthorized worker. As an employer, you must verify the identity, immigration status, and eligibility to work of all individuals hired. You do this by completing the Employment Eligibility Form, commonly known as *form I-9*.

You also need to be aware of anti-discrimination rules. If you have more than three employees, you have to take care to not discriminate against foreign-born job applicants, and you cannot request that an applicant present a particular work-related document. Specifically, the law provides that employers cannot discriminate in hiring or terminating employees based upon their nationality or citizenship status and that it is illegal to forge, counterfeit, or alter documents needed to provide identity and employment eligibility. If you do not follow proper employment-verification guidelines, if you abuse those guidelines, or if you discriminate illegally, you will be exposing your company to substantial sanctions, as well as civil and criminal penalties.

As the employer, you are not required to be a document expert, but you are required to make a good-faith determination that the documents are valid. You must keep all I-9s for at least three years after the date of hire or for one year from the date of termination, whichever is later. In case of an inspection, you will be required to produce these I-9s. That means you should establish and maintain a system for storing and locating executed I-9s and conduct periodic internal audits (or hire proper counsel to conduct audits) to ensure compliance and avoid unnecessary sanctions.

Employment-Verification Checklist

- ❑ Complete and execute form I-9.
- ❑ Physically examine each document provided by the candidate.
- ❑ Check for genuineness, and make sure that the documents are listed on the back of the I-9 form to ensure that they establish identity and employment eligibility.
- ❑ Store form I-9 for at least three years after the date of hire or for one year from the date of termination, whichever is later.
- ❑ Conduct periodic audits to ensure compliance.

Employment Authorization

Authorization to work in the United States is automatically provided if an individual is a U.S. citizen or a Legal Permanent Resident (LPR). Authorization to work is also granted by the INS upon application under certain temporary non-immigrant classifications—for example, H-1Bs, L-1s, Os, Ps, Rs, and TNs. Employment authorization is documented through an employment authorization document (EAD), an EAD card, or through INS's Notice of Approval, form I-797. Generally, individuals entering on a business or personal visitor's visa, a student visa, except during the optional practical training period, or a visa waiver are not allowed to work and receive compensation, except reimbursement for out of pocket expenses.

note Non-immigrants are allowed to work only in certain non-immigrant classifications: H-1B, L-1A, L-1B, O, P, R-1, E-1, E-2, and TN.

Temporary Workers

If you want to hire foreign workers to temporarily perform services or labor or receive training, you may file a non-immigrant visa application. There are a number of non-immigrant temporary worker classifications for admission, the most familiar being an H-1B, which is a temporary non-immigrant worker visa. An H-1B petition is for a foreign alien who will be employed temporarily in a specialty occupation, requiring theoretical and practical application of a body of specialized knowledge with a minimum of a bachelor's degree or its equivalent. An H-1B visa is company, job, and location specific. There are limits as to the number of H-1B visas issued per year by INS. It is important to consult and work with a competent business-immigration attorney to ensure compliance with the H-1B regulations and guidelines.

Following are some key H-1B facts:

- There is an annual limit on the number of H-1B aliens who may be issued a visa or otherwise provided H-1B status.
- The employer petitions and sponsors an H-1B worker.
- The employer attests that it will pay the candidate at least the local prevailing wage or the employer's actual wage, whichever is higher; pay for non-productive time; and offer the same benefits as other U.S. workers. In addition, the employer attests that it will provide working conditions that will not adversely affect the working conditions of workers similarly employed, that there are no strikes or lockouts for that occupation at the

place of employment, that it will provide notice to union or to workers at the place of employment, and that it will provide a copy of an approved labor condition application to H-1B workers.

- There are two aspects to an H-1B process: acquisition of H-1B status upon approval of an H-1B petition with the INS in the U.S., and acquisition of the H-1B visa to travel to and from the U.S. for the period of approved status upon approval of a non-immigrant visa application by the U.S. Consulate in the candidate's home country or elsewhere, as applicable.
- The 2002 H-1B filing fee for the principal candidate is a basic fee of $130, an additional $1,000 fee to employers for training of U.S. employees, plus an additional $1,000 fee for premium processing, which guarantees processing within 15 days of receipt. There are separate fees for family members.
- The processing time varies for H-1B applications from 15 to 120 days, depending on backlog.
- Certain aliens working on Defense Department projects may remain in H-1B status for 10 years.
- An H-1B status is employer, job, and location specific. A material change without appropriate application may result in automatic termination of a candidate's status.
- Any substantial or material change in the job—such as a new job title, changes in required qualifications, significant changes in job duties, changes in location of the job, and so on—will activate the employer's obligation to file an amended H-1B petition, which may involve filing a new labor condition application.
- If an H-1B is terminated, the candidate's H-1B status terminates immediately. There is no grace period provided.
- New portability rules allow an H-1B candidate to start working for a new employer upon receipt of the new application from the new employer to INS.
- An H-1B employee must be paid 95% of the prevailing wage or higher as his or her base wage. INS does not allow payment of the H-1B employee's full salary to be in stock or profit sharing or on bonus.
- *Dual intent* is allowed in an H-1B, whereby the employee can have an intent to immigrate to the U.S. on both a temporary and permanent basis.
- An H-1B employee's spouse and children under 21 are automatically eligible for H-4 status as the derivative beneficiaries. A person with H-4 status may not be employed in the U.S.
- An H-1B employee is granted the same basic rights and privileges as any other employee within a company.

- An H-1B may be granted for a period of three years with a right to renew for another three years, for a total period of six years.
- An H-1B employee can start a company, but the employee should work with a qualified attorney to properly establish the company without jeopardizing his or her H-1B status.

Planning and Documenting Angel and Venture-Capital Financing

In this book, you have learned the fundamentals of how to take your idea from concept to the creation of a viable company to commercialize your idea. You know what corporate form to choose, the state of incorporation for your company, and the basic structure of your board of directors and management team. You know about the different forms of intellectual property and how to make sure that IP is safely embedded in your assets. You've got a good idea about employee issues, including the many regulatory traps and sensitive issues surrounding labor, employment, and immigration matters. The planning is done. Now you're ready to take your company to the next level. For that, you need money. You are ready to approach investors and, with their backing, you're ready to drive your company forward to realize your goals.

What Kinds of Investors Are Out There?

Angel investors traditionally invest in early-stage companies. They're typically the first backers, the people who will put money into organizations before large, established venture-capital firms will show interest, and when only a relatively small initial capital infusion is necessary to get going. Entrepreneurs often meet angel investors through social or professional contacts. They're usually more accessible than venture firms, particularly at this early stage of your company's development. Angel investors also tend to be less hands-on than venture-capital investors; most do not get particularly involved in the company's business. (Of course, there are always exceptions to prove the rule; some angel investors may be very interested in having more involvement with the company.)

In addition, a lot of entrepreneurs turn to family members and friends to help them fund their companies. Be aware, however, that stock sold to family and friends is still subject to the same federal and state securities laws that apply to other types of investors, and certain formalities must be maintained. It's critical to engage sophisticated legal counsel with extensive experience in financing matters and securities-law expertise if you want to avoid some serious consequences.

Other potential investors for the company include venture-capital firms or corporate investors (either directly from the corporation or through the corporation's venture-financing arm). Corporate investments generally follow much the same path as a venture financing but, from a strategic viewpoint, such investments are usually motivated by a need for shared technology or some other business synergy unique to the needs of the corporation. (In other words, they want and need something that you have.)

What Is the Process for Getting Money into the Company?

Most angel investors, and certainly all venture-capital firms or corporate investors, will require a written business plan as a first-level information source for background on you and your company. If the investors read the business plan and are intrigued by your company and its future prospects, you will go through a series of meetings with the investor—in the case of a venture capital firm, first with one or two members culminating in a meeting of several (or all) of the partners in the firm. These meetings are comprehensive and exhausting, but necessary. If the investor decides to pursue an investment, the next step is the presentation of a term sheet. (Term sheets are discussed in more detail later in this chapter in the section titled "Frequently Asked Questions and Answers.")

The term sheet is one of the most heavily negotiated portions of the investment process. Most of the major issues, including the valuation of the company, the structure of the investment, and the rights of the investor are covered by the term sheet. It is not a document that you glance over casually. The terms of the investment will be set here; do not assume that you can go back later and renegotiate terms you do not like when the final documents are being drafted. You and your attorney need to be comfortable with the term sheet before proceeding to drafting definite documents.

After the term sheet has been exhaustively negotiated and executed, the company and investors must still enter into definitive financing documents. The definitive financing documents flush out the broad outline of the term sheet. Having experienced corporate legal counsel to guide you through this process is essential. Poorly drafted legal documentation evidencing the financing will likely cause future problems for the company as well as the investors. It is important that the documents accurately reflect the deal. Future investors will also want to review these documents in their due-diligence reviews.

Finally, keep in mind that throughout the process of documenting the investment, the investor will be conducting an extensive due-diligence review of the company and its business. All the careful planning you did as a result of reading prior and following chapters should pay off in this phase of the process, as closing a financing for a good, clean company tends to happen more quickly than for a company that requires a significant amount of corporate clean-up.

Most deals get done in a fair and standard way. Sophisticated investors have done hundreds of deals with start-up companies such as yours. There is a basic format and process that almost all investors follow. This does not mean that you cannot negotiate specific investment terms based on the needs of your company; keep in mind, however, that at the end of the day, most of the early-stage investments look fairly similar. Investors such as the ones interested in your company are, by definition, risk takers, but they also have some standard protections that they have come to expect.

The following sections will guide you through some of the most typical terms of the early-stage investment term sheet.

Investment Terms

There are some traditional areas of negotiation in virtually all early-stage financings. The following discussion references a sample term sheet attached as an appendix to this chapter. The sample term sheet for the fictitious company, WhiteHot Technology Company, Inc., covers many of the standard terms and conditions requested by early-stage investors, several of which will be subject to negotiation by you and your attorney.

Valuation

The valuation of your company determines how much equity the founders must sell to get the desired amount of financing. For example, if a company is valued at $4,000,000 pre-money (referring to the value before the investors purchase their equity portion of the company), the founders could sell 33% of the company for $2,000,000. Investors will almost certainly negotiate the founders' proposed pre-money valuation of the company. If the pre-money valuation falls from $4,000,000 to $3,000,000, the same $2,000,000 investment will cause the investors to own 40% of the company. Thus, the valuation of the company is often a hotly contested (and sometimes the most important) issue facing the entrepreneur and the investors.

Preferred Stock

Outside investors almost always demand preferred stock. Preferred stock generally enables the investor to receive a return on his or her investment before the founders (who typically hold common stock). Holding preferred stock gives the investors the upside of equity ownership in a successful company, because the preferred stock will undoubtedly be convertible into common stock in the event the company is sold or goes public. It also helps protect the investors if the company doesn't succeed. In a liquidation proceeding, available cash is distributed first to the creditors of the company (secured first, unsecured next), then to equity holders of the company (preferred holders first, then the common). The preferred stock, therefore, gives the investor some additional protection in case the company is not successful.

Although the equity received by investors is almost certainly going to be preferred stock, there are some additional terms related to the rights of preferred stock that frequently get mentioned and/or negotiated:

- **Dividends.** The term sheet will almost always specify an annual dividend for the preferred stock. A dividend looks much like interest on the preferred stock. From a practical standpoint, however, the board of directors usually has a great deal of discretion in declaring and/or paying dividends; therefore, they are rarely declared or paid by start-up companies. Cumulative dividends are those that add up year after year. In the event of a liquidation, keep in mind that most dividends become due and payable.
- **Liquidation preference.** As mentioned previously, preferred stock gets preferential treatment over common stock in the event of a liquidation. The term sheet will usually provide that upon a liquidation, holders of preferred stock will be paid their original purchase price for the preferred stock plus accrued dividends on such shares before anything is paid to the common holders. (The definition of *liquidation* is now fairly standard, and usually includes a merger, a reorganization, sale of all or substantially all the company's assets, and any transaction in which the majority voting control of the company is transferred.) This repayment of the original purchase price is commonly referred to as a *1x liquidation preference*. Multipliers on the liquidation preference are also not uncommon. A multiplier of 2x entitles the investors to receive two times the original purchase price of the preferred stock before anything is paid to the common holders. Note that if the liquidation proceeds cover only the preference on the preferred, the common holders will end up with no proceeds from the sale.

note Companies frequently negotiate the liquidation preference. Although multipliers are common, companies obviously prefer to keep the liquidation preference as close to 1x as possible. A lower multiplier enhances the chance that common stockholders (frequently founders) will see some return in the event of a liquidation. In addition, each subsequent financing will look to the previous liquidation preference as a starting point; the lower it is initially, the better position the company is in to keep it lower for the next round of financing.

- **Participating preferred.** In addition to the basic liquidation preference, some preferred stock is *participating preferred*, meaning that in addition to the preferential 1x or 2x return from the proceeds of the liquidation, such preferred will also be entitled to participate in any remaining proceeds as if the preferred stock had been converted into common stock prior to the liquidation. Remember that, generally, once the preferred holders have been paid their liquidation preference, the remaining money goes to the common holders. If the preferred are entitled to participate, they get counted again and are paid on a pro rata basis from the leftover proceeds with the rest of the common holders.

- **Conversion.** Generally, the preferred stock will be convertible at the option of the preferred holders. In addition, the preferred stock will be automatically convertible upon a public offering or upon a vote of the preferred stock as a class. The term sheet will specify the conversion ratio; keep in mind that such ratio will be subject to anti-dilution provisions and other adjustments (see below). Conversion is rarely negotiated.
- **Anti-dilution.** Most times, the preferred stock converts on a one-for-one basis into common stock. As opposed to general conversion rights, however, negotiation on anti-dilution provisions can be fierce. Investors want anti-dilution to protect against future stock issuances by the company at prices lower than the price paid by such investors. The anti-dilution provision is usually drawn from three alternatives, with the broad-based weighted average provision being the preferred choice of the company. Other choices that tend to favor the investors include the narrow-based weighted average and the ratchet. (See the section "Frequently Asked Questions and Answers" for more details on the anti-dilution weighted-average and ratchet formulas.)
- **Pay to play.** A *pay-to-play* provision is intended to encourage existing investors to participate in subsequent financings by taking away such investors' anti-dilution protection (and/or other rights) if such investors do not fully participate in each subsequent financing. A pay-to-play provision might be contained in the conversion section of the term sheet or in a separate section altogether.
- **Registration rights.** There are generally two types of registration rights addressed in a financing term sheet: demand and piggyback. The *demand* registration right allows the investors (upon a vote) to force the company to register their shares so that they may be traded on the public market. Registering shares is an expensive endeavor, so many companies would prefer simply to give piggyback registration rights. *Piggyback* registration rights allow the investors to participate in a company-initiated offering of shares (so that the company controls the timing of the offering). All such rights are subject to limitations, but more control is reserved for the company under the piggyback scenario.

- **Right of first refusal on sales to third parties.** Investors generally will require that the company and the investors have the right to purchase a founder's stock in the event a founder tries to sell his or her stock. Remember that the investors are not just investing in your company and its products/services. Especially at this early stage, they are also investing in the team/founders. The investors want to be sure that the founders aren't bailing out of the company and disappearing. In addition, in a privately held company, the composition of stockholders is very important. The investors may rather the company spend money to purchase founders stock or the investors purchase the founders stock rather than take their chances with unknown new stockholders. Most importantly, though, especially at this stage in the company's life cycle, founders usually remain key players, and the investors do not want them to be free to cash out and leave the company without some notice and control.
- **Redemption.** Investors may ask for a redemption right for their preferred stock, although generally, the company tries to resist giving such a right. A *redemption right* means that the investors may (upon a vote—usually a two-thirds majority) elect to force the company to buy back their shares of preferred stock. This right can be triggered without the prior approval of the company management. The redemption price is negotiated, but it may be the fair market value of the preferred stock plus any declared but unpaid dividends. Companies obviously don't like this type of right, because it can be an untimely cash drain on the company, and company management would rather have the investors wait for their return until there is an event such as a public offering or acquisition or merger with additional consideration available for the stockholders.

Corporate Governance Terms

Investors also frequently negotiate for certain corporate governance rights in connection with their investment. Frequently negotiated terms with respect to corporate governance include

- **Board representation.** Most investors will generally ask for a board seat. This enables the investors to keep their finger on the pulse of the company and to have a voice with respect to major company decisions.
- **Veto power.** In addition to obtaining representation on the board, most investors will request voting protections against certain company actions. This means that for a specified list of actions, the investors will be entitled to a separate vote. If the majority of such investors' shares do not approve the proposed action, it cannot happen. This is effectively a veto right, and it can apply to a number of different corporate actions (although the company

and its counsel will try to limit this list as much as possible). Among others, the following are typical corporate actions subject to such a "veto" right:

- Changing the rights or privileges of the preferred shares
- Creating any securities senior or equal to the rights of the preferred shares
- Changing the authorized number of directors on the board
- Changing the authorized number of shares of preferred stock
- A consolidation, sale, or merger, or a transfer of all or substantially all of the company's assets or other transaction in which the majority voting control is transferred
- Amending the company's organizational documents—the certificate of incorporation or bylaws
- Redeeming, repurchasing, or declaring a dividend (with certain exceptions)

What Is an Exit Strategy?

Most investors—angels and professional venture capitalists alike—invest in risky venture-capital financings with the primary purpose of realizing an economic return. By investing in a private company, investors have few options in making a return on their investment (referred to as an *exit strategy*). Generally, there are two primary exit strategies for a private company:

- **Initial public offering (IPO).** In an IPO, the company's common stock becomes publicly traded and the original shareholders would then be allowed to sell their stock, in accordance with certain legal limitations.
- **Merger or acquisition.** Upon a merger or acquisition, the original shareholders would either receive cash or publicly traded securities (if acquired by a public company). Unfortunately, an acquisition or merger by a private company for stock would not provide any liquidity for the shareholders.

Other Traps

Often, individuals approach entrepreneurs claiming that they can help raise money for their company. While many such individuals do have access to funds, entrepreneurs should use extreme caution in these relationships. These individuals (generally referred to as *finders*) do not work for free. In exchange for bringing in financing, such finders typically ask for a portion of the cash (meaning there is less for the company), an equity piece of the company, and similar rights for all future financings—sometimes encompassing financings undertaken years in the future.

Investors (such as venture-capital firms) are generally loath to put money into a company that will immediately be paid to a finder; the company does not then get the benefit of the money to move forward. In addition, the long-term nature of such finder agreements—that the finder gets a portion of future financings for a period of years following the signing of the contract—can effectively choke the company and prevent it from getting meaningful outside funding. There are also securities laws that the finder must comply with to provide these services and if they fail to do so it could jeopordize the company's financing. If your company must enter into such an agreement, quality counsel from your attorney will be invaluable.

What Happens After I Get the Money?

Once the company has successfully completed raising the initial venture-financing round, the entrepreneur and the company as a whole can turn the focus back to making the business a successful and profitable enterprise. You will also begin preparing for the next round of financing to bring the business to a new level, but this time, you will bring much more experience and wisdom to the process.

Frequently Asked Questions and Answers

What Is an "Angel" Investor?

Angels are usually wealthy individuals who are interested in leveraging their business experience and participating in a promising company's growth—thereby achieving a rate of return better than they can get by more traditional investments. Angels frequently, but not always, are former start-up entrepreneurs themselves, and can be good resources for industry contacts and solid business advice.

What Is Venture Capital?

Venture capital is money from a firm whose purpose is to invest capital from a fund raised from various institutions and high–net worth individuals. Venture-capital funds are expected to realize a high rate of return within a relatively short timeframe.

What Are the Pros and Cons of Venture Capital?

On the pro side, obtaining venture capital is a significant step in a company's growth progression. It signals to the world that a professional investor has bought into the company's products/services and business plan. This frequently leads to additional rounds of financing and, in some instances, growth to the point of conducting an initial public offering. Venture-capital firms, especially those that specialize in certain industries, may also bring valuable contacts and networking opportunities for the company. Finally, once invested in a company, the venture-capital firm is motivated to help the company become a bigger and profitable entity—so that the firm can reap the rewards of its investment.

On the con side, the most frequent complaint of entrepreneurs is about the assigned value of the company by the investor. The less the company is valued, the more equity the founders must give up in order to obtain the desired dollar amount of funding. Most entrepreneurs are surprised by the valuations given their business by the professional investment community. In addition, most entrepreneurs have concerns about the level of corporate governance control that is relinquished to the investor in connection with the investment. Prior to making the investment, venture-capital investors also conduct extensive due diligence on prospective companies, which takes valuable time away from the operation of prospective company's business—especially if you don't end up with any money.

Which Venture-Capital Firms Should I Approach and How Do I Get an Introduction in the First Place?

First, identify the type of venture-capital firm that might be interested in your business. Does the firm focus on seed-stage investments (generally $50,000 to $1,000,000), early-stage investments (generally $1,000,000 to $10,000,000), or late-stage investments (generally $10,000,000 and up)? Also, although some venture-capital firms are generalists, consider whether your company would be better served by a specialist firm known for investments and contacts in your industry. There are pros and cons to the choice of both generalists and specialists. Weigh all factors carefully; your professional advisor can assist in this evaluation.

Keep in mind that venture-capital firms are inundated with business plans and entrepreneurs seeking funding. Many get literally hundreds of unsolicited plans a week. Your best bet is to have some personal connection with the recipient—perhaps through your business advisors (lawyers or accountants), through a member of your management team or board, contacts at a large and well-known company, or even a personal contact made by you at an industry conference. As in product sales, a cold call is one of the most difficult ways to get your audience's attention. Of course, a cold call is better than no call at all; therefore, be an active member of your industry's community, but don't let the lack of a personal contact stop you. You never know what might come out of a simple phone call.

How Long Does the Average Venture-Capital Round Take to Close?

A venture-capital round will never happen as quickly as the company wishes. Plan on at least three months (and sometimes longer) from your initial meeting with the venture capitalist. Remember, however, that the more prepared and organized you are in terms of having your company's affairs in order, the faster the process may go. Some financings happen in a matter of a few weeks. Through good preparation and solid professional advice, you may be able to reduce the time to close (meaning you get the money more quickly).

What Is a Term Sheet? Who Drafts It? Is It Binding?

Typically, the investor provides a term sheet to the company outlining the basic terms upon which the investment will be made. A term sheet will always include a valuation of the company, the amount to be invested, the equity vehicle the investor wants to obtain for the money, the rights of the equity vehicle, and other rights for the investor.

note See the appendix at the end of this chapter for a sample term sheet for the fictitious company WhiteHot Technology Company, Inc.

The term sheet is typically negotiated between the investor and the company (and their respective lawyers), and provides the basis for the final investment documents. Term sheets are rarely binding upon the parties. Investors will invariably request a *due-diligence out*, which allows them to continue their due diligence review of the company and its business during the negotiation and drafting stages. If the investor finds something (or even if he gets cold feet), he can simply refuse to close the deal. The bottom line is that there is no guarantee until the money is in the bank.

What Is a Broad-Based Weighted Average Versus a Narrow-Based Weighted Average? What Is a Ratchet?

All these terms relate to the formulas used to calculate anti-dilution rights of investors. Weighted average formulas vary from deal to deal, although some basic methodologies apply according to whether the formula is broad-based or narrow-based.

In the case of a broad-based weighted average, when calculating the price to which an existing series of preferred stock converts, the outstanding shares of common stock are treated as though they were sold at the same price as the series being adjusted. This lessens the impact of a down round (where stock is being sold at a lower price than in a previous round).

A narrow-based weighted average, on the other hand, focuses the anti-dilution adjustment on just a preferred-to-preferred comparison, and adjusts downward more rapidly than the broad-based version (thereby explaining why investors tend to prefer the narrow-based and companies tend to prefer the broad-based).

A *ratchet* does not take into account the size of the round (unlike the weighted-average formulas). It allows investors to convert their series at the lower price even if only one share is issued below the price paid by the investors. Companies tend to resist ratchet provisions (unless they have very little leverage in the negotiation), as they are fairly draconian.

Appendix I: Sample Term Sheet

SUMMARY OF DRAFT TERMS

WhiteHot Technology Company, Inc.

[DATE]

This memorandum summarizes the principal terms of the Series A Preferred Stock financing (the "Financing") of WhiteHot Technology Company, Inc. (the "Company"). The Company was incorporated in Delaware on ______________, 200_.

KEY PROVISIONS

Investors	ABC Ventures, L.P. XYZ Technology Partners, L.P. (the "Investors").
Security	Series A Convertible Preferred Stock of the Company ("Series A Preferred").
Price per share	$_____ (the "Series A Purchase Price").
Aggregate proceeds	$___________ (minimum proceeds of $__________ required for the Initial Closing).
Expected closing date	________ ___, 2002 (the "Initial Closing"). Additional closings may be held at the option ofthe Company within ninety (90) days after the Initial Closing, at times selected by the Company.

TERMS OF SERIES A PREFERRED STOCK

Dividend provisions	Each share of Series A Preferred will be entitled to an annual dividend in an amount equal to 8% of the Series A Purchase Price, which dividend shall only be payable if, as, and when determined by the Company's Board of Directors (the "Board"). Such dividends are not cumulative. With respect to any other dividends or distributions, shares of Series A Preferred will participate with shares of the Company's Common Stock ("Common Stock") pro rata as though the Series A Preferred had been converted to Common Stock (an "as-converted basis").
Liquidation preference	Upon a liquidation of the Company, each share of Series A Preferred shall be entitled to receive, prior and in preference to any other shares of Company capital stock, the Series A Purchase Price plus accrued dividends on each share of Series A Preferred. Thereafter, the holders of Series A Preferred and Common Stock will share proceeds on a pro rata as-converted basis until the holders of Series A Preferred have received an aggregate amount of

	$_____ per share. Thereafter, the balance of the proceeds of such liquidation shall be paid to the holders of Common Stock. A merger, reorganization or other transaction in which majority voting control of the Company is transferred, as well as any sale of all or substantially all of its assets, shall be deemed to be a liquidation for purposes of the liquidation preference.
Conversion	Each share of Series A Preferred will be convertible at any time at the option of the holder thereof into one share of Common Stock (subject to antidilution and other adjustments).
Automatic conversion	All shares of Series A Preferred shall be automatically converted into Common Stock, at the then-applicable conversion price, upon the earlier of (i) the closing of an underwritten public offering of shares of Common Stock at a public offering price per share that is not less than three times the Series A Purchase Price and an aggregate offering price of not less than $30,000,000 (a "Qualifying IPO"), and (ii) the date upon which the Company obtains the vote or consent of holders of at least 51% of the then-outstanding shares of Series A Preferred to such conversion.
Antidilution provision	The conversion ratio of Series A Preferred shall be proportionally adjusted for stock splits, stock dividends, and the like. In addition, the conversion ratio shall be adjusted on a broad-based weighted average basis in the event that the Company issues additional equity securities at a purchase price per share that is lower than the Series A Purchase Price (other than shares issued under stock option plans approved by the Board and other customary exceptions).[1]
Voting and protective provisions	Holders of Series A Preferred will vote with the Common Stock on an as-converted basis, but will also have a majority class vote on the following matters: 1) Altering, changing, or amending the preferences, privileges, or rights of shares of Series A Preferred; 2) Authorizing, creating, and/or issuing any shares of a class or series of equity securities that is senior to or *pari passu* with shares of Series A Preferred; 3) Increasing or decreasing the authorized number of directors constituting the Board; 4) Increasing or decreasing the authorized number of shares of Series A Preferred; 5) Any consolidation, sale, or merger of the Company; transfer of all or substantially all of its assets; or other transaction in which majority voting control of the Company is transferred;

*[*1]The antidilution provision is typically drawn from three alternatives, with broad-based weighted average" provision being the most prevalent. Other choices include narrow-based weighted average and ratchet antidilution. A ratchet provision in a term sheet might read as follows: "Conversion ratio adjusted on a full ratchet basis in the event of any dilutive issuance."*

6) Amending or waiving any provision of the Company's Certificate of Incorporation or Bylaws; and
7) Redeeming, repurchasing, or declaring a dividend with regard to any security of the Company, except upon termination of employment with the Company pursuant to the terms of a stock-option plan or other agreement approved by the Board.

TERMS OF INVESTOR RIGHTS AGREEMENT

Right of first offer on subsequent issuances

Each holder of at least _______ shares of Series A Preferred (each, a "Significant Holder") shall have the right in the event the Company proposes to offer equity securities to any person (other than the securities issued pursuant to stock-option plans or agreements or in connection with acquisitions, in each such case as approved by the Board, or other customary exclusions) to purchase on a pro rata basis up to the minimum number of such shares necessary for such holder to maintain its percentage ownership of the Company's equity securities (such percentage ownership being based on the "fully diluted" capital stock of the Company assuming exercise or conversion of all outstanding options, warrants, notes, and other rights to acquire shares of the Company's capital stock). Any securities not subscribed for by a Significant Holder may be reallocated among the other Significant Holders. Any securities not purchased by the Significant Holders may be offered to other parties on terms no less favorable to the Company for a period of sixty (60) days.

This right shall terminate immediately prior to the earlier of (i) the closing of a Qualifying IPO, and (ii) the closing of any merger or consolidation of the Company in which majority voting control of the Company is transferred.

Right of first refusal on sales to third parties by founders

The Company shall have the right in the event either _________, _________, or _________ (each a "Founder") proposes to offer equity securities to any person to purchase all or any portion of such shares (subject to customary exclusions). Any securities not subscribed for by the Company shall be reallocated among the Significant Holders on a pro rata basis. If neither the Company nor the Significant Holders purchase all of such securities, the Founder may sell that portion of such securities that were not purchased by the Company or the Significant Holders to other parties on terms no less favorable to such Founder for a period of sixty (60) days. Such right of first refusal will terminate upon a Qualifying IPO.

Registration Rights

Demand rights	Beginning upon the earlier of five year anniversary of the initial closing, and the six (6) month anniversary of the closing of a Qualifying IPO, holders of at least 40% of the outstanding shares of Series A Preferred and any shares of Common Stock issued upon conversion of shares of Series A Preferred ("Registrable Securities"), voting together as a single class on an as-converted basis, will have the right to initiate two (2) demand registrations by the Company, provided that each such registration includes Registrable Securities having a minimum aggregate offering price to the public of not less than $10,000,000.
Company registration	The holders of Registrable Securities shall have unlimited "piggy-back" rights to participate in registered public offerings by the Company, subject to pro rata reduction of their participation at the underwriters' discretion. The participation of such holders may be completely eliminated in the Company's first registered public offering (an "IPO"), but such holders shall have the right to sell at least 25% of the shares sold in each subsequent registered public offering. If such holders are so limited, however, no party shall sell shares in such registered offering other than the Company or the holders, if any, invoking the demand registration.
S-3 rights	The holders of Registrable Securities shall have the right to initiate up to two (2) demand registrations by the Company on Form S-3 during each calendar year, provided that each such registration has a minimum offering size of $1,000,000.
Termination of registration rights	The foregoing registration rights will terminate upon the earlier of (i) the fifth anniversary of an IPO, and (ii) such time following an IPO when all shares held by an investor can be sold under Rule 144 within a 90-day period. No future registration rights may be granted without the consent of holders of a majority of Registrable Securities unless such future rights are subordinate to those of the holders of Registrable Securities.
Expenses	The Company shall bear registration expenses (exclusive of underwriting discounts and commissions) of all such demand, piggy-back, and S-3 registrations (including the reasonable fees and expenses of one special counsel to the selling stockholders).
Transfer of rights	The foregoing registration rights may be transferred to (i) any partner or retired partner of any holder that is a partnership, (ii) any family member or trust for the benefit of any individual holder, or (iii) any transferee who acquires at least ________ shares of Registrable Securities; provided, in each such case, that the Company is given prior written notice thereof.

Standoff provision	No Investor shall sell shares of the Company's capital stock within 180 days of the effective date of the registration statement for an IPO if all officers and directors of the Company and all holders of greater than 5% of the Company's capital stock are similarly bound. Each holder of Registrable Securities will, at the request of the Company or any underwriter involved in such IPO, execute a written statement in a form requested by the Company or the underwriters reaffirming this obligation to the Company and the underwriters.
Board representation	The authorized number of directors shall initially be ________. Series A Preferred shall have the right to elect _________ directors and the Common Stock (voting as a class) shall have the right to elect _________ directors. Effective upon the Initial Closing, the members of the Board shall be __________, ____________ and _____________. The above Board composition shall be implemented through a Voting Agreement.
Inspection and information rights	Each Significant Holder shall have the right to inspect the Company's premises and books at times convenient to both parties. Such Investor also shall have the right to receive unaudited quarterly financial statements (including income statements, balance sheets, cash-flow statements, and summaries of bookings and backlog) and any management commentary related thereto within thirty (30) days of the close of each fiscal quarter, and audited annual financial statements within ninety (90) days of the close of the fiscal year, in each case showing changes from the applicable budget for the corresponding period. Prior to the beginning of each fiscal year (and prior to the Initial Closing), the Company shall prepare and forward to qualifying Investors detailed monthly financial projections for the such fiscal year. The foregoing rights will terminate upon the closing of an IPO.

TERMS OF PREFERRED STOCK PURCHASE AGREEMENT

Representations and warranties	The investments shall be made pursuant to a Stock Purchase Agreement reasonably acceptable to the Company and the Investors, which shall contain, among other things, appropriate representations, warranties and covenants of the Company reflecting the provisions set forth herein and other standard provisions, and appropriate conditions to the Initial Closing, including a customary legal opinion of Company counsel regarding the Financing.
Expenses	The Company and the Investors shall each bear their own legal and other expenses with respect to the

Financing except that, assuming a successful completion of the Financing, the Company shall pay the legal fees and expenses of one counsel to the Investors, up to a maximum of $20,000 plus expenses. Every effort will be made to minimize these expenses.

FOUNDERS AND EMPLOYEE AGREEMENTS

Stock vesting	Unless otherwise approved by the Board, all stock and stock equivalents issued after the Initial Closing to employees, directors and consultants of the Company shall be subject to vesting as follows: 25% to vest at the end of the first year following such issuance, with the remaining 75% to vest monthly over the next three years. All such stock and stock equivalents shall be subject to repurchase by the Company prior to vesting. Such repurchase right shall provide that upon termination of the employment or other service to the Company of the stockholder, with or without cause, the Company or its assignee (to the extent permitted by applicable securities law qualifications) retains the option to repurchase at cost any unvested shares held by such stockholder.
Restrictions on Common Stock transfers	No transfers of unvested shares of Common Stock will be allowed. The Company will have a right of first refusal with respect to transfers of shares of Common Stock until the closing of an IPO, subject to customary exclusions.
Market standoff	As a condition of his or her purchase of shares of Common Stock or the receipt of a grant of options to purchase Common Stock, each holder of Common Stock or options will agree not to sell or otherwise transfer any securities of the Company during a period of up to 180 days following the effective date of the registration of an IPO and, at the request of the Company or any underwriter, shall execute a written statement in a form requested by the Company or the underwriters reaffirming this obligation to the Company and the underwriters.
Proprietary information and inventions agreement	Each officer, employee, and consultant of the Company shall enter into an acceptable proprietary information and inventions agreement.
Co-sale rights	Each Significant Holder shall have the right to participate pro rata (based upon its portion of the fully diluted capital stock of the Company) in transfers of stock for value by any Founder, subject to customary exclusions.

OTHER PROVISIONS

Management rights	The Company shall execute a "Management Rights Letter" in the form attached hereto as Exhibit A.

Closing conditions The Initial Closing will be subject to negotiation of definitive legal documents and the completion of legal and financial due diligence by the Investors.

Capitalization Immediately following the Initial Closing, there shall be ________ shares of issued and outstanding Common Stock held by the Founders, _________ shares of Common Stock reserved for issuance pursuant to outstanding options and commitments, and an additional ________ shares of Common Stock reserved for future issuance to key employees.

This letter is only a list of the proposed terms that may become part of an eventual agreement (the "Agreement") between the parties and does not contain all matters on which agreement must be reached in order for a transaction to be consummated. This proposal does not constitute a binding contract and the parties do not intend to be legally bound and nothing stated herein expressly or by implication shall impose any obligations on the parties. This proposal shall expire if not accepted by the Company by the close of business on ________________ ___, 2002.

If this letter confirms your understanding, please sign below and return. We look forward to working with you on this transaction.

Sincerely,

[LEAD INVESTOR]

Agreed to and Accepted by:

WHITEHOT TECHNOLOGY COMPANY, INC.

Date:

four 4

CHAPTER

The Human Equation

Co-Chair: Prasad Kaipa, Co-founder - **SelfCorp., Inc.**
Co-Chair: Paul Kimura, Principal - **Avery Associates**
Co-Chair: Raj Sampath Ph.D. - **Heidrick & Struggles**
Sanjana Anand - **People Dynamics**
Ruby Rekhi Bal - **Netlink Consulting Services**
Ron Bohlin - **Knowledge Impact**
K.P. Chaudhuri - **GSI Technology Inc.**
Subhash Chowdary - **Aankhen, Inc.**
Ben Connors - **Ben Connors & Associates**
Theresa Dadone - **Propel Software Corporation**
Firth Griffith - **Beachhead Capital**
Tim Harris - **Clarent Corporation**
B.V. Jagadeesh - **Netscaler, Inc.**
Kenzo Kimura - **Avery Associates**
Thomas Milus - **SelfCorp, Inc.**
Aloka R. Naskar - **Brown Venture Associates**
Vimu Rajdev - **Rajex Inc.**
Paul Sabharwal - **HR Consultant**
Roma Trakru - **Infobridge Inc.**
Kyung Yoon - **Heidrick & Struggles**
Mark Yowe - **Heidrick & Struggles**

Introduction

With your vision clear, technology or service defined, business plan and financial structure in place, and founding team established, there remains one huge fundamental that will ultimately determine your ability to build a sustainable enterprise: how you use your people. Human-capital management is an "inside-out" issue; your chances of success are multiplied to the extent that you maximize your human capital.

While other chapters of this book address acquiring and working with financial capital, licensing, technology, mergers, and other very important issues, this section addresses the "soft"—but extremely important—human-capital issues. Maintaining an equal level of respect for and attention to natural capital (the environment), social capital, financial capital, and human capital is essential in helping you build balance. Achieving equilibrium between the different types of capital will result overall in a stronger organization.

To maximize your human capital, you must develop the following:

- **Soft skills.** Soft skills such as leadership, decision making, conflict resolution, negotiation, communication, creativity, and presentation skills are critical to all facets of your venture. They can provide great energy and cohesion for all members of your enterprise.
- **Management team.** Your success is more secure with an experienced management team at the top. You don't want to gamble on the abilities of you and your cofounders to grow the company at optimal rates through the different stages of the enterprise.
- **Talent-management system.** Focusing on such issues as HR systems; company culture; hiring, retaining, and motivating employees; knowledge-transfer processes; and so on allows you to harvest the creativity of your talent. People leave or lose motivation at different times. Without the proper system, you can keep making the same mistakes.

These are three corners of a triangle; failing to pay adequate attention to any of the three will impede your chances of success.

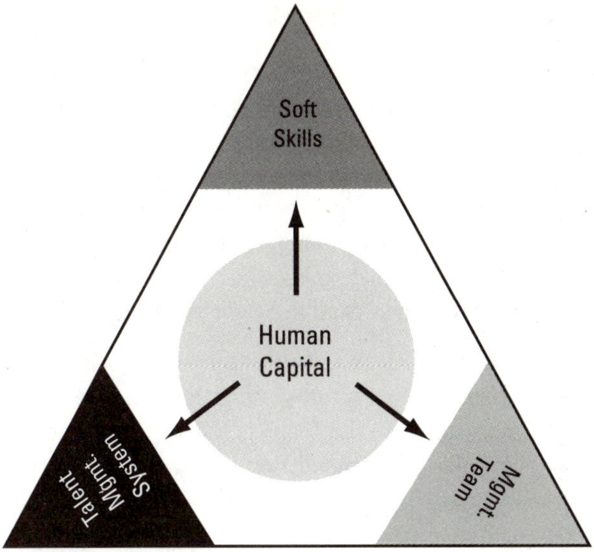

When your enterprise is optimized around the three corners, each corner multiplies the value of other two. Of course, when the enterprise is sub-optimized, then each corner operates at a fraction of its capacity; arguably, this also adversely affects the other facets of your organization. The overall net result may be much less than what you are capable of.

Soft Skills Are Smart Skills

Executive Summary

Soft skills such as leadership, decision making, conflict resolution, negotiation, communication, creativity, and presentation are essential for entrepreneurial success and for maximizing human capital in any enterprise. When balanced with a good management team and an effective human-resource management system, soft skills provide a way to get the highest return on investment in terms of human capital. Although professional skills may open the door of opportunity, soft skills keep you in the driver's seat. In this section, we offer our "Top 10" list of items on which an entrepreneur should focus. We conclude with some suggested competencies, which deserve particular emphasis.

Why Do You Need to Develop Soft Skills?

It's a fact: The vast majority of projects that focus on systems development and deployment in big organizations are late, over-budget, or cancelled. Time and again, studies have shown that the underlying causes of project failures are rarely technical (that is, idea-related). Instead, most project failures can be attributed to breakdowns in communication between executives and the talent, teams, and project managers. When the talent-management system—including executive teams and skill sets (technical, professional, and soft skills)—are not balanced and optimized, financial capital and human capital do not pay the anticipated returns.

Many entrepreneurs with great ideas and great talent fail—often because they neglect to install the appropriate structures and processes that are essential to moving forward. In addition, when the focus is too much on hard technical skills, the dynamics in the workplace become difficult to manage. Many entrepreneurs never see the first anniversary of their companies because they lack soft skills.

Don't underestimate the importance of soft skills. The failure to balance and maximize the human-capital triangle makes or breaks companies. Without the right team in place at the top of the hierarchy, decision making suffers. Markets change and competition grows in unexpected ways. When you're not making the right decisions at the right time to deal with new realities, you're falling behind. Without soft skills, poor decisions are made, negotiations go poorly, communication lacks passion, and leadership withers away fairly quickly. And on a more practical level, failure to optimize HR systems may lead to people going unpaid!

Technical skills get you in the door, but soft skills keep you in the job. Technologies, even great technologies, can only keep you afloat so long. Management determines ultimate success. Eventually, companies sink or swim based on the quality of their management. Soft skills are your life jackets!

note Soft skills are the keystones to success, enabling you to lead people in an effective manner. (The term *people* includes yourself as well as your team members.)

Table 4.1 Value of Soft Skills

Leading people	Leading a team, leading yourself, conflict management, interviewing and selecting new members, delegation, coaching, networking, developing others
Managing activities	Product quality, workplace safety, customer care, fund raising
Managing resources	People, finances
Managing information	Decision making, problem solving, meeting management, persuasion, presentation skills

tip For developing soft skills, focus on a long-term development approach rather than an event-based approach. With regular coaching, mentoring, and action learning sessions supplemented by training and workshops, you can make your entire team effective in giving presentations, negotiating with suppliers, building teams, and innovating products.

Preparation

Planning a venture is like mapping a route before a long trip. Travelers beware! Think through the possible consequences of decisions you make about your destination, your travel companions, your route, and your mode of travel. In a venture, a quality business plan is the roadmap to success. Starting a venture is like initiating a journey. Focus on hiring the right people with the right skill set (and passion). Strive to create a culture of teamwork and commitment coupled with high-quality execution. Only then will you reach your destination safely and successfully.

Think of your venture as a long sea voyage. To be successful, you need strong leadership, experienced officers, an able crew, a plan, provisions, and a seaworthy vessel. You are the captain. Your business plan is your map of the turbulent ocean (the marketplace), and the ship is your organizational system optimized for your journey as well as for getting the best out of your talent.

Your executive team members are your officers, at least some of whom possess prior experience on similar journeys. They're the ones who will know how to deal with the unexpected, including hurricanes and possibly mutinous crews. Your engineers are your crew; they know your system—software, approach, and equipment—the way a nautical crew knows its ship. They need to have the tools and training to navigate it (Java or .NET or other software tools, if you are building an Internet software company). Furthermore, they must have the expertise to fix unexpected problems that are bound to come up while you are at sea.

Anyone undergoing a sea voyage not only needs a map for its journey, he or she also needs to know theories about how the currents work, how wind and weather turn, and even theories about the meaningfulness of the journey itself. Your crew must understand what your company theory is, where you are, how you generate value, and what your key sources are of distinctiveness.

Your plans must include supplies for the crew in the form of rewards and recognition, stock-option plans, and a road map to the first release of your product/service. You must also plan to include enough fuel for the ship to last until your next port/dock—that is, money to pay for salaries and equipment until the next round of funding. If the crew members do not trust each other or do not cooperate, then the culture is unstable, and you may never reach your next port, let alone the destination.

Your ship needs constant care and attention. Holes in the ship above the waterline—such as gaps in the technical and professional skills of the people in your venture—are not critical; they can be fixed without interrupting the journey and without creating long-term issues. (You can help your current employees develop the skills or find new people with those skills.) Holes below the waterline, such as a lack of soft skills, are much more serious—they can cause your vessel to sink. Some of them can be fixed from inside, and if they are small enough, you can reach port safely and then undertake the repairs to the ship. Other kinds of holes under the waterline will sink you.

Leadership

Along with communication, creativity, learning and teamwork, leadership is one of the key soft skills. Leadership involves managing conflicts, interviewing and selecting prospective team members, delegating responsibility and authority, coaching, networking, and developing others. As a leader, you must manage activities such as production quality, workplace safety, customer care, and fund raising. Also, a leader is responsible for managing resources such as people, finances, and information in the form of decision making, problem solving, meeting management, and persuasion. Many of these require presentation skills. In other words, good leadership presupposes refined soft skills.

"Top 10" List for Entrepreneurs

1. Focus on Humility and Self Confidence

You must be committed to making your enterprise successful without having to be in the limelight. Arrogance can blind you. When you see yourself as superior to other founders, smarter than your employees and directors, savvier than VCs, and more capable than professional executives, you and your company lose. It is that simple. Don't show off or have a "holier than thou" or "smarter than you" attitude; that puts off prospective partners (who could be customers, VCs, collaborators, employees).

Humility, on the other hand, enables you to look at life from different perspectives (not just from your own); it allows you to see what others cannot. Humility gives you the perspective to do what needs to be done to make your venture successful. In the conceptual and development stages of your company, you should balance humility with self confidence (not arrogance). Listen to criticisms of your ideas and plan with openness, but don't lose your confidence. To partner with others who have a different set of skills than you do, and to hire and manage people better than you, you need to have a healthy sense of self. You must find the right balance between inner strength and outward humility, combined with a genuine goal of leading a whole team and not just advancing your own personal agenda.

2. Emotional Intelligence Quotient (EQ)

Intelligence Quotient (IQ), representing abstract intelligence, gets the company started. Emotional Quotient (EQ) helps it become successful. IQ addresses "what" gets done; EQ addresses "when" and "how." You cannot do anything to improve your IQ, but EQ can be significantly altered; you can learn and develop soft skills over time.

At every stage of your company's development, your EQ makes or breaks its development and growth. EQ competencies include self awareness, self control, team focus, one's ability to influence others, and one's ability to build relationships. These are especially important in the pre-launch phase of a new venture when you are making many sacrifices and commitments.

note Commitment is critical to a venture's success. This commitment must come from all stakeholders—yourself, your spouse and family, and the friends and relatives who will be directly or indirectly connected with your venture. (Keep in mind that your family and friends will also be making sacrifices as you focus more and more time on your company.)

- *Self awareness* begins with knowing the role that you are expected to play, your strengths and weaknesses, your style of communication and management (how others perceive it and its effectiveness), the context in which you assert yourself and the context in which you listen, your own intentions, and expectations of yourself and others (stated and unstated).
- *Self control* relates to knowing how to present yourself—when to focus on your strengths (and assert your point of view), when to be quiet and listen (even if you are right), when to "pull people up" (focusing on their tasks and making sure you respect them), and when to let go (allowing others to make their own mistakes, thereby developing their leadership capabilities). It is not about running the company in the initial stages as a dictator or know-it-all (see the section on building a management team later in this chapter) or, in later stages, competing with your executives rather than supporting them. Most importantly, it is about controlling your passion as well as your anger, outbursts, and frustrations in public. It is important to remember that what makes you passionate can also make you and others frustrated unless you practice self control.

- *Team focus* demands that you focus on the team accomplishments and capabilities instead of on your own, particularly if you want to build a successful company that keeps growing long after you leave. Be generous and timely in rewarding others and acknowledging their contribution. Acknowledge and appreciate people in public and criticize and identify their mistakes in private. Spread the credit around for successes of your company. Don't look for others to acknowledge you; they may be busy looking for appreciation from you. Regardless of your status within the company, learn to lead by setting an example of humility and cooperation. Focus on influencing others through modeling and practicing what you preach. Particularly in startups, people do what you do instead of what you say. Because of the natural insecurity inherent in a startup arena, word spreads quickly among your company about lapses in your commitments. Focus on relationships instead of specific issues that you disagree with.

Many entrepreneurs are let go because they lack EQ and do not know how to grow with a fast growing company. Many times, egos and attachments get in the way of success for entrepreneurs as well as their companies.

3. Build on Strengths and Mind Your Core Incompetence

As an individual within an organization, you must focus on your strengths and define your role based on those strengths. In addition, organizations themselves must act based on their strengths.

In these days of turbulence, everybody wants to grow rapidly and become number one or two in their market; one way organizations accomplish this is through mergers and acquisitions. Unfortunately, more than 70 percent of mergers fail to achieve their stated objectives, be they economies of scale or people or higher market share. Why? When you combine two companies with very different core competencies, strengths, and cultures, many of the strengths that existed prior to the merger are lost. Put differently, they merged because they wanted to strengthen their weakest area, not because they wanted to build on their strength!

To avoid these pitfalls, discover your core strength. What are some things that your company can do without any new thinking or radical sea change in conceptual organization? What are some areas in which you excel with very limited resources? When you understand what drives your company, what your mission and vision are, and what evokes passion and commitment in your company, then you can create a "company DNA map" that you can use to identify branding possibilities, tag lines, and unique opportunities that you alone can exploit.

There is, however, another critical element: core incompetence. This describes that aspect in each individual that interferes with accomplishing goals. It is the place where your foot is nailed to the floor. Just because you know a lot about cars does not mean you can design or fix them. You might be an expert food critic, but that does not make you a great cook. Just because you can see obstacles doesn't mean you can surmount them. Be aware of your capabilities and be honest with yourself about them. What kind of mistakes do you keep repeating, no matter what the context is? If you don't know, or if you think you don't have any core incompetencies, then you are in more trouble than you know. Ask around and find out where you are stuck. By becoming aware of this significant weakness and paying attention to it, you can remove your biggest obstacle to your success: you!

In the early developmental stages of your venture, you might have to wear different hats, but never assume that you can do all things or be all things to all people. A company is never the work of a single individual. As the company grows, what worked before might not work any longer. You will most likely need to delegate responsibilities to the appropriate people and focus on making a contribution in terms of your core strength. As the environment changes, you might have to search for new ways to use your strengths. For example, the CEO in the startup phase might not be the right person to lead the company when it is ready to go IPO. Get a mentor, consultant, or coach, and work to assist in this process; don't wait until you're in a crisis to work with them.

note Internet-based soft-skills training courses allow you to work with simulations, what-if scenarios, and adventure games to learn soft skills. Of course, face-to-face training is often more effective, provided you can find trainers who can customize their courses to suit your needs.

4. Integrity in Speech and Action

Leaders must model the attitudes and behaviors they expect others to display. Speaking and acting consistently allows others to learn from your example. If what you say is important, then your actions should reflect that. Any gap in speech versus action is referred to as the *knowing-doing gap*.

Often times, in the early phases of their venture, entrepreneurs make promises that they have no intention of keeping. In other situations, they have every intention of keeping their promises, but do not have the resources to do so. They hope that by the time they have to keep their word, the situation will have improved. Making promises might be an efficient way to get past an immediate sticking point; doing so moves things along. That said, it's probably not an effective strategy in the long run. When you or your company make promises, it is important to keep them. Therefore, you must limit promises to those that can be reasonably met. If promises are made inappropriately, then whatever potential efficiencies they might have offered at one time are outweighed by the loss of effectiveness. Efficiency is not effectiveness!

This kind of gap shows up a lot in sales, customer-service, and product-advertisement issues. Many times, what a customer buys is not what he was promised, or does not work as expected, leading to a lack of trust on the part of the customer. When that happens, the customer exits to your competitor. Considering the high cost of customer acquisition, it's smart to keep current customers happy by delivering what you promise!

note Pay attention to cultural differences in this area. Some cultures might not say no because they are trying to save face, but in reality they have no genuine commitment on delivering what they were told to deliver. You have to learn to read body language and validate your understanding by asking a series of yes/no questions if necessary. Bridging the knowing-doing gap is important and an essential skill that every entrepreneur could benefit from because it is so pervasive and difficult to overcome. Without it though, you will lose your credibility.

Although shooting from the hip might work in the initial days of your company, working with contracts, deliverables, clear promises, and objectives are recommended. That way, you don't get into legal difficulties because you are not able to deliver on your promises.

Contracts, in particular, can be effective and efficient mechanisms for codifying relationships. Assumptions about integrity, rules, regulations, outcomes, and so on can lead to problems when it comes to putting things into action; the contract enables two parties to come together when interpreting what was said and what is being done. Leadership behavior will also have a strong influence on the perception of integrity within the enterprise and the real meaning of the contract.

5. Sensitivity to Context: Timing Is Everything

There is time for daring and time for caution, and the wise entrepreneur knows the difference. Leading people is different from managing them. Encouraging risk taking is different than exploring possibilities. Knowing the difference in styles of communication and the context in which you can present them can make the difference between success and failure. Timely communications is the most important trait. Saying the right things at the right time with clarity as well as exposing complex issues in simple, basic, and compelling ways are traits of great CEOs.

Considering another perspective on context sensitivity and timing, remember that you may find prospective employees, investors, and directors from your social circle in the initial days of your company. Poor jokes, inappropriate comments during parties, or insensitivity to people who don't share your ethnic or religious background could create a negative buzz about you in the circles in which you move.

What needs to be discussed in the boardroom should not be discussed in the hallways and vice versa. Appropriateness in terms of content, confidentiality, and courtesy are critical to success. Honesty and transparency do not mean you should tell everything to everybody. Confidentiality in HR, business-leadership, and partnership matters is critical. Often, new entrepreneurs do not pay enough attention to these soft issues. Friendship and social etiquette might require one thing, and entrepreneurship might require something entirely different. Watch for the following signs:

- Berating people in front of others
- Not delegating
- Not trusting others' input

Deal making with Japanese might happen over sake. Negotiations with Europeans might take place on golf courses or in cigar bars. Knowledge and awareness of context, culture, and custom can fill your sails on the voyage to success.

6. Manage Perception

Perception *is* reality, in that people generally act upon their perceptions. That action is very real. If you don't learn to manage how others perceive you, your future can be seriously limited.

When you are one of the founders, people watch what you do more than what you say. Make your public speech consistent with your private behavior in your home, with friends, and in social circles. One can identify differences between what is said and what is done as *espoused theories* (what you say) and *theories-in-use* (what you actually do). Lack of awareness of gaps between these two can lead to major conflicts. They create perceptions in others that you may not be who you say you are. Losing the confidence of others can mean losing everything.

There are a number of roles people play within the team or organization. Each role has a function. Failing to take a person's role into account can create a faulty perception about his or her behavior, which can then be amplified by your misguided response to your perception. In other words, successful leaders must be sensitive to their own judgments and comments about others. Be aware of the consequences of your words as much as your actions. Even if little harm results from individual perceptual errors, their accumulation over time can contribute to difficulties further down the line. Lots of little misperceptions can add up to a complex organizational "reality."

note Cultural differences account for some differences in perception. Something that is said in one culture could mean something very different in another. This becomes very important when teams are multicultural or the supervisors are unfamiliar with cultural perspectives on work, management, personal freedom, responsibility, ethics, and the like.

Finally, it is common for many entrepreneurs to feel that they have not been given a chance to present their reality before an opinion is formed by others about them, their company, and so on. There's not much point in fighting or denying what others perceive, because that is the reality for them. It's far better to develop a plan for acknowledging the prejudices and figure out a way to present an alternative view. This is especially important when you meet VCs, customers, and suppliers, who have probably, in the course of their due diligence about you, already pre-judged you many times. If you can take yourself a little less seriously and develop a sense of humor, you will be more approachable and you may be able to get more and better insight from the people around you about how you are perceived. Managing perception is one of the key skills that you must learn to move forward in the entrepreneurial world.

7. Appreciate the Roles of Others

Give credit where credit is due. Find reasons to show your appreciation. When you acknowledge others' contributions, you encourage loyalty and set the stage for more good work in the future.

It is particularly important to show appreciation (and to receive it) in high-stress situations. That's not easy, especially when you're under deadline pressure yourself. Don't wait for some earth-shattering event to recognize contributions. It is important to boost morale by recognizing the small things and showing clear appreciation for what it took to make those contributions. The culture of your company will begin to reflect your approach if you are diligent about catching people doing something right.

tip Don't forget your friends and family. Without them, your venture would be far less valuable. Although it is easy to push them aside, giving them second best, or forgetting them altogether, is not a good idea. Make sure you show your appreciation for them, just as you do for every other member of your enterprise.

Be specific, timely, and concrete when you show your appreciation. Comments like "You did really well!" don't really indicate to the listener just what about his or her behavior was so impressive (thus reducing the chances of said behavior being duplicated). Here's an example of a more constructive compliment: "Yesterday, I saw you sitting with customer X, who is so judgmental. You noted all his objections, grievances, and requests. Your sensitivity and responsiveness made X happy. Just to let you know, he sent me an e-mail that said how much he appreciated your willingness to listen to his complaints. We have already identified what we can do to continue to satisfy his demands and meet his expectations. What you did raised our customer-satisfaction numbers. Keep up the good work."

At different stages of your company's growth, different ways of appreciation become necessary. Pats on the back might suffice in the concept stage of the company or even during the development stage. But in the execution stage, rewards and recognition, stock options, bonuses, and promotions become much more important. You also have to know what moves whom and when. For example, some executives and engineers might like titles and recognition. Some others don't care for titles, but go for stock options and money. Others might be totally motivated and have clarity of vision, clear direction, and targets. When you appreciate people in different ways, be conscious about fairness and appropriateness: If you ignore financial rewards, which are due to someone because he or she is intrinsically motivated, then it might have a negative impact.

tip Delegate, delegate, and delegate some more. It shows that you really appreciate what people are doing and it communicates your ability to trust. If you delegate based on appreciation, then it can be a win-win. For example, by delegating a task to those members of your charge who are capable of completing it well, it means that you have one fewer task to complete and you know that it will be done well.

Appreciating the concerns of the people in your company is another important way to let them know you care. You might not be able to do anything for them, but listening appreciatively is significant. By empathizing, you build a stronger relationship, which in turn becomes the foundation for further good work.

Appreciation of others' roles is also important. A VC who has just joined your board of directors may criticize you; this is when you have to remember that's exactly what your directors are supposed to do. They are helping you learn from your mistakes. If you can accept their comments with equanimity, you will show your maturity and probably extend your stay in the company. If you can't, then you might be judged as someone unable to learn what you need to continue to add value. In that case, in all likelihood, sooner or later you will be asked to step down.

8. Teamwork Is Key

Regardless of how smart you are, you can't single-handedly navigate and guide your ship from its home port to its destination. Captains are measured on the strength of their crew. Find experts to complement you, and expect to take on a narrower role (see the section on building the management team later in this chapter) as the company evolves. Hire people smarter than you, and reward them appropriately.

note Your team does not begin and end at work. When you started out, your family, friends and relatives supported you with money, time, advice, encouragement, and referrals. As you grow the organization, you must figure out a way to make those people part of the extended team. Your empathy, appreciation, and acknowledgments should extend to your family members and other supporters if you want their continued support.

As the venture community says, a 5% stake in a watermelon is always better than 50% stake in a grape. To take the company from a grape to a watermelon, you will need people who are as passionate and skilled and committed to success as you are. Once you bring them on, it is about sharing the wealth, sharing the authority, and sharing the vision; these are what make the company move at an accelerated pace to success. Your role as founder has value only as long as you show effective leadership. Teamwork is critical to growth and long-term success.

Hoarding power and decision making, as well as treating people like hired hands, can seriously curtail development of their sense of ownership and responsibility. All the credit will be yours, but so will the big failure. Share the rewards and share the work, and they will share the risk. Expect the best from people, and many times you get it from them.

tip Invest in good people! The moment you stop adding value to the company will be the moment you are gone—even if you are one of the founders!

9. Focus On Outcomes and Process

Performance metrics should be established and communicated during the selection process. Executives who resist being measured on tangible or quantifiable performance may not be appropriate for startups and should be screened in the selection process. Once the executive selection has been made, motivating and retaining them and helping them transfer knowledge to other members on the team becomes important. Focusing on establishing and communicating appropriate metrics for quality, process, completion, and delivery will go a long way toward success.

- Value-adding activities such as management meetings and conflict resolution—and applying learning principles to them—are important. Balance your opinions and judgments with openness and authentic inquiry in meetings so that you don't appear as a bore who has an opinion about everything without necessarily knowing what is going on at the ground level.

- Hard work is not equivalent to *smart* work. Although working long hours is a given in the initial development stage of an entrepreneurial venture, the most critical factor is the value that is created. By focusing on appropriate processes and getting the results, you establish a culture of quality, attention to detail, delivery, and accountability. You become less dependent on personalities and more on roles and responsibilities.
- Information is *not* knowledge. Giving information to others does not mean that they understand what to do with it and how to do it. Focus on what others are taking away. Check for understanding and follow up on action.
- Create a line item in your budget for failures and allocate a certain percentage of your budget for them. This is a very novel approach and may seem difficult, especially when you are operating on a shoestring. However, the reality is that failures *do* happen; by allocating budget and requiring that assessment of failures be documented, you encourage responsible risk taking. Moreover, you create an invaluable repository of lessons learned throughout the evolution of your company.

note Entrepreneurs often fail because they don't act decisively soon enough. They also fail because they don't take appropriate risks. Denying failures only allows you to delay learning. Fail big; fail often. Remember to do it consciously, and don't fail in the same game more than twice. If you do, then it means that you have not learned the lessons from the previous failure.

10. Learn

There are two types of learning:

- Continuous. Continuous learning is the incremental, step-by-step type, with no shift in context or point of view.
- Discontinuous. Discontinuous learning occurs when the context or point of view shifts.

It is discontinuous learning that leads to breakthrough innovation. Shifts in perspectives can produce significant insights and inventions, which can change the direction of people's lives.

note Some companies say that if they do not come out with at least one new product every month, they fall behind their competitors. Staying on top of new developments requires continuous innovation; it is the touchstone of competitive strategy.

If you find yourself in a new role, or your venture is bought by a company that has a different culture, or you have new executive team members, you must find ways to learn some new lessons and apply your old lessons to new situations.

Everybody has edges—places where their knowledge is shaky. Be aware of your edges and ask for help. If you are struggling with a new project, bring in others who can help you think it through. Together, you might identify a potentially profitable area you should focus on. Partnering and teaming are most effective ways to learn.

tip Listen to others carefully and completely when they are trying to help. If your mind is planning what to say next while others are talking, then you are not listening. Being silent does not mean you are listening. Asking questions and actively integrating what they said with your responses and plans make you a popular teammate. Each time you miss listening to others, you lose an opportunity to learn.

The smarter you are, the quicker you may be able to pick up concepts and ideas from others. Executing on an idea that you really understand is quite a different game. Do you have depth and tacit knowledge that you can draw from in that area? Do others consider you as an expert in that area? If not, you had better continue learning about the new area.

Conclusion

Every entrepreneur thinks that his or her product or services will change the world. That could happen, but the change has to begin closer to home. By focusing on your behavior, attitude, and soft skills, you begin to inspire others to pay attention; when key people in the company develop their own soft skills, your chances for success increase exponentially.

Table 4.2 Section Summary

Soft skill	*What the Leaders do*	*What Others get*
Humility and self-confidence	The ability to allow others to contribute to the vision while maintaining confidence that the vision is well-founded.	The ability to contribute to the vision in order to generate a sense of ownership.
Emotional Intelligence (EQ)	Sensitivity to the emotional aspects of life.	A personal sense of feeling good at work (and at home) that can assist in managing the influence company success and personal stress of being an entrepreneur.

Soft skill	*What the Leaders do*	*What Others get*
Build on strengths and mind your core incompetence	Focus on using personal strengths enhances the ability to see them in others. This can reinforce the delegation of tasks to those who can do them better.	Working in an area of strength builds self efficacy, self esteem, job satisfaction and loyalty. Who wants to leave such rewards?
Integrity in speech and action	Awareness of the knowing-doing gap enhances the opportunity for integrity. The goal becomes doing what should be done when it should be done.	Trust and security grow in an environment where integrity is the goal. Surprises in this context are pleasant and excitedly anticipated
Sensitivity to context	Awareness of what should be said, to whom, and when are matters of strategy and responsibility—not emotion	Hearing/knowing information intended to be confidential can lead to insecurity, mistrust, decrease in morale, and leaks to competitors.
Managing perceptions	Understanding that perception is reality by virtue of its ability to create reality. What you say and do is critical.	The perception of success extends beyond personal contribution to the product or service. The image of success is created by all members of the enterprise, not just the leadership.
Appreciation for others' roles	Recognition that the function of others is critical to success and that the pride of success is magnified by the organized cooperation of many.	Recognition for good performance enhances the perception of self efficacy as well as pride.
Teamwork is key	Recognizing that others are not merely extensions or duplications of your mind and body parts. The enterprise is the composite of many hearts, hands, and minds. The distribution of profits reflects your understanding of this principle.	Personal satisfaction from individual and unique contribution to the outcome. Satisfaction and pride resulting from the share of the profits reflecting your true contribution.
Focus on outcomes and process	Weighing progress by process and product rather than personal investment.	The security of knowing what is expected and that some amount of failure is expected relative to pursuit of excellence.
Learning	Competent leadership requires never-ending learning. When growth stops, decline begins.	Boredom is not satisfying. The lack of new learning can be felt as status quo replaces innovation.

Addendum: Core Competencies for Success:

Integrating the skills you develop into a systemic practice helps you acquire new competencies for success. Competencies allow you to integrate your skills and knowledge in the context of new projects. The following six competencies are useful in all stages of your company and, in fact, could be very useful in your personal life as well. When you start something new, keep these six competencies in mind and consciously apply them in your work and life; as you do, you will integrate key soft skills with your professional skills over time:

- Be clear about what you want.
- Be aware of what is going on around you and inside you.
- Have empathy for others.
- Appreciate what you have and what others bring.
- Know your limits and stretch beyond them.
- Let go of what does not work.

Bibliography

Argyris, C.; Putnam, R.; et al. *Action Science*. Jossey-Bass. 1985.

Caruso, Brian. "Soft Skills Can Be Hard for Tech Managers—Inability to Deal with People Can Short Circuit a Career." *Information Week* issue 681. May 11, 1998.

Collins, Jim. *Good to Great: Why Some Companies Make the Leap...and Others Don't*. HarperBusiness. 2001.

Collins, Jim and Porras, Jerry I. *Built to Last: Successful Habits of Visionary Companies*. HarperBusiness. 1997.

Cooper, Robert and Sawaf, Ayman. *Executive EQ: Emotional Intelligence in Leadership and Organizations*. Putnam Group. 1997.

Goleman, Daniel; McKee, Annie; and Boyatzis, Richard. *Primal Leadership: Realizing the Power of Emotional Intelligence*. Harvard Business School Press. 2002.

Kaipa, Prasad. *Discontinuous Learning*. Vinayaka Publishing. 2002.

Senge, Peter. *The Fifth Discipline: The Art and Science of Learning Organizations*. Doubleday. 1990.

Building the Management Team

Executive Summary

This section describes how to build management teams in the early startup venture. We look at the needs of different parties—namely entrepreneurs/founders, managers, boards, and investors—and how they change through the various phases of the startup (concept, development, execution, and growth). The entrepreneur will learn what a management team is, when to begin hiring, and what roles to fill. Lastly, we provide anecdotes from successful entrepreneurs, leaders, and venture capitalists on the issue of building management teams in entrepreneurial ventures.

Synopsis:

In this section, you will learn the answers to the following questions:

- What is a management team?
- Why should I build one?
- Whom do I need to hire?
- When do I need to hire each?
- How should I hire?

Here are some of the key things entrepreneurs need to consider when building a management team:

- **DO** hire people smarter than you.
- **DO** communicate with your entire team and staff on a weekly basis.
- **DO** seek out a mentor or advisor from the industry from whom you can learn.
- **DO** formalize all promises to stakeholders in an e-mail or a legal document.
- **DO** diligently seek outside input and check references on all stakeholders.
- **DO** allocate ownership interest equitably among those associated with your success.
- **DO** clarify roles and responsibilities for everyone in writing, including your board members.
- **DO** re-define roles and responsibilities for each contributor as the company evolves.
- **DO** organize the team, including the founders, to anticipate change and accommodate it.

- **DO** always allocate the heaviest burdens and expectations to the founders.
- **DON'T** assume founders will retain control of the company from inception to liquidity.
- **DON'T** assume you have someone's consent or obligation without a written agreement.
- **DON'T** enter into contracts without legal or professional guidance.
- **DON'T** enter into verbal agreements without issuing an immediate e-mail or legal confirmation.
- **DON'T** hire or engage anyone without references from disinterested parties.
- **DON'T** assume anyone's opinion comes without an agenda.
- **DON'T** formalize a relationship with directors, sub-contractors, vendors, or employees without first assessing their capacity to meet your needs.
- **DON'T** assign people to positions whose responsibilities they have never assumed before.
- **DON'T** engage a director or other stakeholder who puts his or her interest ahead of the company's.

Introduction

A *management team* is group of executive-level officers, each with clearly defined responsibilities in the creation and growth of a company. In the startup setting, a common suite includes

- **A CEO.** The CEO is the leader of the organization, the main money or cash manager, the chief fund-raiser, the storyteller and evangelizer, the voice to market, the liaison to the board (and all stakeholders in general), and the ultimate bearer of responsibility for the success of the new company.
- **A VP of Sales and Marketing.** The VP of Sales and Marketing is responsible specifically for growing the customer base, including the beta-testers (or the initial product experiments by the founding technical team and their outside contacts).
- **A CTO.** The CTO is typically the entrepreneur/founder with the original idea, who is in charge of developing and customizing the new product/service in step with the increasing requirements of building the business and entering the market.

note As the company grows, these roles may change, and different individuals may end up assuming different roles over time.

Strong management teams can make or break a venture; it is that simple. If your business concept requires no infrastructure in order to sell and be successful, then you may be able to build a company without a management team. Founders may act as leaders when the company is young. But founders can actually stymie growth in a company if they cannot attract the players needed to expand the market or elicit the trust required to build a significant business. In other words, beyond the original idea, you will still have to produce, market, and build your business. Eventually your vision will have to realize itself in the complex yet practical world of commerce and finance. Investors will not fund a project without able hands to manage the entire process of building a successful company. The main goal of a startup is to produce a great business, which will yield great returns for all parties involved in the venture. More often than not, it is strong management that guarantees the realization of the main goal of the enterprise.

Only companies with strong management teams survive in the long run. Even companies entering rapidly growing markets will need a strong management team to thwart new entrants from eroding market share. If a company chooses a weak management team and grows beyond its capacity to service demand effectively, the moment it faces stronger competition it will surely falter and may even fail. Indeed, many argue that the strength of management is the decisive factor that makes or breaks a new venture (see the bibliography at the end of this section).

This section looks at four phases of the startup, and lays out the requirements, options, action items, and challenges of the primary stakeholders of the incipient venture during its various phases. Primary stakeholders are

- Founders
- Management
- Boards (typically are comprised of early investors, such as VCs, angels, and so on)

The four phases are

- Concept
- Development
- Execution
- Growth

Phase: Concept

Founders

The concept stage is in many ways the most exciting time of a company. Even the smallest achievements are cause for celebration, and the air is rich with infectious enthusiasm. Often, the founding entrepreneur is still employed somewhere else, and is debating the merits of leaving a secure, if uninspiring, job for the adventure and uncertainty of starting a new company.

In the early stages of the company, the founders are exploring their idea compared to market requirements, market size, target customer segments, and existing product/service offerings from incumbent competitors. At this stage, the founding team is essentially the total company staff. As such, each member of the team must wear many hats, and divide his or her time between every functional role. They must provide leadership, vision, teamwork, and execution. The founding team must set the tone for other team members to follow; this is especially true at the early concept phase, when the company culture is being formed. First-time founder-entrepreneurs can learn to communicate a passionate vision in plain language if they take the time to vet their ideas with insiders.

Table 4.3 Challenges/Suggestions for Founders in the Concept Stage

Challenges	*Suggestions*
Division of responsibility	Make everyone accountable. Play to your strengths; do not act as a dilettante or a know it all; do not try to be all things to all people.
Prioritizing	Track companywide progress at least weekly. Ensure that most-important issues are addressed first. Manage cash conservatively (winning your first round of funding is not cause for unbridled celebration, but judicious planning, decision-making, and execution).
Focus	What is the company's mission? Stick to it.
Equity allocation	Consult trusted advisors or attorneys.
Early staff attrition	Execute confidential information and employment agreements early, before trouble arises.

Management

Because you will need help exploring the technical development of the product in this phase, the key hires at this juncture are typically technical collaborators. Later, you will supplement the technical team with sales, marketing, and other business functions.

The management team is accountable for all facets of the business and must be especially hands-on at this stage. This implies that no one is above any task, from strategizing to handling janitorial duties. Be careful of hiring team members who are expecting big-company infrastructure and resources such as secretaries, executive assistants, office managers, long-term planning horizons, and so on. You should expect long hours, cancellation of personal activities, and other stressful and unpredictable situations. Make sure that the team members you choose are people who can ride these rough waters with a cooperative spirit. Everyone must understand the context and environment in which he or she works.

Team selection is one of the most difficult and important tasks you will undertake. Founders should hire managers and team leaders who can take initiative and deliver results. Often, a startup's early success hinges on its ability to deliver on short-term goals to penetrate niche markets. Do not assume that if a manager succeeded in a large organization, he or she can build a company around discrete intermediate requirements. Furthermore, today's industry leaders do not abandon their positions for a startup job unless they are convinced of the viability and liquidity of a plan or idea. *Liquidity* means that an idea with financial promise can generate actual, cash returns. (Similarly, venture capitalists do not fund a plan unless it inspires confidence among industry leaders.)

When possible, use your network of business associates to find candidates. This is free (or, at worst, inexpensive if you offer a referral bonus) and draws from the experience your trusted colleagues have with the candidate. This will tell you far more about the candidate than a brief interview with a candidate who came to you through a less trusted source, such as a job posting, tradeshow meeting, recruiter, and so on. If your network is not vast, then look to seasoned industry experts for guidance. They will know who will have interest in your vision and your value proposition. In creating a network of interested parties, you will be led by other founders, advisors, and employees. To find qualified candidates look to

- Friends
- Your extended network
- Competitors
- Trade shows
- Recruiters
- Advisors
- Online recruiting sites
- Partners

note You should involve your current management and founders in the interview process for two reasons: Multiple opinions are better than one, and you want to ensure that the candidate's personality and work style will fit with your existing team.

No matter how the candidate was introduced to you, check references carefully. Ask the candidate for names of managers, peers, subordinates, and others who know him or her professionally. Where possible, check blind references—that is, check their references with people whose names the candidate did not provide, but whom you may know well at their former employer. Be discreet, and use only those contacts who you trust to keep confidence; after all, candidates may not want staff at their current employer to know they are looking for a new job. For important hires (and early in the company, nearly everyone is an important hire), ask your outside board members and/or advisors to interview candidates who pass initial screening.

When it comes to the mechanics of the hiring process, here are some red flags to watch for:

Red Flag	***What to Ask***
Rapid job changes	Inquire why each change occurred. Verify if possible.
Resumé inflation	Verify titles. Ask specifics about assignments.
References from long ago	Get references from most recent job. Require at least one reference from a previous manager.
Rigidity during interview	They must be able to adapt. They should show flexibility in assignments, schedules, and so on.
Recruiters pushing for close	Decide according to your needs and schedule. Be aware of candidate's impending deadlines (for example, response to their other job offers), but don't get forced into a decision with which you are not comfortable.
Time gaps in resumé	Ask what the candidate did during those periods. Be alert to vague answers such as "did consulting work" or "took some time off," and probe details of position just prior to gap.

It is important to understand that building the right team is critical even at the concept phase. If you build the foundation right, then you will not face as many unforeseen obstacles down the line. (See Table 4.17 for details on the hiring process.)

Table 4.4 Challenges/Suggestions for Management in the Concept Stage

Challenges	***Suggestions***
Division of responsibility	Play to strengths. Make responsibilities clear, and hold staff accountable for them.
Founder/management relationship	Play down founder/management distinction. Everyone has to earn respect and status, including founders. Founders typically have larger stock awards; they should understand that putting the most qualified person in management (founder or not) is to everyone's benefit.
Recruitment	First pick other team members who can attract capital and key hires on the basis of their own track record and experience. Show that you are a winning, high-quality team that others should want to join. Give the company a larger-than-life appearance via visible manifestations like quality Web site, office banners, T-shirts, and so on. You must sell the opportunity to prospective hires or employees.
Team selection	Get multiple opinions on candidates. Don't assume that experience is the same as expertise. Don't be afraid to hire people smarter than you.

Board of Directors

The board of directors is initially composed of only the founders, sometimes with a friend or close associate from the industry. Its role at this stage is usually administrative (signing formation documents). With funding come changes in the board's composition, with investors often requiring a board seat. Board size is typically three members, one of these being the outside director who is the angel investor (assuming you chose angel investment as your early financing). You should avoid the temptation to seek a silent outside board member; instead, seek out a board member who can add value through his or her relevant expertise. Ideally, this will be an angel investor who has been successful in the area of the company's focus.

As the venture goes to market, prestige and name recognition of board members play a critical role in selling the new product to a larger customer base. If you raise money from a venture-capital firm, outside investors will comprise the majority of the board, or there will be an equal number of board members from management and investors with one board member who is unaffiliated with either of these groups but whose nomination is accepted by both groups. (See Table 4.16 later in this section for more information.)

Table 4.5 Challenges/Suggestions for Board Members in the Concept Stage

Challenges	*Suggestions*
Attention and commitment	Consider board members' available time and resourcefulness before inviting them to join. Make sure they complement the team and do not detract in any way. Keep them involved via frequent updates.
Guidance	Solicit advice on a routine basis.
Effective resolution of issues	Ensure that the board has a balanced composition, and an impartial protocol for discussion of issues.

Phase: Development

Founders

At this phase, the founders may have been reassigned to narrower roles as experienced non-founding managers have taken on senior executive positions. Indeed, some of the founding team may have left the company altogether, and the remaining team must work to fill the void a founder's departure creates. Founders must get comfortable with the concept of having a smaller slice of a larger pie, and taking on different roles. Founders must understand the difference between controlling an idea to the point of overkill and realizing a great market opportunity through shared commitment and *business* decision-making with non-founding executives. That is to say, although they cede control and percentage ownership as their company grows, founders are usually still better off to be part of this larger, more successful company compared to the alternative of the more resource-constrained startup they can only fondly remember.

First-time entrepreneurs need to be sufficiently introspective to know when to lead and when to follow or cede control. Investors look initially at the founders to determine how flexible they are about their own positions. Investors expect founders to assume their positions in the company until the position outgrows their skill set.

Founders often assume they have a big role to play in the development of a company. Investors, however, are able to determine early whether a founder's leadership skills extend no further than the launch of a company or the acquisition of a few niche customers. Entrepreneurs need to understand that their roles as founders in the growth of the company are necessary only as long as they can lead effectively.

Investors and board members will decide to replace a founder with a more seasoned, professional manager when the task of growing a business becomes beyond a founder's capacity. In some cases, the task of securing a new and more desirable user base may be beyond the reach of a founder. In other cases, the founder will need to raise post-seed capital to enter or expand a new market or attract more talented staff. In such cases, the investment community may only fund a seasoned CEO with a track record building such a business.

When it comes to recruiting a seasoned CEO, entrepreneurs/founders have the option to retain a professional executive search firm. These firms charge a retainer fee to launch the search (usually paid in three equal installments over a defined period). This retainer fee is up front and independent of the commission won from the successful placement of a candidate. Upon placement of the successful candidate, search firms take one-third of that CEO's first-year salary and equity/compensation. The decision to hire a search firm depends on a number of factors, including the life cycle of the startup, the executive talent pool in a given industry, VC and board recommendations, and so on. You should consult your VCs, board members, and industry experts on whether a "retained" search firm best suits the needs of your startup.

Table 4.6 Challenges/Suggestions for Founders in the Development Stage

Challenges	*Suggestions*
Loss of control/freedom	Remember the Big Picture: equity growth, wealth creation for stakeholders, financial realization of concept, capturing a greater share of your industry's market, and so on.
Company culture change	Support the new management team as you would want to be supported if roles were reversed. Recognize that managers are now a critical part of the identity of your company/venture. You are all in it together, and everyone must work accordingly for the benefit of the whole organization.

Management

As the company reputation and resources grow, it will attract higher-quality management candidates. More operational issues arise with the increasing number of internal and external participants. Recruiting seasoned managers to the team who have been through the process before will help you avoid mistakes that rookies often commit.

Typically, the board at this point will install an experienced CEO to replace the founding CEO, and this new CEO will frequently have a trusted team of colleagues whom he or she brings into the company. This can sometimes lead to friction between the original founding and new teams. Mature participants will seek to maximize the value of the company, with each team member benefiting from his or her share of the resulting increased value of their stock options.

note Investors will continue to fund a seasoned executive capable of taking the company beyond the next definable milestones. It is very rare that a founder is also the executive who builds the business into a behemoth. Bill Gates, Larry Ellison, Walt Disney, and Sam Walton are the exceptions that make the rule.

Egos may be required to formulate a big dream. Egos may be required to launch a company. Egos may even be required to secure talent and customers. But egos have no place in the evolution and development of a company. In a successful company, inspiring trust always wins over satisfying ego requirements. Investors are only interested in rewarding the former.

It is absolutely critical that the company finds a true leader in a CEO, who can take the company to the next phase. Following is a sample interview (geared for a technology company) to help you weed out CEO candidates.

CEO Interview—*Candidate Name*

First, we would like to explore your leadership potential.

- How would you characterize your leadership style?
- What performance indicators do you believe are relevant?
- How would your team, board, and subordinates characterize your leadership qualities?
- How do these qualities translate to a private startup product business?
- How do you motivate people in your organization?
- How do you develop people around you?
- What level of energy do you bring to the company?

Next, we would like to put some dimension around implementation skills.

- What are your specific accomplishments in your various jobs?
- What concrete examples of your execution skills can you provide?
- What product businesses have you brought to market?
- What successes have you achieved in creating new business models?
- What went wrong at your last company? What would you have done differently?
- Have you ever managed a software team?
- How would managing a software team be different from managing a service provider?
- How much money can you raise on your name alone?
- How well do you set priorities?
- How do you make decisions? Who do you involve in the decision process?
- How will you go about scaling a business from a small startup staff of engineers to a much larger staff of perhaps 10×?
- What makes your specific qualities relevant to a private, startup product/service business?

What entrepreneurs often fail to recognize is that the caliber, strength, and effectiveness of CEO leadership is probably the single most critical factor in the continued success and growth of the venture.

Table 4.7 Challenges/Suggestions for Management in the Development Stage

Challenges	*Suggestions*
Friction with original team	Be sensitive to the difficult situation the original team must navigate as they cede control. Look for ways to help them save face and participate in solving problems.
Original founders' resistance to change	Managers must communicate reasons for the change. What is obvious to you may not be to others. Be open to suggestions.

Board of Directors

The board takes on a more operational role at this phase, assisting in key hires; customer and partner introductions; developing marketing, sales, and operational strategies; navigating financing issues; and more. They should be viewed as a resource, and not kept at a distance. You should provide them with early insight to both good news and bad news and avoid late surprises. A good board can be a valuable extension to the management team, but only if its members are kept involved in the process early enough to be of help in an issue.

Table 4.8 Challenges/Suggestions for Board Members in the Development Stage

Challenges	*Suggestions*
Conflict resolution	Board should be a coach, among other roles. Seek out their counsel to frame problems properly to get to the optimal solutions.

Phase: Execution

Founders

At this phase, the company has launched its product, and the staff has grown substantially. Founders are often filling roles as visionaries and specialists, while experienced managers now carry out the broader company operational issues. It can be gratifying to witness your product emerge from whiteboards and prototypes to market exposure, press and analyst reaction, and most importantly, customer acceptance. Founders will find that the pace of their day becomes more organized and somewhat less chaotic as the organization ramps up to challenge the incumbents and other competitors in the market.

Table 4.9 Challenges/Suggestions for Founders in the Execution Stage

Challenges	*Suggestions*
Focus	Let go. Allow others to develop the company and themselves.
Repositioning your role in the company	After product is developed, learn to contribute altruistically to other facets of the business.

Management

The management team may take the product and company in a modified direction from the founders' original plan. This may entail recruiting team members from somewhat different backgrounds than the original vision would have suggested. If the company is progressing well, there will be a palpable sense of momentum building. Large corporate or brand-name customers will start appearing on the company's welcome board in the lobby. The management team must be qualified for the task of making the company a serious contender in the big leagues (i.e., already established, brand-name, corporate giants).

Some management attrition should be expected as job requirements are increased during this process; it can be healthy for the company. Outward-facing staff, such as sales, business development, and marketing will increase dramatically.

The company will often need to create remote offices for sales and possibly other functions. This will require more formal communication and reporting systems, which will feel uncomfortable for some. Managers who have had experience with both large and small companies are often well suited to help navigate the company through these transitions and implement the more formal processes and systems necessary for the company's continued growth and success.

Table 4.10 Challenges/Suggestions for Management in the Execution Stage

Challenges	*Suggestions*
Demands of first customers	Foster a strong sense of customer focus, while staying mindful of strategic direction to avoid being pulled off course. Constantly evaluate original company direction in light of customer feedback. Do not overly customize your offering unless its applicability is wide enough to dominate a substantial market niche.

Board of Directors

The board members may become less involved in the smaller issues with which they previously spent time. They will now be increasingly focused on positioning the company for expansion financing. Often, new members with well-known professional reputations are added at this point to help elevate the company to its upcoming role as a public company.

Table 4.11 Challenges/Suggestions for Board Members in the Execution Stage

Challenges	*Suggestions*
Ensure the company gets "traction" in the marketplace	Leverage existing board relationships to accelerate early customer adoption.
Avoid non-CEO management	Arrange meetings with managers to understand issues outside the boardroom setting. Look for validation/consistency of one executive's perspective from multiple other executives.

Phase: Growth

Founders

The founders will take on roles as contributors in a more focused area of concentration, and enjoy the fruits of their years of hard work. Founders become the informal company historians who help pass the company's core values and culture to the ever-growing team. Several of the founders may depart by this stage, either due to discomfort with a company that they barely recognize, or else to seek the excitement of starting another venture from early stage elsewhere.

Table 4.12 Challenges/Suggestions for Founders in the Growth Stage

Challenges	*Suggestions*
Doesn't feel like home anymore	Evaluate and reset your expectations. It may be time for you to move on if the company has become too big for entrepreneurial excitement.

Management

Management at this phase should be of the highest professional quality. Your company will be viewed as a desirable place for startup staff, and will attract the best talent. This team should be ready to provide the consistent execution that will be required as you move toward IPO and beyond.

Table 4.13 Challenges/Suggestions for Management in the Growth Stage

Challenges	*Suggestions*
Fiefdoms	Visibly emphasize/reward teamwork.
Communication/coordination	Institute formal mechanisms to keep all informed (for example, internal newsletters, Web sites, company meetings, and so on).
Clean up old messes in systems, contracts, policies, people, and so on	Recognize issues created by growth. Fix problems, don't fix blame.

Board of Directors

During this stage, members of the board will be focused on ensuring that company financial performance will meet requirements for an IPO. They will be very involved in interviewing investment bankers to select the team to perform the IPO underwriting.

Table 4.14 Challenges/Suggestions for Board Members in the Growth Stage

Challenges	*Suggestions*
Supporting IPO process	Board members should make themselves available to provide extra assistance during this process, which may be unfamiliar to company executives.

Summary Tables

Table 4.15 Team Building by Company Phase

	Concept	*Development*	*Execution*	*Growth*
What company needs	Visionary	Engineers	Operating expertise in all areas	Discipline
Who is needed	Tech collaborator Marketing	Engineers Finance Business development Sales	All areas	Professionals All areas
When needed	Vision ready to share	Alpha ready	Product launch	Ramp up
Where to find	Close colleagues	Network/friends Trade shows Job ads	Network/friends Trade shows Job ads Recruiters	Big company Network/friends Trade shows Job ads Recruiters
Cost	Pre-existing relationships (free)	Referral bonus Advertising	Referral bonus Advertising Recruiter fees	Referral bonus Advertising Recruiter fees

Table 4.16 Board Size and Composition by Company Phase

Phase	*# Board Members*	*Typical Composition*
Concept	3	2 founders + investor
Development	3–5	Founder + investors
Execution	5	Management, investors, 1 neutral
Growth	5–7	1 management, investors, professional board

Table 4.17 Flow Chart for Recruiting Process Steps (Define Job Description All the Way Through to Employment Offer Issues)

1. Assess hiring issues.
   - Company needs
   - Company budget for staff
2. Create job description.
   - Title
   - Responsibilities
   - City location
   - Reporting structure
   - Required experience/skills
3. Gather compensation guidelines (for internal use only). Be realistic, and ask recruiters/others.
   - Salary
   - Stock options
4. Determine when job starts (usually immediately).
5. Advertise position.
6. Screen resumés.
7. Conduct phone interview (optional).
8. Conduct face-to-face interviews with management team.
9. Conduct second round of face-to-face interviews.
10. Check references.
11. Determine candidate's interest.
12. Prepare job offer and get it approved by management.
13. Get the candidate more excited about the position/company.
14. Deliver offer, and request response within less than one week.
15. Place follow-up call to inspire candidate to join.

Anecdote: Kumar Malavalli, Board Member, Former CTO, and Co-Founder of Brocade Communications Systems, Inc.

Brocade Communications Systems, Inc. is the industry leader and was the first to establish the standard for network storage and transfer data reliability. It is the recipient of numerous awards in its field, and is widely acclaimed as a model for business growth and execution for startups in the high-tech sector. Kumar Malavalli is the visionary and driving force behind what would become Brocade's central technology product. He provides a superlative example of an entrepreneur/founder who responded with grace, elegance, intelligence, and efficacy to the vicissitudes of the startup life cycle.

Kumar was the creator and the technical leader who inspired, catalyzed, and actuated the development of the product, but he had great self understanding and acute awareness of the extra demands involved in creating a successful company. He realized that between an ambitious technical vision and practical execution resided the need for an interim CEO, or someone who could get the product to market in a timely fashion. Because of executive management brought in by the investors, Brocade was able to avoid the syndrome that usually plagues the engineering world: the incessant and obsessive need to continually tweak a technology to the point of missing the market opportunity.

The visionary possesses the idea/IP and creates the product. He or she typically augments the product. But management is responsible for the growth and structuring of the business, the entrance to the market, the erection of barriers to entry, strategic partnerships, and so on.

The startup life cycle typically begins with innovative engineering and architecture prototyping. With market entrance comes the need for PR and more advanced sales/marketing strategies. Increase in customer base necessitates manufacturing, distribution, and thus operational mechanisms. Kumar sensed that the transitions and continuities to these various phases were not always clear to the founding engineering team. By deferring to a new CEO, the burden of staffing and responsibility for company creation was lifted from the technical teams.

Brocade's critically acclaimed success is due to *both* the original innovation or idea and the keen awareness of the founders and investors to bring in management at the right time to productize the idea, enter the market, and actually create a new industry. Dominance of that industry was further solidified when a business-savvy CEO was allowed to take the company public and manage Wall Street perceptions. In 1999, Brocade was the second-best IPO underwritten primarily by Morgan Stanley (Morgan Stanley Dean Witter at the time) and secondarily by Alex Brown (now part of Deutsche Bank).

With the example of Brocade, a fine balance was struck between perseverance of the technical and scientific superiority of an idea and the acute business awareness to recognize the timeliness of market entry. It is no exaggeration that this balance was the result of the interpersonal dynamics between the founder/entrepreneurs, the initial investors/VCs, and executive management, which was brought in from the outside. To some companies, this synchrony or equilibrium is mysterious or serendipitous. To Brocade, however, wealth creation became possible precisely because the needs of all parties were assessed; self understanding on the part of the parties was the cause and effect of the process of overall value creation, and the inherent willingness of individual egos to sacrifice their different demands for the good of the whole became increasingly apparent over time. Brocade provides an excellent example of the moment when entrepreneurs/founders let go of the process and embrace the big picture of creating a successful company.

With executive management in place, the startup with a promising idea became an industry-leading company with real results to verify its stature. Kumar, the founder, also represents the quintessential evolution of a successful entrepreneur through the various phases of leadership: He went from technical leader to non-executive or non-managerial spiritual leader to non-leader or advisor and member of the board. It was because of Kumar's ability to let go that his stature in the tech world along with Brocade's industry dominance grows day by day. As a member of the board and advisor to the company, Kumar is now applying the same principles for creating the company to the next era of the company's innovation and ambitions; by setting up a constellation of satellite R&D programs outside the company, the burden of continuous innovation—propelled by hawkish Wall Street firms—is shared with outside centers of gravity for innovation. Together, the *ecosystem* (as Kumar defines it) allows Brocade to learn from protocols and principles that it does not itself develop, but that it has the power to scale and take to market. Inversely, the satellite programs are virtually guaranteed a framework for success and maturation already pioneered by Brocade's historical examples of wise decision making. It is a win-win situation, and it all comes down to trust, the ability to share power and decision making, and being sensitive to the customer's increasingly fine-tuned needs.

As the Brocade User Group shows, the whole process of corporate governance and corporate strategy/policy formation can undergo a positive transformation, which is healthy for Brocade, its competitors, and hence the industry writ large. The input from customers has a direct effect and impact on the ratification of standards for network storage and data-transfer reliability.

The concept of the ecosystem and the Brocade User Group reflects a new mentality and a new vision for the *mode* of wealth creation and value creation in the tech world. Indeed, this new mentality is only the tip of the iceberg. New thinking about management in the world of startups will create ever-better technical products, and thus better-performing companies and more robust industries with greater competitive differentiation. It all begins with creation of value-generating relationships and cohesive understanding between entrepreneurs/founders, investors/VCs, and executive management.

Anecdote: Purnendu Chatterjee, Chairman of The Chatterjee Group.

Purnendu Chatterjee is the founder and chairman of The Chatterjee Group. Formerly of McKinsey, and before that Stanford Research Institute, Dr. Chatterjee engaged clients in everything from electronics to information technology to chemicals to the manufacturing industries. As an investor, current ventures include biotechnology, petrochemicals, healthcare/IT, and software development. Having led major strategy and organizational assignments for CEOs of large U.S., European, and Japanese industrial companies, Dr. Chatterjee now serves on the boards of R&B Falcon Corporation, Indigo, N.V., and Global Power Investments (a joint venture with GE Capital and International Finance Corporation). He is also a member of the Council of Foreign Relations.

For Dr. Chatterjee, the first test a potential investment opportunity must pass is whether the idea itself has a compelling market rationale. In most cases, this is a very analyzable, tangible issue. It is based on factors relating to market need, market potential, competitive positioning, technical risk, and so on. But in his opinion, these are not the most difficult questions to address. Instead, in Dr. Chatterjee's words, "The biggest risk in the venture business is whether the team will gel or not. Every facet of a venture is analyzable except this." Effective management teams are rarely found intact. More often, they are made through an extended process of integrating ideas and skills, adjusting roles and agendas, assimilating new people and inputs as the business evolves, and continuously redefining and building consensus toward a powerful shared vision for the business.

When asked about the issues of leadership and management, Dr. Chatterjee offered two guiding views. First, as a rule of thumb, he is more comfortable with a situation in which a clear leader is apparent rather than a team of equals. Second, he believes that the ultimate measure of the effectiveness of the business leader is whether he or she can create an environment that is conducive to the development of an effective management team. According to Dr. Chatterjee, the most effective leaders he knows spend a great deal of their time understanding the skills and personal agendas of the other members of their team, facilitating an integration of interests and building broad-based consensus for the key initiates required for success, and thinking proactively about the way in which the team needs to adjust to best meet the needs of the business.

Obviously, there is room for style differences between leaders, but allowing for those differences, the most effective leaders tend to have several traits in common:

- They put considerable thought into whether the organizational environment is yielding effective interaction between the key members of the management team.

- They are often consensus builders rather than controllers.
- They tend to have an extraordinarily clear focus on the critical issues facing the business and tend to be an energizing force for the organization to see and address those issues.
- They tend to have a tolerance for diversity of opinions and approaches and are more inclined to bring in people to fill critical holes in the team than to focus on how well those individuals fit with current team dynamics.

With the benefit of enlightened leadership, strong management teams can effectively form and translate their vision and energy into a *mode* of productive behavior, which creates real value and facilitates the scaling the company. By creating an optimal environment, management teams can gel and organizations can function at their peak levels. As importantly, the organization is in the best position to adapt to new developments as circumstances evolve.

Anecdote: Snapshot Views on the Need for Strong Management and Criteria for Investing (The VC Perspective)

Justin Perreault, General Partner, Commonwealth Capital

Management issues are stage-dependent; each stage requires a different solution to the management problem. In an early-stage setting, VCs do not assume that a complete team is in place from the beginning. The trick is to spot the holes and balance those risks, which are worth taking. Early-stage emphasis is usually on the quality of the technical team. Focus on sales capabilities and on financial capabilities comes later.

Some criteria for investing are

- Relevant prior domain expertise of the founders
- Presence of a visionary, or someone able to take the story externally
- The team must understand that its great idea is eminently practical—customer-facing, customer-solution oriented—and not just a fascinating technological achievement

The company should have the ability to round out the management team as it goes along. In an early-stage investment, there is often a clear understanding that the technical founders may not be the CEO, and that an outsider will have to be brought in. It is very rare that a rock-star team is in place at the inception of a venture and stays the same through all the phases leading to growth and IPO. Rare exceptions are the Siebels and the Sycamores.

Marcia Hooper, General Partner, Advent International

Management team building strategy differentiates the competitive strategy of different venture-capital firms. It is rare for VCs to take the management risk; in other words, most VCs fund only individuals who have done it before. However, that does not mean that the entire team, or even the team leader (CEO), must be intact (present) at the outset of a venture. If there is a core group of experienced managers present at the time of the investment, then it is okay to have gaps. In as many as one-third of the companies funded, investors understand and expect that a new CEO will be brought in to build the company to the next stage. When looking at a CEO, VCs usually take in to consideration these prerequisites:

- Prior experience being a CEO
- Learned through failures as well as successes
- Keen appreciation of the cost of time and cost of money
- Strong sense of what they can and can not do

Some VCs do not like situations with a single, dominant, overbearing leader. You have to have a CEO who can make a decision on a timely basis; wavering consensus is not an excuse for not being decisive. Make the decision, move on, and then evaluate the outcome. That said, it is important for leadership to build consensus on the vision of the product and the company strategy. Goal setting must be congruent. People need to be pulling on the oar in the same direction. Often, VCs look at the relationship between leaders and their technical teams. In later-stage investments, reference checking on CEOs should be done more broadly and deeply in the company. As the company grows, the CEO's relationships in the organization become more complex.

The most important trait of the CEO is timely communication—saying the right thing at the appropriate time, and communicating with the utmost clarity to the entire organization. A good CEO understands the value of communication and building consensus. A great CEO has the ability to take the most complex issues and situations and state them in a simple, basic, and compelling way. This ability to help the entire organization focus on core issues can be the difference between a team that never gets on a track and a team that excels.

Mike Cronin, General Partner, Weston Presidio

On management: We like it when only one key person is driving the team and setting the tone. We consciously look for someone with mental or psychological problems but who understands the positive effects of being obsessed with driving the performance of the business. If there is confusion in the team, and no central voice, then no one can feel responsible for that. But that does not prevent healthy delegation. Good leaders also find great people and let them go. Leaders are motivators, energizers, and liberators. They have a passion for results. It is not possible to overdo it when it comes to motivation and energizing. We focus as much or more of our attention on the leader as on the technological innovation or product.

Bibliography:

Anthologies

Harvard Business Review on Corporate Governance. Harvard Business School Press. 2000.

Harvard Business Review on Entrepreneurship. Harvard Business School Press. 1999.

Harvard Business Review on Leadership. Harvard Business School Press. 1998.

Major Studies

Flamholtz, E. and Randle, Y. *Growing Pains: Transitioning from an Entrepreneurship to a Professionally Managed Firm*. Wiley and Jossey Bass. 2002.

Khurana, Rakesh. "Finding the Right CEO: Why Boards Often Make Poor Choices." *MIT Sloan Management Review* vol. 43, no. 1. Fall 2001.

Standard Works on Leadership By

Warren Bennis

Jim Collins

Jay A. Conger

Manfred Kets De Vries

John Gardner

John P. Kotter

Jay W. Lorsch

Henry Mintzberg

Nitin Nohria

Abraham Zaleznik

Human-Resource Management

Executive Summary

In this section, we look at all the fundamental challenges of human-resources management. These include forming a core team and defining roles and responsibilities; determining staffing needs in line with growth strategies; exploring the recruitment process and its various types; executing the interview process and offer of employment; determining compensation strategy; implementing employer-employee relation guidelines and benefits; establishing human-resource information systems; dealing with company size reduction or downsizing; and risk management and workplace safety.

Introduction

> "People are the primary source of competitive advantage. At the end of the day we bet on people, not strategies."
>
> —Anonymous

This section will help you navigate the human-resource challenges as you lead your company through the various startup stages (concept, development, execution, and growth). The human-resource philosophy of a company is typically not as concrete and specific as the other areas of the company. Indeed, entrepreneurs often express frustration with the lack of absolute and defined rules. Although everyone agrees upon the importance of hiring and creating an exceptional team, cultural considerations are often an afterthought or are left to evolve by default.

We have attempted to present these critical aspects of human-resource management in a practical and chronological manner based on the evolution and the resulting needs of your company. In some instances, we'll repeat previously discussed issues or revisit key HR considerations articulated elsewhere in this chapter. This is reflective of the critical importance relating to those topic areas and the need to reinforce those subject areas.

The Concept Phase

Making your dream a reality requires necessary tangibles like a business plan and funding. Your most powerful resources, however, will be the people you attract to your new venture. The previous section covered the critical importance of selecting and hiring the right people for your business; here, we'll focus on the areas of human-resource philosophy, practices, and operations. The people factor is always the hardest for entrepreneurs to predict. People are dynamic. They react to situations, changes, and each other. The people you bring into a new venture—those who form the core of your business—ultimately shape your company culture.

Form the Core Team

> "Organization doesn't really accomplish anything. Plans don't accomplish anything, either. Theories of management don't much matter. Endeavors succeed or fail because of the people involved. Only by attracting the best people will you accomplish great deeds."
>
> —U.S. Secretary of State Colin Powell

The core team will help put your plans in motion. The ideal team will have highly complementary skills, a common passion for your business, and the ability to work together toward making your plan a reality (shared values). Founders will often look to family and friends for help. This can be an excellent resource, but ensure they have the right skill sets.

Define Roles and Responsibilities

Evaluate every need that will contribute to the organization's success and clearly define the roles and responsibilities of every member on the core team. Try to avoid redundant professional skill sets and make sure the core team has the ability to shore up the organization's weaknesses. This will minimize ambiguity and help to ensure key priorities don't fall through the cracks. At this point, it is important to clearly define reporting relationships and the decision-making process. These decisions at the early stage ultimately will be factors in determining your corporate culture.

The infant company will need a strong development team and a finance team to oversee administration. You may also need a product-management, sales, and marketing focus. After you've defined your needs, select wisely and hire the best talent you can afford. A bad hire will be expensive in terms of time, money, morale, and opportunity costs. When you hire, look for soft skills, professional skills, and attitude.

tip When you hire talent, irrespective of how much effort you put in the interview process and due diligence, you will inevitably make some mistakes. When that happens, don't regret it. Take quick action and see whether that person has the right attitude and fits in any other role. Otherwise let go of that person appropriately. One person with negative attitude can create havoc in a small company as well as de-motivate others.

- **DO** realistically evaluate the needs of the company and hire only for critical positions.

- **DO** understand the strengths and weaknesses of your core team in terms of talent, competencies, and soft skills, and know what expertise is need for further hire.
- **DO** hire the best person for the role based on your budget. Remember the maxim: "A players hire A players, B players hire C players!"
- **DO** define roles and responsibilities of each person on the team, including the founders.
- **DO** create a 3-6-12 month plan and project hiring needs.
- **DON'T** ignore or under-invest in recruitment. Every person you interview is potentially an ambassador for your firm, a future client, or a future employee.
- **DON'T** provide inflated titles. At a later stage of your growth, this will create issues with your organizational structure and can become a source of unnecessary conflict.
- **DON'T** make rash, impulsive hiring decisions. Proceed with urgency, but make informed decisions. Bad hires are costly!
- **DON'T** hire friends/acquaintances if they do not have the skill sets you need.

Additional considerations during the concept phase include the following:

- How will decisions be made? Who has the final authority?
- Is the equity structure of the company defined? Are contracts and commitments documented and in place? (Refer to Chapter 3, "Legal Issues," for more information.)

Work with the core team to define the shared mission and vision of the organization. Solidarity on these points is critical to the success of the organization. Potential investors will want to see a powerful, shared vision coupled with a strong core team.

Developing a Corporate Culture

> A task without a vision is drudgery.
> A vision without a task is but a dream.
> But a vision with a task is the hope of the world
>
> —Inscription on a church wall in Sussex County, England

Corporate culture can be a powerful impetus toward creating a success-driven organization, or it can undermine the success of your company. The key is your ability to effectively articulate the vision in a compelling manner that will capture the hearts and minds of the workforce.

This vision—along with a sense of purpose; strong and mutually respectful relationships within the company; and work that is fun, exciting, and challenging—combine to create a vibrant and motivated staff. This sets the standard for organizational excellence that will enable you to attract and retain the best and the brightest employees available. Similarly, the mission statement will define the organization's objectives to help achieve the overall vision.

Many of the decisions made during the concept stage will also help shape and define your culture. The nature of corporate decision making (consensus or autocratic); the level of authorization delegated to the various levels of management; the choice of facilities, office setups, and other workplace amenities—all these decisions will determine the ultimate culture embodied by your firm. In addition, many of the skills needed in this stage are not professional and technical skills, but soft skills such as the ability to manage conflict and arrive at a consensus that people are still passionate about. Your ability to negotiate and not dictate will set the tone of how the core team will deal with people who work for them. Be fully aware that your company's culture can be something that makes or breaks its status as one of the best companies to work for (be it according to industry buzz or *Fortune* magazine).

Corporate culture will evolve through the various phases of corporate growth. That makes the vision, mission, and values of your company the critical avenues for maintaining the desired culture.

Closing Thoughts on the Concept Stage

Following are a few closing thoughts about the pre-launch stage:

- **Commitment.** By now, you've already realized your new venture has a life of its own. It will continue to take time away from your spouse, your children, and your friends. Be sure that you have everyone's blessing to undertake this venture, and you are willing to make the commitment and personal sacrifices to see it through. It's not just about you anymore.
- **Management, management, management.** Venture capitalists have always bet on people first and ideas second. Align yourself with people who have a successful track record, and don't be afraid to bring in an industry heavyweight who can provide critical access.
- **Adaptability to a changing environment.** Entrepreneurs must be able to adjust to volatile economic markets, an uncertain global situation, and natural or precipitated external forces. Adaptability, flexibility, and change must become part of the daily vocabulary.

- **Alignment of goals.** Ensure that the core team has a common understanding of the vision, mission, and corporate culture of the new organization. Without it, you may as well turn back now!

The Development Stage

Congratulations!! If you are still reading this chapter it means you are close to getting a term sheet or have already secured one. Now comes the challenge of building your company.

Determine Your Staffing Needs

> "You can't spend too much time or effort on 'hiring smart.' The alternative is to manage tough, which is much more time consuming."
>
> —Gary Rogers, Chairman & CEO, Dreyer's Grand Ice Cream

Effective hiring is a result of planning, preparation and execution. In assessing your immediate and short-term personnel needs, you'll need to define the work to be accomplished, the timeframe in which it must be accomplished, and the number and type of staff you'll need to do so. In doing so, you develop a staffing plan; your next step is to determine how to fulfill your hiring requirements.

Your core team includes those people who are already signed up for the venture. You should also have a second wave of supporters who are interested in joining the venture upon funding approval. As the organization grows, there will be increased demand for human-resources talent, and you need to anticipate the need and plan for it beforehand. As momentum builds for this business venture, it is important to keep moving forward without having to delay progress while searching for additional support.

tip Hiring mistakes often occur due to the urgent need to have a position filled yesterday. When possible, project your staffing requirements in advance. This provides you the ability to adequately identify and assess potential hires.

When it comes to fulfilling your hiring requirements, one option is to solicit referrals from friends and family. When these resources are tapped out, or your management team must dedicate its time to the development of product, it may be time to consider utilizing the services of recruitment specialists. Following are your options:

- In-house recruiters
- Contract recruiters

- Head hunters
- Retain search firms

In-House Recruiters

In-house recruiters are full-time regular employees who are paid a fixed salary regardless of the hours worked. They are an economical choice when the company needs to fill multiple positions and needs help ramping up quickly. In-house recruiters can manage several open positions at one time, and can get the pipeline full of potential candidates. In addition, in-house recruiters are often equipped to handle human-resource activities beyond recruitment only. It can be disadvantageous, however, to hire a generalist versus a specialist when recruitment is a critical need.

Contract Recruiters

Contract recruiters are consultants who work for your company on a full-time or part-time basis for a specified period of time. They are typically paid on an hourly basis, and are not employees of the company. If your company has multiple junior- to senior-level positions to recruit and needs help ramping up quickly, then contract recruiters are the most economical choice—in part because they can be hired on an as-needed basis, without taking up head count, and can be terminated in the event your business situation changes. In addition, contract recruiters can manage several open positions at one time, and can get the pipeline full of potential candidates. One downside of contract recruiters, however, is that they are often limited in their knowledge of human resources in general. Their focus is primarily recruitment.

tip Contract recruiters are ambassadors for your company. Make sure yours are able to represent your company well to the candidates.

Head Hunters or "Contingency" Recruitment Firms

A *head hunter* is a recruiter who works for you on a success basis. That is, you pay a fee only when you hire the head hunter's referred candidate. If you hire a head hunter, you should not assume you have an exclusive agreement with him or her; head hunters will "shop" their candidates to several companies simultaneously. Head hunters recruit at all levels, including executive levels, which can make them effective in helping you recruit multiple positions—although their placement fee is typically 20–30 percent of the new hire's annual salary, making them an expensive solution for multiple hires. That said, head hunters can often provide a company with a wide variety of candidates, and can provide excellent value and service for the most hard-to-find positions.

tip Head hunters are most effective when they screen candidates to your specific job requirement. Don't use head hunters that just throw resumés your way without screening candidates first.

CAUTION: Using head hunters can create significant paperwork for hiring managers, and can lead to fee disputes. Some level of oversight to this activity must be maintained.

Executive or "Retain" Search Firms

Typically, an executive or "retain" search firm's core focus is senior management, executives, or highly specialized technologists; you should use a retain search firm only for your senior-management team (VPs and other C-level positions). A retain search firm maintains an exclusive work agreement with you; due to the exclusive nature of this relationship, you should expect regular communication and a greater level of service. The terms specify the services provided, fee structure, and terms of payment. Typically, retain search firms charge an amount equal to one-third of the new hire's total cash compensation for year one of employment. Payment terms typically include equal payments of one-third the projected fee due at search initiation and at 30 and 60 days into the search. Some firms will ask for equity (stock) in lieu of cash for a portion of the fee.

tip Interview the search firm and the specific consultants who will be working on your assignment. Conduct reference checks on the consultant with his/her current/prior clients, and make sure the firm has the domain expertise as well as the functional expertise to successfully fill your position.

Table 4.18 outlines the advantages and disadvantages of using in-house recruiters, contract recruiters, head hunters, and retain search firms.

Table 4.18 Recruitment-Specialist Options

	Advantages	*Disadvantages*
In-house recruiter	As an employee, the in-house recruiter is committed and dedicated to the company. In-house recruiters are also less expensive than contract recruiters.	Fixed expense of full-time headcount. Less flexibility during economic downturn.
Contract recruiters	No headcount necessary, no benefits, can be terminated without cause.	Less knowledge of company/ positions than in-house recruiter. Highly compensated relative to in-house recruiter. Lack of commitment to company

	Advantages	*Disadvantages*
Headhunters	Broad access to various types of candidates.	Service level.
Retain search firms	Effective in hard to fill placements customer-service level.	Cost. Usually fills only senior-management positions.

The Recruitment Process

Hiring great staff is not simple, but represents some of the most important business decisions you'll make. Your success depends on making the right choices in hiring the right people.

note If you've hired a contract recruiter, he/she will coordinate many of the activities discussed in this process.

Full Time Versus Contract Staff

Emerging startups often face the decision of hiring full-time staff versus hiring contract staff. Although there are many considerations for these decisions, the most compelling argument may be availability and necessity. Rapid growth often exceeds the capacity available. In the case of hiring staff, the organization's capability to recruit and hire may not conform to the critical need. The ability to supplement or substitute contract staff may provide the ideal solution, especially if the deliverable is a one-time event. Look to your HR consultant to identify the various advantages and disadvantages of each option.

Outlining Position Specifications

The person who is responsible for the hiring should be very clear about what business needs must be met through the hiring process. This can be done in the form of a specific job description or personnel requisition that includes the following information:

- A brief overview of the company
- The main job responsibilities
- The key initial objectives
- The critical activities of the position
- Specialized skills required
- The desired level of education and experience

CAUTION: The position must be justified and approved up through the executive chain of command before recruiting efforts are initiated. Failure to do so can result in employment and legal complications that can adversely affect the organization.

The Interview Process

Many of the key interview questions were identified in the "CEO Interview" section earlier in this chapter. A similar comprehensive approach should be adopted for all other positions being filled within the company. There are three main purposes for conducting an interview:

- **Discovery.** Discover all the past and present job-related information about the applicant that will help you in making a decision.
- **Co-relation.** The information that you gather from the applicant should be related to the company's present and future needs. This helps you assess cultural fit.
- **Prediction.** The past is an indicator of future behavior. Armed with all the information that you have collected, you can make an unbiased judgment of the applicant's potential as an employee.

note If you use a contract recruiter, he/she should have the ability to coordinate the entire interview process for you.

Planning the Interview

Before you conduct interviews, you should determine who will be on the interview team. Generally, the nature and level of the position in question will determine who is included. Minimally, it's recommended that the team include between three and five members, including the hiring manager, a key internal customer, a teammate(s) or peer(s), a second-level manager, and a human-resources representative (or contract recruiter).

The team should achieve consensus about the main knowledge, skills, and abilities (KSAs) being assessed, and should formulate open-ended job-related questions that require the applicant to give behavior-based examples. (Good examples of these types of questions include "Tell me about the most frustrating boss you ever had. How were you able to effectively work with him/her?" and "What was the most difficult team project you undertook? How did your efforts help towards ultimate success of the project?".) Once the interview begins, ensure that each team member asks different questions designed to evaluate different aspects of the applicant's qualifications. It is imperative, however, that interviewers ask only those questions that are job related. The human-resources representative and the hiring manager should coordinate this process.

Once the interview is finished, do plan to debrief immediately as an interview team (as opposed to debriefing. individually). This helps you avoid miscommunications and misinterpretations, provides an opportunity for the team to determine areas that require further evaluation from reference checks, and allows for rapid follow-up in determining offer status.

Creating a Positive Interview Environment

Just as the interview offers you an impression of a candidate, it offers the candidate an impression of your company. Creating a positive interview environment is crucial for attracting people to your company. Keep the following in mind:

- **Be sure there are minimal or no interruptions.** Continued interruptions can be perceived as an insult to your candidate. Equally important is the fact that constant interruptions reduce your ability to focus and assess the candidate's qualifications.
- **See that the applicant is comfortable.** This isn't an inquisition; it's an opportunity to gather information about the applicant's expertise.
- **Plan for enough time.** Cutting an interview short has the same effect as subjecting the candidate to frequent interruptions.
- **Stay on schedule.** Going under/over on time will disrupt the order of the interview schedule.

Conducting the Interview

Once the interview begins, you'll want to consider the following guidelines:

- Schedule interviews beforehand and stay on time.
- Introduce yourself to the candidate. Let him or her know your position in the company and how it relates to the job for which the candidate is being interviewed.
- Ask behavioral and open-ended questions. *Behavioral questions* are simply questions that ask how a person has acted, responded, or addressed a situation in the past. They force the candidate to share how they have actually reacted, rather than hypothetically stating how they would act. Good examples of these types of questions include "Tell me about the most frustrating boss you ever had. How were you able to effectively work with him/her?" and "What was the most difficult team project you undertook? How did your efforts help towards ultimate success of the project?"
- When the candidate does not understand a question, paraphrase or ask the question in a different way.
- Do not be afraid of silence. The candidate may be formulating an answer.
- If a candidate goes off on a tangent, tactfully guide him or her back to the question at hand.
- Seek disconfirming evidence. Often, a candidate will provide the answer he or she thinks is the correct answer, or the one you want to hear. By asking behavioral questions, you'll be able to validate responses or hear disconfirming evidence from the candidate.

- Control the interview, but listen more than you talk. Remember, you're trying to find out about the candidate. A good rule of thumb is to listen 70% of the time. The majority of time spent selling the candidate on your organization should occur after you've determined he or she is one you want to hire.
- Leave sufficient time at the end of the interview for the candidate to ask questions. This will enable you to sell the candidate if you've determined a desire to hire.
- Convey to the candidate to whom he or she will report, who will make the hiring decision, and who will explain compensation and benefits issues.
- Inform the candidate about the rest of the interview/hiring process, and provide contact information should the candidate have further inquiries.

Evaluating the Interview

The most effective way to evaluate an interviewee is by use of a standardized evaluation form that provides for objective measurement of the candidate's accomplishments and expertise versus the requirements of the position. Common success factors for any work environment include adaptability, creativity, problem-solving skills, and commitment. You should also look for people who can communicate, share ideas, and interact across generation gaps.

CAUTION: Avoid hiring in the perceived image of yourself or an existing group member—a phenomenon called the *halo effect*. Often times, the best hire is someone who brings something different to the table.

Documentation

The host of the interview should ensure appropriate time is set aside to secure an employment-application form and a background-authorization form to conduct some level of background check.

The Employment-Application Form

The employment application is necessary because it's a signed document whereby the candidate states that the employment and personal information listed is true and accurate. If the background check results in an inconsistency, this signed document is the basis of retracting a formal offer or for terminating employment. An employment-application form must

- Stipulate the "at-will" nature of the work relationship
- Be filed with the California Division of Labor Standards (if hired in California)
- Include a voluntary self-identification disclosure form (gender, ethnicity, veteran status, disabilities)

The Background-Authorization Form

The background-authorization form grants permission to the company or its agent to access various aspects of the candidate's personal background that may be relevant to the work environment. Possible checks include educational background, employment background, driver's-license check, public filing records, evaluation of criminal conviction records, and credit history. These checks are often conducted by a contract security firm specializing in background evaluation.

note The nature of the position will often dictate which checks are appropriate. For example, it may be relevant to perform a credit history on the CFO or other finance managers, or a driver's-license check for someone who is provided a vehicle for company use.

Golden Rules for the Recruitment Process

When it comes time to conduct interviews, it's important that you do the following:

- **DO** prepare for the interview.
- **DO** respect the candidate's time.
- **DO** schedule the time and location of interviews beforehand and stay on time.
- **DO** make sure that you have read the resumé and all pertinent material on the candidate prior to the interview.
- **DO** review the current position and update if necessary.
- **DO** make a list of interview questions that will help you to determine the information you need to make a decision. (Make sure they are job related.)
- **DO** follow up with the candidate on any issues left on the table at the time of the interview.
- **DO** secure a signed employment application and a completed background authorization disclosure form prior to extending a formal offer.

That said, here are a few things to avoid:

- **DON'T** cancel the interview at the last minute.
- **DON'T** ask questions that exclude persons on the basis of protected categories.
- **DON'T** ask inappropriate questions.
- **DON'T** talk excessively.
- **DON'T** evaluate the candidate on any basis other than qualifications for the position.

The Offer of Employment

The Offer of Employment is a critical document that dictates the terms and conditions of employment. Offers should be coordinated through a central administration point—preferably human resources, if the function already exists. Offers must be in writing and should be signed by the employer and employee; signed offer letters should then become part of the employee's personnel file (this minimizes any chance of misunderstandings at a later date). In addition, offer letters must include at-will language, as well as a statement to the effect that the terms of the letter can be modified only by a company officer or director. Finally, offer letters should have an expiration date, and should state compensation information in bi-weekly, semi-monthly, or monthly terms (not annual). Signed offer letters should become part of the employee's personnel file; this minimizes any chance of misunderstandings at a later date.

Due Diligence

In today's complex legal world, there exists extensive legislation and regulation related to employment law. These concerns range from terms and conditions of employment to documentation and record keeping, and even liability regarding referencing and background checking (of the lack thereof). By this point in your growth, it's absolutely critical to pay attention to these issues. If you do not have a full time personnel presence at this time, we recommend you utilize a personnel consultant and/or legal representative to identify and develop the necessary procedures.

The Compensation Strategy

The compensation system that you establish for employees is one of the main engines that will drive your business; at the same time, it will be your largest fixed expense. For this reason, you must formulate a strategically driven compensation philosophy that becomes the basis of compensation decisions. This philosophy should take into account your company's mission and strategic goals.

Some of the questions that will determine your philosophy are as follows; be advised that no specific answers are right or wrong for every situation:

- Will your base salaries be competitive with employers in your area and in related industries?
- Will you establish a structured pay scale for specific positions in your company, or will you set salaries on an individual basis, based on the experience and accomplishments of the person filling the job?

note The larger your organization becomes, the greater the need to set up a structured pay scale.

- To what extent are the monetary rewards you offer employees going to take the form of merit increases, performance bonuses, or benefits?
- What will be the basis of salary increases?
- What is the bonus philosophy? Is it calculated based on individual performance, departmental or project-based performance, company revenue, some combination of these factors, or other factors?
- How important is internal pay equity and how will you ensure you maintain it?
- What part of total compensation will stock options play?

tip The area of compensation is complex and detailed. If your company lacks the internal capacity to develop a compensation system, consider seeking assistance from a human-resources/compensation consultant or firm.

Payroll Considerations

Payroll of the company must be completed consistently, accurately, and in a timely fashion. Typically, this responsibility rests with finance, but there is a heavy reliance on human resources because individual salary data is initiated and adjusted through the personnel records function. Payroll administration is one essential function that lends itself to an effective outsource model. You can easily obtain information about payroll-outsourcing companies from your bank or accountant.

Performance Management

This all-inclusive term incorporates a number of concepts and programs related to maximizing workplace performance. The basic concept is to ensure regular two-way communication and feedback regarding expectations of performance and deliverables. There are many formal and informal tools to facilitate this process; following is a classical and fundamental "top-down" process for facilitating the performance-management process.

1. Annual or semi-annual company objective(s) is established by the management team. Objective(s) should be consistent with the vision, mission, and values of the company. At this level, the objective is fairly broad and general. Examples might be product to market within a specific timeframe or *x* percent of market share by a certain date.

2. Each of the department areas (Engineering, Marketing, and so on) determines its key contributions and deliverables to achieve the corporate objective(s).
3. Within each department area, objective-setting discussions take place between supervisor and subordinate to determine individual performance goals and timelines.

note Note that at this stage, supervisors and subordinates are demonstrating significant soft skills such as creativity, leadership, negotiation skills, presentation skills, conflict resolution, and so on. Now is also a good time to set personal development objectives for soft skills.

4. Some form of documentation, such as a project plan or other project document, is completed to formalize agreed-upon objectives including timelines, success criteria, and reward systems for achieving success.
5. Regular discussions take place to assess employee and/or department progress with goals.
6. A formal discussion of performance at the end of an agreed-upon timeline (monthly, quarterly, semi-annually, or annually) occurs.

There are numerous performance-management models; the key aspects of each are the identification of objectives that are consistent with company goals and the performance measurements outlined for attaining them. There are numerous benefits to utilizing a formal performance-management system, including the following:

- A performance-management system provides a way to measure performance and to justify merit increase or bonus recommendations.
- It provides a mechanism to insure consistency of corporate goals to individual goals.
- The process ensures that regular communication occurs at all levels of the organization.
- The process drives many of the positive aspects of corporate culture including communications, reward and recognition for top performers, and alignment to company mission.
- It allows you to identify performers who are not measuring up to company standards.

Personnel Administration

Due to the numerous mandated and legislated reporting requirements of a business, it's highly advisable to develop a personnel record-keeping system for the company. Among the documents to maintain are

- A personnel file that includes salary and classification information, offer letters, and any other work-related status changes regarding the employee
- A benefits file containing confidential information related to medical, dental, and other personal issues
- A confidential file containing information related to employee-relations issues, disciplinary actions, harassment allegations, and so on
- I-9 forms to document an employee's legal authorization to work in the United States

tip There are so many reporting and record-keeping requirements, it's highly advisable to have a personnel consultant assist in creating your records infrastructure.

Corporate Culture

The American model for successful companies always incorporates open communication as a key part of corporate culture. Conversely, the lack of communication—or top-down, one-way communication—is often cited as the greatest weakness. Effective communications emerge when there are regular and ample opportunities to interact and exchange information at all levels of the organization.

By now, a definite culture will be emerging within your company. The various activities that occur in your company help shape and define the culture. Following are some activities that may be appropriate for or are already taking place:

- **Communication activities.** These include monthly or quarterly "all-hands meetings," brown-bag lunches with cross-organizational management, company or departmental lunches, and company newsletters or e-mails. It's also a good idea to maintain a suggestion box, and an open-door philosophy.
- **Company celebrations and social activities.** These include company picnics, company field trips (to movies, concerts, and so on), quarterly or annual company "birthday" parties, employee anniversary recognition, pizza parties, and weekly stress-relief activities (such as beer busts).

- **Team oriented activities.** These include fielding sports teams in various leagues (such as softball, basketball, and the like) and participating in intramural competitions (such as ping-pong, foosball, tennis, jogging, and so on).
- **Miscellaneous company-sponsored benefits.** These include massage therapy, aerobics classes, health tips, investment advice, home services (such as dry-clean pickup and delivery and on-site automotive servicing), Weight Watchers, Toastmasters, and so on.
- **Lunchroom amenities.** These include complimentary beverages; refrigerators and microwaves; comfortable seating accommodations; donuts, muffins, or bagels on Friday; and other amenities that would make the lunchroom a desirable informal meeting place.

Significant Personnel Considerations

In today's global economy, we have seen two significant trends:

- Increasing reliance on internationally based resources for engineering, product development, and manufacturing.
- Continued reliance on foreign-born, non-naturalized technical personnel who are sponsored to work for technology corporations in the U.S.

Both of these trends require significant attention and support by the human-resources function.

Outsourcing of Engineering and Product Development

Technology companies often create subsidiary firms internationally or contract with international third-party companies. While a tremendous opportunity, this activity requires significant oversight because the employment laws and cultural norms of the country must be recognized and observed. Although this arrangement is quite advantageous to the company, this business relationship should be closely monitored on an ongoing basis to ensure the company doesn't create unnecessary risk and exposure. Consultants are often used to facilitate this process.

Hiring of Foreign-Born Non-Naturalized Employees in Your U.S. Operation

The practice of hiring foreign-born non-citizens/non-permanent residents has been an institutional practice in high technology for many years. The process of securing temporary work visas and sponsoring employment-based permanent residency is an important administrative and legal process that requires a high level of knowledge and awareness from the human-resources staff. With concerns emanating from September 11, a whole new level of scrutiny over immigration has become the norm, which means properly adhering to the laws and regulations surrounding it has become oven more important.

The new attention to temporary residency and travel abroad by non-citizens/non-permanent residents makes it absolutely critical for companies to ensure that their employees do not violate terms and conditions of their visas. Whereas pre-September 11 violations may have resulted in the inconvenience of one to two days of delayed travel, violations today may result in the suspension of visas or the inability to return to the U.S. The heightened attention to immigration-related issues calls for extreme diligence by company management and the HR staff.

The Execution Stage

By now, you will have probably hired a full-time human-resources administrator to oversee this function. This person must be capable of further developing your HR programs. The issues now relate to the refinement and improvement of your HR infrastructure. Listed in this section are areas previously discussed that are now ready for further attention:

Recruitment Strategies

Recruitment strategies include the following:

- Maintaining a formalized interview, assessment, and selection processes.
- Maintaining ongoing recruitment support (ideally, a full-time contract or permanent in-house recruiter).
- Maintaining and expanding a candidate database and applicant-tracking mechanism.
- Creating some semblance of a staffing plan that projects hiring needs through a defined time horizon.
- Developing some sort of a corporate branding strategy designed to bring name recognition to the firm. This is typically initiated by a marketing or a public-relations firm and can be adapted for application in the recruitment market.
- Implementing a new-hire orientation program.

Performance Management

A formal process of evaluating performance may be desirable for this stage. Normally, this is accomplished by an annual performance-review system that incorporates many of the elements identified in the development stage. In addition, future equity (stock options) grants should be related to employee performance, especially if the company has an "evergreen" philosophy (annual or bi-annual re-grants of stock options).

As part of a broader performance-management system, an overall system of salary management and performance management can be introduced. This includes the following:

- A budgeted merit increase program
- A performance-review system
- An allocated stock-option pool.
- Disciplinary and termination procedures to address performance problems

note This type of program is most effective during a fixed "focal" point (a specific date each calendar year).

Training and Development

Training and development is critical to employee retention and succession planning. Employees must be given the opportunity to maintain and upgrade their existing skill sets for their personal and the organization's professional growth. The company can identify authorized training per job function, level, tenure, or other means.

Organizational-development initiatives focused on soft skills such as teamwork, collaboration, communications, and other key factors affecting company performance can be a valuable asset to the company.

Training and professional-development opportunities can take many shapes. Among the low cost means to provide resources in this area are

- Brown-bag or lunchtime mini-training activities
- Off-the-shelf desktop-training programs
- On-site group training classes and activities

Management training is especially important, especially as you begin promoting people from within the ranks to managerial positions. Typically, good engineers are promoted to managers, but aren't provided the necessary management tools to succeed. The company must invest in the development of a strong management team, and this is one significant way to do so.

tip Training and development is a highly outsourced and heavily populated field. It's quite easy to secure an independent consultant to deliver a range of services to meet your company's needs.

Compensation Systems

You will eventually need to establish the cycle for salary evaluations. Typical cycles are by anniversary date of hire or at established points in time on a quarterly, semi-annually, or annual basis. This cycle is called a *focal point review system*. Generally, salary increases coincide with the performance-evaluation cycle; salary-increase budgets can be pre-determined and budgeted on an absolute percentage of payroll or by way of minimum/maximum increase guidelines based on performance.

Salary ranges should be evaluated on a regular basis to ensure consistency with your compensation philosophy. In a time of tremendous economic expansion, the market forces will make it virtually impossible to maintain ranges reflective of current activities. Although there is not a pat solution for this challenge, human resources must ultimately make the proper analysis and recommendations based on business requirements.

Human Resource Information Systems (HRIS) and Records

- **Human resource information systems (HRIS) and records.** Accurate record keeping is of critical importance. As the company grows, it must meet mandated reporting requirements (for example, by submitting affirmative-action reports and the like) to local, state, and federal entities. These requirements involve high levels of information that can be generated through use of an automated system. There are numerous off-the-shelf personnel-information systems; generally, an integrated system that has various modules for benefits administration, personnel-records administration, and recruitment systems is ideal. Of course, you'll want to perform a cost-versus-benefits analysis before buying such a system, but there is no doubt these systems are the best tools to monitor personnel-related administration.

note The myriad of local, state, and federal ordinances, regulations, and legislation generates a lot of work without a level of perceived return. Be aware that this challenge exists, and don't overlook the importance of this area. Consider it a cost of doing business. The alternative, of course is to ignore it, but be aware of the potential negative consequences of a lawsuit, audit, or investigation if your organization does not comply with these rules.

Benefits Administration

Benefits administration should be considered a part of the overall compensation strategy, which should provide a balance between cash compensation and benefits consistent with the culture of the company. Typically, the vast majority of benefits development and administration is outsourced. This model should continue, although there is a need to provide an in-house benefits specialist to ensure proper oversight and program administration. Most likely, your HR VP, Director, or Administrator will have the necessary level of knowledge to oversee this activity.

Employee Relations/Conflict Resolution

As the employee population grows, there will inevitably be conflicts in the workplace. In the ideal environment, all managers are highly trained and capable of addressing and resolving conflicts with their staff. The reality, however, is that there will always be a level of conflict that requires the attention of an arbitrator; you want to ensure that third party is someone within the company.

Integrity and ethics are the cornerstone to most companies' value systems, and the manner in which conflicts are addressed internally reflect of the company's corporate culture. There will be a need to determine your philosophy and approach in dealing with workplace conflict and performance problems. As with many aspects of HR, your direction here helps shape the culture of the company. Issues in this area represent some of the most difficult challenges within the corporate environment. The various shades of gray and the potential legal ramifications of employee and management actions call for extreme diligence in handling these issues.

The use of a performance-management system, regular communications, and various aspects of corporate culture all play major role in minimizing conflict. For example, the institution of an open-door policy enables disaffected employees to consult with higher levels of the management chain or with HR to discuss ways in which to alleviate a situation. Likewise, a manager faced with a difficult employee situation can seek assistance from management or HR. Indeed, there appears to be a direct correlation between the use of or lack of these systems and the level of conflict that exists within the workplace.

The Growth Phase

As the organization grows, many of the functions and activities related to human resources become more formal. Activities that previously occurred on an ad-hoc basis now become part of a human-resource system, and the nature of the HR business partnering expands significantly.

Corporate Culture

As the company continues to grow, the established means of communications and the intimate nature of employee gathering may no longer be sufficient for the company. Listed here are various ways to share information with employees as the company grows larger:

- Regularly published information newsletters distributed at work or sent to homes
- E-mail "blasts" for quick turnaround conveying significant company accomplishments
- Corporate phone messages to announce key events or accomplishments
- Birthday cards or employee anniversary cards signed by the president or executive management team
- Holiday cards with a year-end thank you message and reaffirmation of vision
- Year-end holiday party or fiscal–year end party
- Formal monthly or quarterly "communication" meetings
- Service recognition awards
- Department specific events (luncheons or outings attended by a member of the management team)
- New-hire orientation (where new employees meet key management personnel and gain exposure to the vision, mission, and objectives of the company)

Recruitment Strategies

In this stage of the company, recruitment has evolved to a continuous activity in which potential candidates are identified and contacted regularly. This form of strategic recruitment is most effective when coupled with a formal staffing/headcount plan developed in conjunction with the short-term operating plan. The desired result is to have recruitment activity concurrent with the opening of a new position or the replacement of an existing position. Additional activities might include

- A college recruitment program, including internships
- An expanded outreach program that capitalizes on the company's branding effort
- An internship program to identify potential future hires and to assist on lower-level, low-visibility projects

Performance-Management and Compensation Systems

With the evolution of a performance-based compensation system, you will have integrated a total system that can effectively automate the process. Additional aspects of the compensation system include

- Salary families and ranges for myriad positions including marketing, sales, product development, engineering, finance, and administration
- Competitive analysis of pay ranges on a regular basis
- Formalized performance evaluation, goal setting, and disciplinary action processes
- Formalized performance bonus incentive programs based on corporate and/or individual performance measures
- Specific compensation programs for sales and related personnel (if appropriate)

Training and Development

The focus on training and development continues to expand with the growth of the company. This activity can play a key role in helping solidify the corporate vision and mission, as well as other critical communications and programs throughout the workplace.

A well run training and development program will administer training in line with departmental and overall organizational goals, and will assist in retention and succession planning. New-hire orientation will also be developed and facilitated under the auspices of this function. This presents an opportunity to deliver a wide variety of information related to the company and can typically run from one half day to several days.

There are a number of organizational tools that can be developed and utilized to facilitate communications or assess the organizational mood. Common tools include "skip" level interviews and organizational assessments. These types of processes have significant value as well as significant risk, and should be introduced only after discussion and agreement by the key decision makers and stakeholders.

Human Resource Information Systems (HRIS) and Records

The business will need regular headcount reports, along with open personnel requisition reports and a number of other personnel-related benchmarks. In securing an automated personnel system, there are many options. Some of the key considerations will be the potential integration of a payroll and finance system, the integration of the recruitment database for purposes of driving new-hire paperwork, the ability to drive effective organization charts and headcount reports, and the integration of benefits and records information. Whatever the ultimate solution, ensure that the information is gathered and entered in a consistent, secure, timely, and accurate fashion. Experience has shown that far too much time is invested in non-productive efforts to secure and develop accurate and up-to-date information.

Employee Relations/Conflict Resolution

This represents another area where a correlation exists between the number of conflict situations and the number of employees in the workplace. Under the best of circumstances, it may be a direct correlation; under the worst of circumstances, the number of problems can increase exponentially. Unfortunately, there is no magic to solving this equation. It's simply a function of management and leadership (the soft skills), communication, and management/skills training. The disconnect is often a result of managers not making or not investing the time, energy, and commitment to manage staff.

New Human-Resource Challenges for the Growth Stage

Two new dynamics may come into play during the growth stage of the business:

- Merger and/or acquisition
- Downsizing.

Mergers and/or Acquisitions

This activity regularly occurs in the technology world. If you are the acquiring company, there are significant aspects of due diligence that should be conducted by your HR lead prior to consummation of the deal. These include

- Evaluation of compensation practices including bonus and merit-increase commitments
- Potential liabilities in the area of retirement programs, defined benefits, and deferred compensation
- Dilution of equity (i.e. stock options) and/or accelerated vesting schedules resulting from acquisition
- Potential liabilities regarding employment agreements and existing golden parachutes
- Potential liabilities regarding medical/dental/ workers'-compensation claims
- Potential liabilities regarding employment law–related actions or suits

Following approval of the deal, the following are important action items to ensure your company gets maximum value from the acquisition. Keep in mind that a key component in an acquisition is the purchase of human capital. The following will assist in an effective transition of the two entities (you'll want to continue all these practices throughout the integration process):

- Establish a series of communication meetings in which your management team can introduce your company to the new employees.
- Create a frequently used written-communication tool specifically addressing issues related to the merger. Remember, your audience includes both your current and your future employee population. Concern and apprehension exist on both sides.
- Over communicate to both sides. For employees, the primary concerns are "What happens to me?" and "What happens to my salary and benefits?" It's okay and even important to let everyone know when no decisions have been made or no action has been taken. Remember that in the absence of information, people will create their own—and it will be negative.
- Find ways to integrate the two workgroups via mixers, joint communication meetings, and celebrations. Explore mechanisms to have executive exchanges—for example, the VPs of Development from your company and the acquired company meeting with both development teams.
- Establish and implement the new programs as quickly as possible. Delaying decisions creates more apprehension and concern.
- Be clear, firm, and specific in communications. Ambiguity allows for interpretation and misinformation.

Downsizing

Unfortunately, at some point in the growth and evolution of your company, expenses may very well exceed your funding and/or your revenues. When projections for the deficit reflect the need for a reduction in staff, ensure that the human-resources department is intimately involved in managing the process. Here are some crucial considerations when faced with this decision:

- If mishandled, reductions in force can generate significant negative exposure for the company.
- Typically, temporary and/or contract personnel should be the first to be released prior to reduction of full-time, regular employees.
- Performance-management documentation is a key tool in making the determination of who is selected for reduction, underscoring the need for accurate (and truthful) reference evaluations.
- Criteria for selection should be documented and tracked for all decisions. This provides your defense in the event complaints or litigation is filed. Adverse impact analysis will need to be done to ensure non-discrimination.

- Arbitrary and capricious decisions are dangerous precedents to establish during this process.
- The reduction process should be well thought out and cohesively planned prior to implementation. Poorly coordinated implementation will result in miscommunication and adverse circumstances for an activity this is already a negative situation.
- Be prepared to communicate with those who are not affected by the action immediately following notification of those laid off.
- Engage legal counsel regarding the selection of employees and the criteria utilized.
- Be aware that employees on visas will be severely affected through this action. At the same time, this is not a viable consideration for purposes of the selection criteria. In fact, the opposite will generally be true.
- Be prepared for a public-relations "hit" on your company. This action will adversely affect your future recruitment efforts and will affect the perception of your company.

Risk Management and Safety

Due to concerns about workplace-caused disabilities, the areas of risk and safety become important considerations, especially as they relate to company liabilities. This liability takes several forms, ranging from the impact of legislation such the Americans with Disabilities Act (ADA), to the rehabilitation cost of workers'-compensation re-training, to issues related to Carpal Tunnel Syndrome. Typically, these activities can be handled on an outsource basis, but the key consideration is the potential financial liabilities and the necessary accommodations that are dictated by legislation.

Handbooks and Policy Guidelines

In today's world of legislation and litigation, it becomes necessary to have established and defined codes of conduct and guidelines for the workplace to protect the integrity of the organization. A comprehensive Standard Operating Procedure manual will also provide useful information for employees, reduce time commitments from HR personnel, and establish consistency across the organization. Some of the important components of these guidelines are

- The reaffirmation that you are an employment-at-will employer
- Expected behavior in the workplace, including violations, such as sexual harassment, that can result in termination
- Sharing of your vision, mission, and values

- Articulation of the various aspects that create your corporate culture, such as your open door policy, communications practices, and other programs that reflect your culture
- General company information including pay cycles, benefits explanation, and your commitment to a diverse workforce and workplace
- Rules and regulations regarding the terms and conditions of the workplace

Conclusion

The overview contained in this section represents just a portion of the attention and detail required of today's human-resources function. Your commitment to the human-resource role in the company will pay significant dividends toward the ultimate success of your venture. The contemporary HR professional is focused on performance as a true business partner while providing the service of the corporate conscience. This does not represent a contradiction in terms, because the prevailing wisdom dictates that sound business decisions are often solid personnel decisions as well.

five 5

CHAPTER

Business Presentations

Guy Kawasaki, CEO - **Garage Technology Ventures**

Kumar Malavalli, Founder - **Brocade Communications**

Tyzoon Tyebjee, Prof, Entrepreneur studies - **Santa Clara University**

Introduction

Every entrepreneur needs to learn the Latin phrase "*Adicio, ergo sum.*" Roughly translated, it means, "I pitch, therefore I exist." Good entrepreneurs are either pitching or sleeping—and when they're sleeping, they should be dreaming about their next pitch.

Making an effective pitch—that is, business presentation—is one of the most valuable skills that an entrepreneur can master. Entrepreneurs use pitches to raise money, close customers, sign up partners, and recruit employees. Ironically, however, even the most seasoned entrepreneurs often neglect their pitching skills.

So, in this chapter, you will learn

- How to prepare for a pitch
- The essential topics to cover in a pitch
- How to avoid the typical pitch pitfalls
- What lies you should never tell
- When to shut up and leave a meeting

Some of us suffer from a medical condition called tinnitus. It is a constant ringing in the ears. Doctors aren't sure what causes it. The treatment, like a dotcom's business model, is to throw everything at it and hope the problem goes away.

In our search for the cause and the cure, we've been told to reduce salt, miso soup, chocolate, wine, and cheese intake; to get allergy shots; to sleep more; to determine whether there's a tumor in the brain; and to buy a $3,500 digital hearing aid ("Siemens Inside").

A far simpler explanation for this medical mystery: We have listened to thousands of lousy pitches from entrepreneurs trying to raise money. It's a wonder that we haven't developed something more serious than a little ringing in the head.

Ingredients of a Successful Business Presentation

Every good business plan contains a few key ingredients:

- **Vision.** The vision should be practical and affordable, and should meet customer needs. At the same time, the vision should clearly explain the value that differentiates you from your competition. The investors are not looking for vision that marginally improves the products already available and that leads to a small incremental market share. They are looking for potential to capture a leadership position and proposals that have unfair advantage through either the company's cutting-edge technology or its unique services addressing a large market.
- **Total commitment.** The commitment to succeed should be strongly backed up by clearly defined priorities and narrow and easily understandable objectives.
- **Strategy.** Include execution-plan, product, and "go to market" strategies. You might have the greatest vision in the world, but without good execution, you do not have a business! Concentrate more on strategy and less on tactics, and show how you can implement and execute on the vision in a reasonable time frame. Also make sure that your presentation gives a very clear and unambiguous description of the product/service that you are going to provide, as well as an understanding that the product/service is aimed at solving a real-life problem that customers are presently experiencing.
- **Time to market.** In addition to "fit to market" and "price to market," the product strategy should also address "time to market." The initial product offering and the feature set should fit the window for general availability of the product. This involves prioritization of the features. It does not mean that you have to forget about the features that fall outside of this window, but to include them in the product road map. This will show the investors

that you have paid attention to the company's growth plan/prospects and this company is not a one-trick pony.

- **Management team.** You should be able to convince the investor that you have a winning management team with depth and experience to lead you to successful business, that you are uniquely qualified to execute the plan, and that you will provide additional members to enhance the team in tune with the progress of the company.
- **Passion.** Fire in the belly and a strong belief in the self and the business plan from your team builds confidence for the investors to take the next step
- **Customer testimonial.** This becomes a very key point during the later stage of interaction with investors. Do your homework well and make sure your product and solution offering are supported by prospective referencable customers. Even if you do not have a memorandum of understanding to buy your products/solution, a simple endorsement, subject to the availability and timing of the product/solution, will take you a long way in convincing investors.
- **Competition.** In thoroughly evaluating your competition, you should identify both its strengths and weaknesses. Explain what differentiates your company from the competition, and what barriers there are for others to enter the market you are going after.
- **Capital need.** Your funding request and future capital needs should be carefully orchestrated to be consistent with the product plan, market strategy, and financial forecast. For example, if you need $5,000,000, ask for $6,000,000 (with a factor of safety to cover any unforeseen slippage or expense)—not $10,000,000 or $3,000,000! This is true whether you are at the seed round or later rounds.
- **Milestones.** Both near-term and long-term milestones should be clearly laid out. The milestones should identify when the company's technology will be ready for beta testing, and when the company will begin shipping product. In addition, if you can also indicate how many customers the company can realistically sign up after general availability, it will be very advantageous.

Top Tips for Pitching

#1 Do the Research

The seeds of a great presentation are not in an ability to make up stuff on the fly. The foundation of a great presentation is research that's done before you step up to the projector. The first step is to learn what is important to the people who will be in the meeting. You can get this information from your "sponsor" in the firm. Ask questions like these:

- What are the three most important things your firm would like to learn about our company?
- What attracted your firm to our business plan?
- Are there any special issues, questions, or landmines I should be prepared for in the meeting?
- Which partners will be at the meeting? (If you want a particular partner there, don't be shy to suggest it.)

Second, go to the venture capitalist's Web site and gather some core information:

- Partners
  - What companies did they work for?
  - What schools did they attend?
  - What companies have they invested in?
  - What boards do they serve on?
- Partnership
  - What does the "About Us" say?
  - What sectors are they interested in?
  - What do their latest press releases tout?
  - What private companies are in their portfolio?
  - What public offerings or acquisitions "made" the partnership?
  - Who contributed capital to their funds?

Third, go to Google and enter the name of the firm and the names of the partners to see what you can find about the people you'll be meeting. Once you're finished, try a different search engine. You may find some new nuggets of information.

Fourth, sit down with your team and brainstorm. You're looking for connections, links, and hooks to engage the people in the meeting:

- You went to the same school or worked for the same company.
- Your spouse, relative, or friend works at a portfolio company.
- You agree with a partner's stance on not expensing stock options.

Also, try to develop insights into why this firm would be a good investor and, more importantly, why you would be a good investment:

- You'd complement, or be complemented by, their portfolio.

- You're in a space that they truly understand.
- You're in a geographic area where other portfolio companies are located.

The fact that you have done your research on your audience will be evident in your interaction with them. It will convey your respect for your audience. After all, they will sure do, if not already have done, their due diligence on you. Moreover, it will inspire the confidence that you will approach your customers with the understanding and insight based on diligence also.

#2 Observe the 10/20/30 Rule

We've never heard a pitch that was too short. We've heard many a pitch that was too long. In practice, there simply aren't any pitches that are too short because an interested investor will ask questions and lengthen the meeting. If an investor is not interested, you can't bludgeon him or her into investing with more bull secretion.

Take out your highlighter and use it now: Ten (10) slides delivered in twenty (20) minutes with no font smaller than 30 points. These are the ten slides that your pitch should contain:

1. **Title slide.** Provide your company name, your name, title, and contact information.
2. **Problem.** Describe the pain that exists for people or entities with money. Try to get "buy in" with this slide, or you'll be viewed as a problem searching for a solution later.
3. **Solution.** Explain how you alleviate this pain. Ensure that people clearly understand what you sell.
4. **Business model.** Explain how you make money.
5. **Underlying technology.** Describe the technology—and there better be technology—behind your company.
6. **Traction, sales, and marketing.** Demonstrate that the "dogs are eating the dog food." You'd better at least have beta sites. Also, explain how you are going to reach your customer and your marketing leverage points.
7. **Competition.** Provide a complete picture of the competitive landscape. Too much is better than too little.
8. **Management team.** Describe the key players of your management team, board of directors, and board of advisors. Don't be afraid to show up with less than a perfect team. Generally, all startups have holes in their team—what's truly important is whether you understand that there are holes and are willing to fix them.

9. **Financial projections and key metrics.** Provide a four-year forecast containing dollars but also key metrics such as number of customers and conversion rate. Do your forecasting from the bottom up as opposed to the usual top-down method of taking a small percentage of a huge market forecast.

note Making people understand the underlying assumptions of your forecast is as important as the numbers you've fabricated. VCs are not accountants; they are not interested in the numbers per se but rather how these numbers reflect your understanding of how the market and your participation in it will evolve. Be prepared to defend your revenue generation forecasts over the next 18 months, beyond that nobody gives much credence to your numbers any way. Expect questions about how many customers are needed to support your forecast and your sales strategy to acquire these customers.

10. **Current status, timeline, and use of funds.** Show how the company has developed and will progress with adequate funding. Lay out the major milestones that will chart your company's development from receiving funding and the next round of investment that you will seek. Also, use this slide to close with a bias toward action and success.

The point is to get to the point. We've sat through the first 30 minutes of dozens of pitches where we couldn't figure out what the company was selling. We learned that the company was "revolutionary," and that "Jupiter says there will be a $75 billion market," and the management team "is proven," but not what it sells.

tip At the back of your deck of ten slides, keep a few more slides that go into greater depth about your technology, marketing, and other key strategies. If asked, use these slides. The fact that you can whip them out in real time is often very impressive—actually more impressive than having them included in the standard presentation.

Why 20 minutes if you have a one-hour slot? First, you may not get one hour if the previous meeting is running late. Second, you want lots of time for discussion. Whether it's 20 minutes of presentation and then 40 minutes of discussion or slide/discuss, slide/discuss, slide/discuss isn't critical. But there's no scenario under which the 30-slide presentation you now use will work in an hour.

We know what you're thinking, "This must hold for the hoi polloi, the great unwashed masses, and the bozos. They should use only ten slides and twenty minutes but not us. We have curve-jumping, paradigm-shifting, first-moving, patent-pending technology."

Yeah, and your business model is to give people the dog of their choice in exchange for signing up for a monthly dog food subscription. We are referring to you. We don't care if you sell dog food, MEMS, optical components, or the cure for cancer: 10 slides and 20 minutes.

Finally, the 30-point font requirement: Any VC who's survived the dotcom carnage is probably over 40 and has deteriorating vision. (This may be why no one saw the dotcom collapse coming.) Thus, a good rule of thumb is to divide the oldest partner's age by two and use that font size.

Also, if you have to use an 8-point font, you're putting way too much detail on the slide. Use slides to lead, not read, because people can read faster than you can talk. Paraphrase and enhance the words of the slides. If you put too much detail on the slide, they'll be ahead of you and not listening to what you're saying. Plus, you're probably not pitching to a 16-year-old VC.

Bonus: Want to shock your audience? Make your Competition slide look like this:

Company name	Your strengths	Their strengths
1. 2. 3.		

Why the third column where you could risk making yourself less compelling? Because the third column shows whether you have a clue about the competition in your market and whether you're intellectually honest. Never underestimate competition. Even if there is no direct competitor today, if the market opportunity is as compelling as you are, hopefully, making out to be, there will be competitors in the market soon enough.

#3 Perform a Sound Check

Review your presentation to ensure that you are communicating the essence of your business plan. A good checklist to run on your pitch is to see if you have answered six important questions: Who, what, why, how, when, and how much:

- **Who?** Who is the customer? Who in the customer organization will decide whether to buy your solution? Who will influence this decision? Who will have to sign off on the sale?
- **What?** What are you offering the customer and at what price? In the current economic environment, you will get more traction if you are offering painkillers rather than vitamins. Customers are reticent to spend on vitamins to improve their general health but more likely to part with their precious cash to ease a massive headache.

- **Why?** Why will the customer choose you over other competing options, including doing nothing? Write a value proposition that articulates the customer's compelling reason to do business with you.
- **How?** How will you go to market? Spell out your channel strategy (direct, indirect, hybrid) as well as your revenue-generation model (purchase, lease, license, recurring).
- **When?** When do you plan to meet major milestones in product development and revenue generation? Be prepared to answer questions about implementation barriers that threaten to de-rail your plan.
- **How much?** Don't forget why you are there. How much money are you asking the VC to invest? Hopefully, you have already established that this funding range is within the parameters of this VC firm.

Another useful checklist to use is the one PR folks and journalists use to judge a story: the 4C checklist. A pitch is, after all, story-telling with a purpose. The 4C checklist is based on how diamonds are valued: carat, clarity, cut, and color. *Carat* stands for the size of the market opportunity you are pursuing, *clarity* represents your ability to articulate what value you bring to the market, *cut* represents the cloth from which your management team is cut, and *color* represents that extra sparkle that makes your story stand out in a sea of stories.

The content of the slides, together with the voice-over that you bring to the pitch, must withstand the test of these checklists. Do a few dry runs with a friendly—but not too knowledgeable—audience, and ask them to evaluate your pitch against these checklists. (More on the virtues of dry runs later.)

#4 Set the Stage

If you show up and there's no projector or the projector and your laptop won't work together, it's your fault. Some entrepreneurs show up assuming that there's a broadband connection in the room so that they can do a presentation off the Web.

If you start slow, disorganized, and disheveled, it's almost impossible to recover, so get there early and set the stage. Bring your own projector. Bring two laptops both loaded up with your presentation. Bring power adapters for your laptops. Bring printouts of your presentation in case all hell breaks loose and nothing works.

If you do hand out copies of your presentation, collect them back at the end of the presentation. The printout is a sterile version of your power pitch and only increases the chances of being buried in the "deal-with-later" stack. If your pitch has done its job effectively, the only thing that the VC needs to move to the next step is your business card.

The first thing out of your mouth in the pitch should be:

- How long do I have?
- What are the three most important things I can communicate to you? (You should have gotten this in advance, but it doesn't hurt to clarify this again.)
- May I quickly go through my PowerPoint presentation and handle questions at the end? (Caveat: VCs are an undisciplined lot and likely to butt in with questions anyway. Take this as a positive sign of their engagement but don't let the questions take you off on a tangent. Use your presentation slides as a roadmap to regain control of the pitch.)

You should have obtained this information before the meeting from the partner that's sponsoring you, but it doesn't hurt to ask this again. If you set the stage so that everyone has the same expectations, you're way ahead of the game.

And one more thing: Don't expect the VCs to sign a non-disclosure agreement. They evaluate far too many opportunities for it to be practical for them to know what information they got where. In any case, they are reticent about being "contaminated" by your information, which limits their ability to engage with other portfolio companies in market spaces close to you. And there in lies the rub. You have every right to be concerned that your IP, which is after all your crown jewel, is at risk if freely circulated within the VC community. Your best protection lies in keeping the content of your pitch at a very high level without revealing details about your technology. Mark your slides as "XYZ confidential" (no real protection from the latter, but at least you communicate your expectations).

#5 Let One Person Do the Talking

It is just great to go to our kids' school plays and ballgames. Every kid gets a piece of the limelight. Kids love it. Parents love it. There are lots of photo ops.

Meeting with a VC is not a school play or Little League game.

Keep the number of your team present at the pitch to a total of two or three. Your team's size should not overwhelm the size of the audience. At the opening, let team members introduce themselves very briefly: their role, their background, their skill set. Then everybody except the CEO should fade into the background. Not everyone on your team has to speak. You won't "prove" you're a team by having everyone click through a few slides. A pitch is the CEO's show. If your CEO can't handle it, practice until he or she can—or get a new CEO.

The rest of the team can supplement the CEO with details about the technology, marketing, finance, and so on. They can help out if he or she gets in trouble. But they're there "just in case," not as part of the main act.

Expect that most of the questions from the VC will revolve around markets, customers, marketing, and business model. Your techie, if present, will probably chomp at the bit to take the discussion into bits and bytes, speeds, and feeds. It is up to the CEO to control the participation of the rest of the team.

tip If a member of your team senses that the VCs receiving the pitch have a problem with some aspect of the presentation, the temptation is to offer a different solution: "Jane (the CEO) said that we will use channel partners, but I think we should sell directly." This is not a good idea. Never show team dissension. In the face of such a situation, the CEO should say to the VCs, "Based on your feedback, my team and I will revisit this issue," and move on. (We hope your team can keep a straight face when your CEO says this!) In addition, if the VC voices disagreement with your views, do not challenge them head on. As Mark Twain once counseled with regard to arguing with the press, "Never pick an argument with anybody who buys ink by the ton." The same applies here: Don't argue with people who write checks in millions of dollars.

#6 Catalyze Fantasy

A good pitch makes the audience fantasize about the potential of your company. You can't bludgeon the audience into thinking there's a market for your product by citing consulting studies. Instead, the plain and simple logic of your pitch is all the "proof" they need.

Unfortunately, this is a fantasy because entrepreneurs usually try to "prove" there is a market by citing consultants: "Jupiter says that there will be a $50 billion market for shrimp-farming software ASPs by 2005."

Nobody believes these projections—not even the people who make them. Instead, tell simple stories about the pain that your prospective customers are experiencing. Then explain how you will ease this pain. A good VC can extrapolate from this.

Ideally, a pitch proceeds like this:

- This is a painful problem that companies with money need to solve.
- There are many companies with money with this painful problem.
- This company has a really interesting painkiller for this problem.
- Management has executed in the past, so they can execute in the future.

Frame the size of the market opportunity in the upper-middle range. A small market opportunity will be viewed as anemic. If the market opportunity is enormous, however, there will be concerns about your ability to capture a defensible position before the Microsofts and Intels enter the arena. The upper-middle range promises a realizable fantasy.

#7 Get High and Stay High

Many entrepreneurs, particularly those with technical and engineering backgrounds, focus on the whiz-bang technology of their products. They want to get down to 1s and 0s or sub-atomic level if possible. They love to talk about the "how"—the tactics—at about a 500-foot level.

This is based on two assumptions: first, that the VCs can comprehend what they're talking about; second, that VCs care about the minutiae of the technology at this stage of the game. Both of these assumptions are wrong.

Generally, the right level of detail in a pitch is 50,000 feet above the ground. Therefore, you should focus on the "whats" and "so whats" of your company: What does your company do? What is your business model? So what if your product has x, y, and z cool features?

Do not focus on the "how" of your technology. If the pitch goes well, there will be a long period of due diligence during which you will have ample opportunity to talk about the bits and bytes. The purpose of the pitch is to get to this stage. Just hook the fish in the pitch. Reeling it in comes later.

A good rule of thumb is that the pitch should be a C-level presentation. This is the level at which the VCs think. They need to be inspired by your vision and leadership potential. With these, concerns about execution and implementation details fall away. Moreover, the early success of your venture hinges on the ability of the CEO to make a sales pitch to C-level executives (CEO, CFO, CIO, and so on) rather than to the purchasing department at prospective customers. (If the decision-maker at the customer site is a purchasing agent, you are probably touting an incremental opportunity of little interest to VCs.)

#8 Tell New "Lies"

Understand the context of a pitch: You are the 11:00 meeting. There was one at 9:00 and 10:00, and there will be three more in the afternoon. You are not the center of the universe. You're like a contestant in a beauty pageant—just another pretty face in a sea of pretty faces. And just as most beauty-pageant contestants declare their intention to work for world peace, every pretty face pitching to a VC pretty much tells the same tales.

Entrepreneurs have their own "world peace" type answers. Here are the ten most common ones—we provide them so that you can at least tell new lies.

1. **"Our projections are conservative."** The truth is that you don't have a clue what financial results you'll achieve. No one does. The issue is not whether you're lying, but the basis of your lying. For example, if you need 25% of the people in China to buy your offering in order to meet your projections, you can pretty much kiss off an investment.
2. **"[Big name consultant] says our market will be $50-billion by year 2003."** This was covered in "#6 Catalyze Fantasy," but merits repeating: Don't do this. Everyone does it, and no one believes it. Bottom-up is the only way to go. Your "reachable market" is never what the consultants forecast for the entire market.
3. **"[Big name customer] will sign our contract next week."** We've never seen this come true. Next week becomes the week after, and then the month after, and then the decision maker has left the prospective customer. Similarly, don't insinuate alliances that are little more than the exchange of business cards. The time to play the card that a big-name company has become a customer or partner is after the ink is dry on the sales contract or partnership agreement.
4. **"[Big-name competitor] is too slow to be a threat."** This lie indicates arrogance and naïveté. There's a reason that Larry Ellison can keep the San José Airport open just for his private jet to land, and you and I fly United in coach. It's not because Oracle is too slow to be a threat.
5. **"We're glad the bubble has burst."** Nobody is glad the bubble has burst. You can't tell me that you like lower valuations, longer due diligence, and smaller IT budgets. The bubble has burst (or more accurately, the tide is out), but a good company can still raise funds and be successful. But no one is glad the economy is in a funk. And although it's tempting to position your company as providing solutions to headaches of customers brought on by the burst bubble, be careful; it's hard to build a business on customers with big headaches but no cash in their pockets.
6. **"Patents make our business defensible."** Other than for biotech and medical-device companies, patents are meaningless as a form of defensibility. Frankly, you don't have the time or money to litigate, and there's not a VC who wants to fund litigation. As a rule of thumb, if you use the P word more than once in your presentation, you're hosed.
7. **"All we have to do is get 1 percent of the market."** There are two things wrong with claiming that all you have to do is "get 1 percent of the market." First, it's often very hard to get 1 percent of a market. Second, VCs want to fund companies that are aiming for 99 percent of the market, not 1 percent. In general VCs don't like to fund legal costs, but most would make an exception to anti-trust defense expenses.

8. **"Key employees will join us as soon as we get funded."** This is a very easy story to confirm—and it will be confirmed. Be sure that your big-name candidate isn't going to say, "I kind of remember meeting them at a cocktail party," because this is what usually happens.
9. **"No one else is doing what we do."** VCs draw two conclusions when you say this: Either there is no market or you're clueless. Neither conclusion is conducive to closing a deal. If you have a good idea, five companies are doing the same thing. If you have a great idea, ten companies are doing the same thing. Competition validates a market; you have to show why you're going to be the winner.
10. **"Other VCs are already interested."** This used to work back when the tide was in (or the bubble was intact). It won't work now (circa 2002), however, because there's no VC that's in a rush to invest. This is a buyer's market. You can't bluff any VC into believing otherwise.

#9 Pitch Constantly

Very few people are natural pitchers, and even the naturals work hard to be better. You can take this to the bank: Good pitchers may be born, but great pitchers are made.

If you want to be a great pitcher, you've got to pitch all the time. It won't be until the 20th time that you'll be any good. Unfortunately, this is a very difficult thing to do. Herein lies the Paradox of Pitching: the more you hate to pitch, the more you need to do it.

If you hate to pitch, it's because you feel stupid doing it. You feel stupid because you know you suck at it. And since you suck at it, you don't do it. And since you don't do it, you continue to suck at it.

If you didn't suck at it, you wouldn't mind pitching. Thus, the key to good pitching is pitching all the time, so practice with your employees, your spouse, your dog, or a video camera. There are no shortcuts—good pitching, in a meeting and in baseball, requires practice.

Training helps too. Seek out a reputable trainer who can coach you on building presence into a presentation. Even a one- or two-day seminar will do the trick, as long as it is hands-on. Simple things such as eye contact, body language, and voice modulation can transform a compelling pitch into a riveting one.

#10 Shut Up and Get Out

Of all the ways to blow a pitch, the dumbest is to sell past the close. Some people just won't take Yes for an answer. So if things go well, shut up and get out then follow up with your contact in a few days. If things go badly, talking more isn't going to change anyone's mind, so stop wasting your time and theirs. Learn from every pitch, build your company, and go back to pitch again when you have "proof" because it ain't over until the fat VC signs.

EcoSystem

Knowing the portfolio companies of the investor/VC firm and the synergy among them, you should be able to visualize an ecosystem composed of some of these companies, as well as visualizing your company as a member of this ecosystem. You will have a tremendous advantage if you can demonstrate, during your presentation, such an ecosystem and the synergy that exists within it. This is a very innovative technique to make several small companies a virtual large-scale company. The ecosystem concept will help you to create a holistic view to the investors, who will be able to visualize the following:

- Where their companies fit in the entire ecosystem model
- A large virtual company with individual ecosystem member companies still maintaining independence in their special area of expertise and product development
- The companies sharing common tools that are outside of their intellectual property and working toward providing optimum solutions to the end customers
- The interaction between the companies leading to the development of their products synergistically to serve common customers

In addition, you should be able to convince the investors that the ecosystem provides the opportunity to eliminate barriers of adoption by end customers who have a history of looking to large companies for solutions. This will also eliminate the fear and doubt to customers in considering incorporation of products from start-up companies.

six 6

CHAPTER

Funding

Chair: Doug Leone, Partner - **Sequoia Capital**
Co-Chair: Mark Dempster - **Sequoia Capital**
Ravi Chiruvolu - **Charter Ventures**
Shamini Dhana - **Silicon Valley Bank**
Prashant Shah - **Hummer Winblad Venture Partners**
Naeem Zamindar - **Intel Capital**

Introduction

First-time entrepreneurs are everywhere. They are sitting deep in the bowels of corporations and high in ivory towers. They are providing some form of professional service to a corporation or nearing completion of their education. They are right down the street in Silicon Valley and halfway across the globe.

You are one of them.

As such, wherever and whoever you are, you share some common characteristics with other entrepreneurs. You're harboring an idea that may well be the foundation of the next great company with the solution for major business and technology problems. But you have a problem: You don't have a clear idea about how to get started. You probably don't have a clear understanding of the subtleties of how the investment process works.

That's what this chapter is about: helping first-time entrepreneurs, like you, progress from inspiration to getting the first investment from a professional investor. In this chapter, you will travel from the broad (marketplace and relationships) to the step-by-step (materials and process) to the detailed (financing). In this chapter, you will learn

- About the different types of investors
- How an investment firm and its partners operate
- What investors' expectations will be
- What to expect from the prospective investor
- How to prepare materials for the prospective investor
- The subtle messages that the prospective investor will be looking for in the business plan, presentation, and due-diligence materials
- The do's and don'ts of interaction with prospective investors
- The step-by-step process that the first-time entrepreneur can expect
- How to interpret when investors are interested and when they're passing on the opportunity
- How to structure a financing—the amount to raise, the number of investors to recruit, how valuations get calculated, and how ownership of the company gets distributed
- How to understand a term sheet
- How to ensure the check gets to the bank after signing the term sheet

note There exists inherent overlap between this chapter and other chapters in this book. Because the investment process is horizontal by definition, it will ultimately cross over vertical topics such as business plans and legal issues. Therefore, the intent here is not to repeat or contradict other chapters, but within the context of how a company gets funded, to help entrepreneurs understand the degree of preparation and perseverance required, and the subtleties of both stated and inferred messages that are sought and delivered throughout the investment process.

Investor Marketplace

What ARE some of the basics about investors that I need to understand?

Each investor type and investing organization has a different level of ability to gauge the potential of a market, team, or technology, and each has a different level of ability to manage the risks in building a start-up company.

To help control these risks, each type of investor will have different ownership requirements, which will be evident through the terms and conditions. Put simply, higher levels of investment lead to higher levels of ownership, which lead to higher levels of control over the company. This will tend to dictate how actively the investor is involved in defining strategy, recruiting the management and engineering teams, defining product management/marketing/sales, and so on.

Ultimately, based on the perception of risk involved, each investor will have varying expectations for the kind of return on investment expected, which will ultimately affect the valuation of your idea.

So, before attempting to meet with a potential investor, it is important that you first have a clear understanding of the different types of investors who could fund your company, the expectations that specific investors will have, and what you'll want to get out of the relationship.

Where's the Money?

It may seem obvious, but it's not as easy as it sounds: Entrepreneurs need to be certain they choose the right investor set. These days there are many different choices and sources for entrepreneurs; the four major sources of funding are

- Individual investors
- Institutional capital
- Business partners
- Venture capitalists

Each type of investor offers a different kind of relationship for the entrepreneur. The investor set you choose will most likely have a big influence on the path taken toward success (or failure).

What follows is a snapshot of the four sources of investment, with accompanying pros and cons. The pros and cons are constructed with an eye toward what's in your best interest given the stage of your company. It's important to view these grids as a guide rather than as absolute truth. They should help orient you in the right direction so that you can start targeting specific investing organizations and investing partners.

Individual Investment

Individual investment capital is the usual starting place for entrepreneurs. It comes from one of two sources: personal savings (friends and family) and angel investors.

Personal Savings

Personal savings, including those of your friends and family, represent an investment by people who are motivated by their belief in your abilities and who are betting as much (if not more) on you as on your business plan.

Pros and Cons of Using Personal Savings as Investment Capital

Pros	*Cons*
Money is easily accessed	Typically unable to add business value
Minimal due diligence	Typically unable to assist in business building activities
Valuation insensitive	Negligible industry contacts
Loose terms and conditions	Often unable to support follow-on fund raising rounds (dilutes their ownership)
Doesn't require an option pool	Things could get personal

Angel Investors

The second individual investment source comes from angel investors. These tend to be wealthy individuals who have experience operating similar companies and who now want to leverage their expertise. Often, matchmakers arrange these investments. They're lawyers, bankers, or accountants for whom this is not a primary occupation, but whose contacts and interests are such that they like to occasionally facilitate such deals.

Pros and Cons of Angel Investors

Pros	*Cons*
Active company advisors	Valuation sensitive
Often able to help in business-building activities	Only want preferred stock
Numerous industry contacts	Expect high rate of return
Rarely monitor company or exercise control	Limited ability to support follow-on fund raising rounds (dilutes their ownership)
Money can be accessed easily	Fewer available investors relative to two or three years ago
Minimal due diligence	
Loose terms and conditions	
Doesn't require an option pool	

Institutional Funding

This type of funding comes from commercial banks, leasing companies, and other agencies such as the Small Business Administration. This funding is normally in the form of loans or leases for equipment purchase or for working capital.

It's important to note that this type of funding, called *debt financing*, is an adjunct to other early-stage funding. It's not really a form of equity as much as it is a source of follow-on financing. You usually can't get debt financing until you have already successfully received other kinds of funding. That being said, it is important to understand debt financing; you'll find important details related to seeking out, obtaining, and managing institutional funding later in this chapter.

Pros and Cons of Institutional Funding

Pros	Cons
Valuation insensitive	Puts pressure on cash flow
Investment is mostly in the form of debt	Typically unable to assist in business building activities
Doesn't dilute entrepreneur's equity structure	Negligible industry contacts
Less expensive than equity	Equity investment from outside investors required first
"Stretches" equity dollars in order to meet product and financial milestones	Restrictive terms and conditions
Ability to finance asset growth (e.g., capital expenditures, accounts receivable, business acquisitions)	Often unable to support, or help find, follow-on fund raising rounds

Business Partners

Potential customers, suppliers, corporate partners, and even former employers are a very good source for start-up funding. Customers may want to invest if they see a potential value-added supply source—one that might give them some competitive advantage, reduce their costs, or help them differentiate their own products and services. Suppliers may want to invest because they have an interest in developing new markets or sales channels. Corporate partners may be interested in developing an ecosystem, complementary technologies, or enabling technologies for their products and services.

Pros and Cons of Business Partners

Pros	Cons
Able to add meaningful business value	Restrictive terms and conditions
Able to assist in business building activities	Require certain preferences to the business partner
Source for technology, market, or business model validation	Can sometimes limit the attractiveness of the company for future investment
Numerous industry contacts	
Valuation insensitive	
Expect lower rate of return	

Venture Capital

Because venture-capital firms represent the bulk of the private-equity market for financing start-ups, we're going to concentrate, in this chapter, on how to meet VC needs. That said, the principles on how to interact with VCs apply equally to any of the other groups of first-round investors.

Venture-capital firms are typically organized as limited partnerships, with pools of capital provided by professionals. They are looking to invest in young, rapidly growing companies representing an opportunity for a high rate of return within five to seven years.

Venture capitalists can be generalists, investing in various industry sectors, or in various geographic locations, or at various stages of a company's life. Alternatively, they may be specialists in one or two industry sectors, or they may seek to invest in only a localized geographic area.

Pros and Cons of Venture Capitalists

Pros	*Cons*
Investment validates business plan	Investor is a professional whose experience in negotiations may work more to his advantage than to yours
Investment gives company credibility	Extensive due diligence
Able to add significant business value	Heavily monitor company and can exercise control
Able to significantly assist in business-building activities	Start-up company could get a less-experienced partner on the Board of Directors.
Numerous industry contacts	Expect high rate of return
Well-structured terms and conditions (balance management incentives with investors' governance)	Valuation sensitive
Almost always able to support, and help find, follow-on rounds of funding	Take 20–30 percent ownership per firm at the early round
	Only want preferred stock
	Require an option pool

Are There Different Types of Venture-Capital Firms?

Venture capitalists will invest in companies at various stages of the business life cycle. A venture capitalist may invest before there is a real product or company organized (so called *seed investing*), or may provide capital to start up a company in its first or second stages of development (known as *early stage investing*). Alternatively, the venture capitalist may provide needed financing to help a company expand beyond a critical mass to become more successful (known as *late-stage financing*).

Seed Stage

These VC firms usually invest between $50K and $1M in a company. Seed-stage VC firms are typically staffed with partners who come from the executive ranks of public companies. They have time, money, and experience to offer. The funded company will typically use the proceeds for research, assessment, and initial-concept prototypes. The VC helps to define the opportunity, structure the business, sort out the corporate documentation, and put in place basic operational components. Its objective is to ensure that a basis for a business is established. This means the entrepreneurs must develop their ideas to include a market definition and a product requirements document (PRD). When these milestones have been reached, the seed-stage VC firm will promote the new company and make investor introductions for further rounds of funding.

Early Stage

Most VCs are early-stage investors, ready to put $1M to $10 M in a company. (The funded company will typically use the proceeds to hire an engineering team, hire initial executives, develop the technology, and build the first product to alpha or beta stage.) Partners in early-stage VC firms usually come from an operating background, where they've had hands-on experience building businesses and running P&Ls. Early-stage VCs have significant expertise and play a major role in the strategy development and business development. Their objective is to minimize, if not eliminate, business risks associated with market definition, management, technology concerns, and competitive pressures. When these issues have been resolved, they will aggressively promote the company and raise additional rounds of funding. Many of the more reputable early-stage VCs have Entrepreneur-in-Residence (EIR) programs. These are like "in-house" seed stage VCs, providing early services and advice. The primary difference is that the entrepreneurs will initially work out of the VCs' offices and use the VCs' operational resources to work on their business/technology idea.

Be aware, however, that not all VCs are created equal. There are considerable differences among firms, and even among partners within firms. Some VC firms operate as basic deal makers; they'll cut a check and about the only exchange with them will be at the board meetings. This may be fine if you want to be left alone to pursue business as you see fit. Other VCs will effectively move in with you once the check has cleared. Again, this may be fine if you want deep involvement from the VC to help shape and direct the business. The point is, make sure you know what kind of firm you're dealing with and have a realistic view of how much or how little they'll be investing in time and energy as you go forward.

Late Stage

These VC firms usually invest between $10M and $30M in a company. Partners in late-stage VC firms typically come from financial-services backgrounds where they've structured investor deals and positioned companies for a liquidity event.

The funded company will typically use the proceeds to scale the business and stage it for an ultimate liquidity event (even if that's a number of years off). At this point, a company has proven the technology, validated the markets, and demonstrated operational capabilities. These VCs help the company obtain even broader market credibility, global reach, and the attention of analysts, investment bankers, and potential acquirers.

Corporate

Many corporations have established VC subsidiaries to invest in companies whose solutions address industry issues and complement or extend the corporation's strategic direction. These VCs will invest at any stage of a start-up company. Corporate VC investments are often made in conjunction with other business arrangements, such as license or royalty agreements, research contracts, or volume purchase agreements. Sometimes, corporations invest in a start-up company with the pre-wired intention of spinning-in the team and technology after specific milestones are met. Normally corporate investors will be interested in your company only insofar and as long as your interests coincide. If you share a legitimate market, customers, and technology, they may want to invest, in part, to discourage their competitors. They may also want to move out if your company's strategy or business direction changes.

How are VC Firms Structured?

Venture-capital firms are organized as limited-liability corporations. They typically raise their funds from limited partners such as pension funds, university endowment funds, foundations, insurance companies, and high–net worth individuals. Because of the risk, length of investment, and limited liquidity involved in venture investing, and because the minimum commitment requirements are so high, venture capital–fund investing is generally out of the reach of the average individual. The venture fund will have from a few to almost 100 limited partners depending on the target size of the fund.

Once the firm has raised enough commitments, it will start making investments in portfolio companies. The venture-capital fund is accountable to these limited partners on a quarterly basis, but has these funds for, typically, a 10-year period.

Venture capitalists may look at (and pass on) several hundred opportunities before deciding to invest in a company. Far from being passive financiers, venture capitalists foster growth in companies through their involvement in strategy, management, product development, and sales of the companies in which they invest. They are entrepreneurs first and financiers second. Venture capitalists mitigate the risk of venture investing by developing a portfolio of young companies in a single venture fund. Companies such as Cisco, Digital Equipment Corporation, Apple, Federal Express, Compaq, Sun Microsystems, Intel, Microsoft, and Genentech are famous examples of successful companies that received venture capital early in their development.

How Do VC Firms Operate?

VC investment activity is divided into four stages:

- Sourcing
- Investment
- Building
- Liquidity

Sourcing

Sourcing means selecting and evaluating investments. The VC firm must have strong networking skills, access to deep industry knowledge, and a deep understanding of business dynamics.

Usually, one partner in the VC firm champions the company evaluation process. Associates may help in conducting due diligence, including reference checks, making technical assessments, contacting potential customers and suppliers, assessing market size, and completing competitive analyses.

Investment

The second stage involves selecting and making investments, although how investment-approval decisions are reached varies from firm to firm. In some, only two general partners must approve the investment; in others, the consensus agreement of all general partners is required. Despite due diligence, this investment process remains an imperfect science. What it does require is knowledge of market trends, understanding of technology, and good people judgment.

Seed and early-stage investors typically expect to own about 20–50 percent of the company. That's about the level necessary to ensure that the VC will be able to yield the desired returns to the limited partners and control enough voting rights to exert a significant level of influence over the company.

For this level of ownership, each VC would require one seat on your board. (If there's one VC firm involved, it's one seat; if there are two, it's two seats.) One or two of the remaining seats go to the founders and management, and the fifth will go to an independent board member—usually someone who is an expert in the specific industry, or who has a high level of influence and credibility within that industry.

VCs typically require the company to include an option pool big enough to attract and motivate the management team and employees. An option-pool size will take into account future hiring considerations. A common allocation is 20 percent of the fully diluted ownership.

Because the company goes through multiple stages of funding as it moves along the path to profitability and ultimately cash-flow breakeven, a VC firm normally plans to invest pro rata in multiple rounds of funding in order to maintain its ownership position. It has become an industry norm that follow-on rounds are led by new investors, who further validate the business model and bring new skills and resources to help build the company. Their involvement, in effect, sets the market price.

Building

The third stage involves monitoring investments. Through active participation on the board of directors of the companies, investors can help provide the company with operating expertise as needed.

Generally, on a day-to-day basis, VC investors divide their time between business-building activities for companies currently in their portfolio and networking with contacts to source new deals that might become part of the portfolio. There is a great deal of interaction between investors and entrepreneurs, ranging from nearly daily at first, to once a week as the company forms, to once a quarter once a company starts generating revenue.

note Typically, a partner will be on the BoD of eight to 12 companies. Therefore, it is important to get to know the associates as well as you know the partner to ensure that you get as much as you can out of the relationship.

Liquidity

The fourth stage is exiting investments, which involves taking the company public or selling it privately. This is an integral part of the investment process. The general partners are compensated for the fund's performance. The general partners get a management fee of 2–3 percent of the fund's capital and then 20–30 percent of the gains on the funds investments. Therefore, their interest is aligned to the success of the companies in which they invest. Naturally, they make every effort to maximize that return.

What Are The Expected Outcomes for a VC Investor?

Investors in a company expect to get a liquidity event (an *exit*) within two to seven years of initial investment. Specifically, early-stage investors seeks a 10× return on investment within five to seven years, and a late-stage investor seeks 3–5× return on investment within two or three years.

A start-up company can expect one of four outcomes. The two ideal outcomes, an initial public offering and mergers and acquisitions, are highlighted next. The two least desirable outcomes—staying a small company or closing your doors—are self-explanatory.

Initial Public Offerings

The IPO is the most glamorous and visible exit for a venture investment. In recent years, technology IPOs were in the limelight and IPO requirements were relaxed. A company could go public before it started making a profit or had even demonstrated a viable market opportunity. After the 2001 NASDAQ collapse and the failure of so many such companies, however, the IPO market retrenched. Today, a company planning to IPO needs to have:

- Revenue run rate
- Profitability for at least two quarters or a proven business model
- Proven market opportunity
- Growing market segment
- Defensible competitive position (barriers to entry)
- Minimal regulatory burdens (i.e., should not be facing regulatory burdens)

Mergers and Acquisitions

Mergers and acquisitions represent the most common types of successful exits for venture investments. In the case of a merger or acquisition, the venture firm will receive stock or cash from the acquiring company, and the venture investor will distribute the proceeds from the sale to its limited partners.

The drivers for mergers and acquisitions (M&As) are

- Acquisition of technology to effectively compete and retain market positions
- Entrées into new markets segments
- Product extension within the acquirer's market

It's important to note a basic premise here: A company is not sold—it is bought. When a buyer wants, or better yet, needs the management team, product, technology, or access to customers and partners, then interest, relevancy, valuations, and prices are higher.

The Investor/Entrepreneur Relationship

What Is The Nature of a Good Entrepreneur/VC Relationship?

A relationship between a VC and an entrepreneur usually lasts at least a couple of years and often stretches out five years or more—although the business plan may well have changed and the entrepreneur may have switched roles in the company. It's like a marriage (while the relationship with your investment banker through the IPO process is more like dating). As with any marriage, there will be lots of ups and lots of downs. The only way to survive will be through good communication and trust. Without these two, see you in divorce court!

Setting expectations is vital. Not all VCs expect their entrepreneurs to call them five times a week, while not all entrepreneurs feel an active VC is a value-add. It's essential to determine up-front what your relationship will look like: how often you will interact (communicate) and for what level of issues. There will be iterative work involved to hone the process, to ensure that both sides get the needed value and nurturing. Like marriage, it is hard work, but the rewards are sure worth it.

What Level of Agreement Among Founders Is Necessary Before Embarking on this Process?

Before you take an investor meeting, you and your co-founders have to have fundamental agreement on two issues. The first begins with an honest self-evaluation. You need to look long and hard in the mirror before deciding what your role and responsibility should be in the company. Ask yourself what your true contribution and commitment will be. Don't fool yourself into thinking that you're a CEO or CTO if in fact your true gift is as an engineer or product manager (in which cases, you should carry the Vice President title). If you insist on holding a title you're not ready for, you'll end up at the short end of the stick. Having said this, the role you're seeking might indeed be the next logical step in your career. Make sure you have the credentials and confidence to back it up.

Second, agree on which co-founder will be on the board of directors. (There'll probably only be one of you there.) Decide who the best person is to represent the founding team, and then be prepared to back that person up completely. Never undermine his or her authority.

In the end, try not to get hung up about these issues. As a founder, your ownership is the same whether your title is CEO or Director. In either case, you have to perform to expectations and achieve results or you won't be in the company.

What Should I Expect/Want from an Investor?

Here are the top eight contributions your investor should be making, in reverse order:

8. **Business sounding board.** Great VCs play roles of cheerleader, minister, security guard (protect cash), psychological counselor, teacher, and student. "Know what you don't know" and bring on people who will help you cover your blind spots. For instance, if you as CEO have never been through the IPO process, there'll be great value in finding an experienced investor who has. Or, if your background is engineering, finding an investor with a marketing and sales background would be very helpful.
7. **Product management.** Often, product management is the most important and most weakly staffed position in a start-up. It is the ugly, gray void between your technical efforts and customers. Hire well here because you don't want your VCs having to play the role of product managers; their expertise is elsewhere. Having said this, capable VCs actually do a good job in helping to focus PRDs and product roadmaps to fit current business climates and realities.
6. **Customer/partner introductions.** If your VCs do this, great! But don't rely on them to do so. All VCs in the honeymoon period will say they have contacts into the top 15 [insert your category here], but when it comes down to making the deal happen, the contacts may not be as strong as advertised. They may get you an introduction, but it's you and your inherent value proposition that will make the real difference.
5. **Hiring.** Quantity and quality of the VC Rolodex, while sometimes touted, is grossly overrated. At the same time, a seasoned VC with good people judgment is a vitally important resource for the entrepreneur. VCs willing to participate in interviewing candidates are even more helpful. Additionally, VCs who are able, on short notice, to meet with and convince potential employees to join the company provide a great service.
4. **Follow-on financings.** Investor help here is critical: The higher the level of existing VC participation in the new round, the stronger the signal of confidence to potential new investors. In tough markets, a company often needs a

VC to lead an inside round, or at the very least participate pro rata in a financing. There are some VCs other investors will follow, and there are those who other VCs like to avoid. Know which you're getting.

3. **Board of directors seat.** Choosing the right members for the board of directors is essential to the success of your company. And yet, all too often, entrepreneurs make this decision passively. A bad board member can be a distraction at best, and at worst, can actually kill your company. Start-ups are like newborn babies: In the early days, all the caregivers need to be aligned with the baby's best interests at heart. Additionally, as there only are a few board seats, the opportunity cost is high when there's a sub-optimal player around. Choose wisely. Check references carefully (this is no time to be shy). If the references are checkered, turn the person down, just as you would with any key employee hire.

note A bad board member is not someone who is tough or who does not regularly agree with your ideas. In fact, such a person is a good board member. Dissension often creates great results. A bad board member is one who has fuzzy ethics; who is not committed to the business (i.e., doesn't come to meetings, doesn't know what the company does); and/or whose interests are not aligned with the best interests of the company.

note It is common for an investor who is not on the BoD to request board observer rights. Such requests need to be evaluated on a case-by-case basis, along with the level of information that will be disseminated. Official BoD members have the right and obligation to know every opportunity, challenge, issue, data point, and blemish facing the company. A board observer does not. These expectations must be established up front. For instance, only official board members should participate in closed sessions to discuss management problems, legal issues, or potential M&As.

2. **Positioning/exits.** As you worry about taking a company from here to there, VCs are usually quite good at helping from "there" to the finish line. Given that VCs usually sit on multiple boards, interact with other investors and bankers, and have connections with potential acquirer firms in your space, the good ones can be useful in devising pragmatic exit strategies. Sometimes VCs and acquiring corporations co-invest in a start-up company with a pre-wired deal. In such cases, there is no uncertainty about the exit strategy. As long as pre-set milestones are reached, there's a pre-set price agreement on the cost of acquisition.

1. **Trust.** Trust is the watchword for success. As in a good marriage, the best way to develop trust is through communication—and nothing is more

important than how you, the entrepreneur, communicate *bad* news to your VC. Are you direct, timely, and can you deliver critical information devoid of spin? As an entrepreneur, your mantra should be "No surprises!" When there are down cycles, and your relationship is fundamentally tested, this trust will be the insurance policy that will get you through the disasters or at least mitigate the damage.

What Does an Investor Expect/Want from Me (The Entrepreneur)?

Here are the top six things that an investor looks for in a great entrepreneur (again, in reverse order):

6. **Maturity.** Start-up life is tough enough, even without a steady captain at the helm. Do your best to balance the ups and downs. As CEO, you should be the counter-weight whenever possible. Be positive when others are down, and be negative when others are up. Insulate your investors from these emotional highs and lows, and always take five minutes to think before reacting to anything. As the founder, understand the power you have. Be mature.
5. **Focus.** Do not boil the ocean. Have a laser-beam focus on your target customers, know their problems, and understand what single product they need that no other provider can offer.
4. **Hiring/culture building.** The ability to select, attract, and retain "A" players is a key talent. Creating a start-up culture, which places a premium on hard work, frugality, and profitability is critical. Many CEOs can do a lot with a little (on a shoestring when necessary). What is required is a unique blend of charisma and leadership by example.
3. **Meet expectations/deliver results.** A classic example of managing expectations is what every start-up does one to four times a year in creating its operating budget. Even though 100 percent of entrepreneurs call their forecasts "conservative," at least 90 percent miss their numbers. How high achievers accustomed to winning repeatedly miss this dismal 10-percent success rate is a mystery to many investors, and one of the untold little secrets of the start-up world. There is big psychological value to hitting the numbers; you should not be afraid to under-forecast and over-deliver. Aggressive revenue numbers are too often just an excuse for aggressive spending.
2. **Deliver bad news quickly.** We've already suggested that "No surprises" be your mantra. Investors know that you will make mistakes. They also expect you to recognize the mistakes and set corrective action. Communicating a problem to a VC builds trust, and provides you with resources to help cor-

rect the problem. Having said this, the VC does expect the kind of leader who will get things done and not rely on the VCs' every word before making a move.

1. **Be a money maker.** Put simply, VCs want a company that makes money. To get there, the company needs to deliver a proprietary, differentiated product to an untapped market where the sales cycle is less than six months. Making money requires no basic change in customer behavior. The solution must integrate seamlessly into IT environments to solve an unmet need.

Materials Needed for the Investor

All your planning efforts have paid off. You've set appointments with the right firms and the right investors. Now it's time to make sure you're armed with the right information to get the prospective investors engaged in the conversations and seriously considering investing in your company. The materials outlined next will come in handy throughout the process that is mapped out in the next section. Get them prepared so you can use the right materials at the right time.

How Should I Approach Putting Together and Delivering the Materials that Will Be Needed?

There are three guiding principals as you organize your thoughts and materials for the investor.

- Remember that you're selling shares, not product. Many entrepreneurs end the process before it even gets started because they just want to brag about the bits and the bytes of the technology.
- Remember that you're not trying to close the deal in the first presentation. You're trying to get the investor into the due-diligence step of the process. Whet their appetites for the main course and the substance you have prepared for them.
- When delivering the pitch, recognize that you have two slides and 10 words up front to get the investor's attention or the meeting is over. In fact, you may be on slide 15 and not realize that the meeting is long over. If you fail to pull the potential investors into your world immediately, all you'll have is a very long meeting with an inattentive audience.

What Is the Single-Most Important Piece of Information that I Can Provide to the Prospective Investor?

The one-liner.

We're not suggesting a glib tag line or a superficial sound bite. Nor is the one-liner a substitute for the substance that ultimately must be provided. The one-liner is a way to very quickly position your company in the investor's brain with an immediately relevant frame of reference. Remember, by the time of your appointment, the investor has just surfaced from five presentations or board meetings in businesses having nothing to do with yours, and they have five more such meetings after your appointment.

The definition of your business and its purpose should fit on the back of your business card. Your ability to succinctly articulate this will communicate volumes about your understanding of your business. It says that you have the potential to successfully recruit, lead, and sell. It also has the added affect of helping them see the market-size opportunity. Put simply, they want to understand what they might be investing in.

Is a Business Plan Required?

Yes, absolutely! As for the structure and content of the business plan, refer to Chapter 4. What follows here is designed to help you anticipate the messages that the investor is looking for when going through your business plan. Time is a precious commodity and investor attention spans are not long. Knowing how to make the business plan stand out is essential.

Business Definition/Company Purpose

We've gone over this, but the one-liner belongs here too. Be prepared to articulate what you do and why, at every step along the way.

Business/Technology Problem

Who cares?

Who in the customer's organization really suffers from this ailment? (Hint: it's not the CIO or CTO.) Know the people who will be recommending, approving, and/or using your product. Make sure your company is selling to the people who really control the budgets.

So what?

Is what your company will be building and selling a must-have or a nice to have? Demonstrate that the customer/user has an acute pain that causes real agony. Put it in terms of wasted CAPEX/OPEX, missed application/service revenues, manual/complex/error-prone/time-consuming processes, and so on.

Company/Product Solution

Given the pain, yours must be the 10,000mg antidote. Developing a product or service that a customer absolutely needs—so much so that they'd be willing to pay you as a development partner— is a good way to build the foundation of a long-term business.

Market Size

The number of customers, with the kind of pain diagnosed, should add up to at least a \$1-billion market (or have the potential to grow into this). Demonstrate a total addressable market (TAM) and served addressable market (SAM). While you can't go after the whole pie on day one, show that the first slice you'll go after locks you into the customer for the rest of the pie. Subsequently, show the Share of Market (SOM) that your company can reasonably achieve over this same five-year period.

note The *TAM* is a top-down analysis of the total number of customers divided by the number of seats in the entire market who could buy the product, multiplied by total spending for your product category in the market. This is typically projected over five years with current spending in the first year and projected spending based upon a category growth rate percentage (CAGR). The *SAM*, on the other hand, is an estimation of adoption—that is, the number of customers divided by the number of seats in your segment of the market multiplied by the estimation of total spending for your product category in the segment over five years. Finally, the *SOM* is a percentage projection of what your company will get of the SAM relative to competition and in-house projects.

Competition

If the pain is agonizing, as you've claimed, then yours is not the only company with a prescription. Competition is good. It validates a market. Just don't be fifth to market in a field of five. There are incumbents, start-ups, and internal customer projects. Demonstrate your differentiation versus each and your barrier to entry versus each. Show that you know exactly what you want and have a burning desire to achieve it.

Product Development

Demonstrate that your solution is hard to do, but that you've figured it out because of the team and the IP. Unveil the solution. Start with the product configurations; then go to the underlying architecture, the component parts and finally, the IP/patents. Also, show that you know the development milestones and that the product releases are realistic.

Sales and Distribution

Show that you know how to build the business, price the product to value (not cost of goods sold), and ramp revenue. Product configurations, pricing, the sales model, and partners must be mapped out. Keep in mind that the model you serve up will be compared to the market size, the type of customer, the sales process, and financials.

Team/BoD

Demonstrate that the co-founders and early employees possess deep domain experience and have a record of success in the market you're going after. Their personal styles should be confident, but modest. Founders should know what they don't know. A-list founders are sought after because they tend to recruit an "A" team and have the ability to set the DNA right in the first 100 days. A void in the management team is better than having a B player who insists on a title.

Financials

This is truth-telling time. Do the financials reflect the plan just described? Include it all. Hide nothing. You need a profit-and-loss statement over three to five years, a cash-flow statement, and a capitalization table (also called a *cap table*). Are you frugal and do you know when, where, and how much to spend in order to get to cash-flow positive? Do you know how to ramp up revenue? Are you realistic about the challenges of building a company and the obstacles to market penetration? In short, do you know your business?

Investors know that years three to five are a model, but they like to see how you think in that model. You'd be surprised at the number of entrepreneurs who put up a model that would make them the most profitable company in the history of business.

How Do I Organize a Presentation?

Basically, you want to organize your presentation along the lines of the preceding business-plan discussion. This flow represents what the venture-capital community has become accustomed to and the kinds of messages it's seeking from the entrepreneur.

There Seem to Be a lot of Nuances at Play in the Presentation. Are There Some Basic "Do's" and "Don'ts" That I Should Subscribe To?

Investors are indeed looking to extract information from any source that they can. That's because there's a lot of money at stake, and sorting fact from fiction is a difficult task. Investments get made on imperfect information. So think of your presentation as delivering both stated and inferred messages. We've already discussed the stated messages. Here are a few inferred ones to be aware of:

- **DO** perform your own due diligence on the VC and customize the pitch accordingly. Know if your company fills a gap, complements, substitutes for, or threatens other companies in the VC's portfolio.
- **DO** "skinny the plan." That is, before you start out to raise money, make your company as lean as possible. Eliminate jobs if necessary. Stop outsourcing. The lower your burn rate, the stronger your negotiating position is. You have to communicate frugality and responsibility. Clearly, you need to know how much you need to raise, and you need to have reasonable valuation expectations. Particularly in austere times, convey that you know how to deliver a fully funded plan. Show that you're focused on the right hires, the right development, and the right customers to get to cash-flow positive.
- **DO** learn and practice good presentation skills. Center the audience's attention on listening to you. The slides should complement your spoken words and hold the audience to a central point.
- **DO** stay fresh. Even though you'll give the pitch dozens of times, sometimes to the same investor, a passionate fervor says you'll be committed. Likewise, don't be discouraged if you find yourself answering the same questions every meeting. It's just the investors' way of making sure they understand the story.
- **DO** prepare due-diligence materials prior to engaging VCs. Having these materials ready to hand over says that you're thoughtful, prepared, and serious—and not about to lose momentum!
- **DO** be honest when answering questions. Investors sense when an entrepreneur is hiding something, and they'll stay on it until they find the truth. Also, the investor will be comparing your answers to those obtained during the due diligence.

- **DO** know your (and your co-founder's) long-term roles. If you have the background, track record, and passion to be the CEO (pick you favorite title), then stand by your choice. Short of this, know what your true competence/contribution/commitment is to the company and assume that role. Keep egos in check. Otherwise, expect to be asked to step aside (or out).
- **DO** demonstrate incredible focus and business acumen. Show that hiring, product development, customer acquisition, and capital expenditures are pursued with an eye toward profitability.
- **DO** ask for the order. Show that you want to do business by stating exactly how much you want and at what valuation. Otherwise, you're turning over the driver's seat to the VC, effectively saying, "Well, that's what I'm about: How much do you think I'm worth?" It's far better to show confidence and knowledge of your own potential and market.
- **DON'T** make the audience read your presentation. Some of the worst presentations are composed of a series of bulleted sentences in 12 pt type. That kind of presentation is a guarantee the investor won't understand your business and won't invite you back. Remember, pictures are better than words.
- **DON'T** bring more than two or three people to the presentation. Only those who have a meaningful speaking role in an area that can't be covered by someone else should attend. Initially, investors want to deal only with the core founders.
- **DON'T** Make the investor feel like one of dozens of appointments you have. A dead giveaway is when another VC's name is on the first PowerPoint slide.
- **DON'T** have more than 25 slides in your presentation. If you need more, you probably haven't done a good enough job filtering the details, identifying key issues, or conveying compelling points. If you can't do it all in a one hour meeting, how well will you do it when running a company?
- **DON'T** use certain phrases that signal you are naïve or desperate. (Even if you are, avoid the appearance.) Specifically, don't say:
    - "I'd like a non-disclosure-agreement."

note Don't ask for an NDA until you know the VC is serious about doing due diligence. Besides, you're not going to unveil the jewels of the company anyway...at least, not at this point.

- "I'm raising $30–50M."
    - "Money only gets us to an alpha product."
    - "We're targeting a 'many-months-out' close."
    - "The market will value the deal."
- **DON'T** use any other indicators that you don't have a clue about how to run a business. (If you don't, by the way, then say so. Honesty always wins you points.) Specifically, don't use any of these terms or phrases:
    - "Office of the President"
    - "No competition"
    - "Head count ahead of plan"
    - "Lack of financials"
    - "These are conservative projections"
- **DON'T** let the VC keep stringing you along for information.

What Should I Be Prepared for During the Due-Diligence Process?

All your efforts to date have been to get to the due-diligence stage. Now that the investor is seriously interested, you need to demonstrate that you're ready to do business. Don't wait for the investor to start asking for specific due-diligence materials Be prepared to hand over the following items (keep in mind, however, that investors are suspicious by nature and will pursue information separate from the materials you provide):

- **Business plan.** This should be based upon the outline provided in Chapter 4.
- **Presentation.** This should be based upon the outline provided earlier in this chapter.
- **Financials review.** Include well-organized data pertaining to P&L, cash flow, balance sheet, and cap table. Also, demonstrate that you've done sensitivity analyses and know how to adjust the plan if certain assumptions don't occur when expected. Know the quarter in which you're company will be cash-flow positive and profitable, and related revenue-recognition issues.
- **Team resumés/references.** Include those of the founders, executives, and top engineers. Keep in mind that the investor will check these and others, so make sure you're completely upfront. You'll be giving personal, technical, and business references that the VC will check. Realize that it's a small world. The VC has lots of connections and will definitely call around to

people not included on your list.

- **Market sizing.** Be prepared to show the math for how the TAM, SAM, and SOM were developed. Provide the market research and raw data. Highlight where assumptions were made. Make this information as tangible as possible.
- **Customer testimonials.** Choose the best from what you've got whether they're full paying, beta, alpha, or merely an LOI. In any case, you'll want them to make meaningful business-oriented statements about their business/technology problem, required solution, product merits, how it is deployed into a production environment, what the ROI is (expected to be), and results or positive changes to the business. Keep in mind that the investors will likely follow up and speak directly with these customers in order to find out what's not going so well with your company, team, or product.
- **Competitive assessment.** Competition comes from every direct and indirect provider vying for the customer's dollars. Include incumbents, replacement products, start-ups, and even home-grown efforts within your target customers. Be thorough in your evaluation in everything ranging from markets to technical features. In fact, embrace the competition's strengths as a means to differentiate your company and products.
- **Technology assessment.** Profile product configurations, underlying architecture, proprietary IP, and patents (either issued or pending). Investors will fund proprietary IP, not an engineering project based on someone else's IP. Having said this, don't disclose the deep technical details of the company until the seriousness of the investor has been established.

Do I Just Hand these Materials Over and Wait for the Phone to Ring or My E-mail Inbox to Ping?

Absolutely not. This should be an engaging and interactive process. You should be prepared for, or encourage, the following to happen at any time:

- Site visits.
- Product demonstrations.
- Numerous presentations in front of potential customers and technical experts whom the investor knows and trusts.
- A patent portfolio review from a lawyer the investor knows and trusts.
- Scrubbing of the numbers that anticipate revenue-ramp falling short for 6–12 months.
- Honest conversation about roles of current team members going forward.

(Be prepared: If three of you start the company, not all three will have equal roles through its development. You must keep your ultimate goal in sight and be prepared to yield power for the good of the company as a whole.)

The Investment Process

What Are the Fundable Milestones that the VCs Want to See?

Although this chapter is largely designed to get first-time entrepreneurs their first funding from a professional firm, there is also a long-term horizon that should be kept in mind from both a business-planning and financing perspective. As a general rule of thumb, use the following as a guide:

Fundable Milestones

Stage	*Use of Proceeds*	*Milestone to Next Financing*
Seed	Incorporation	Completion of business plan
	Market research	
	Recruit co-founder(s)	
Series A	Hire VP, Engineering	
	Hire engineering team	Completion of product conception and development
	Hire Director, Product Development	
	Develop intellectual property	
	Finalize product requirements document (PRD)	
	Test/tape-out/demo product	
Series B	Hire CXOs	
	Hire VP functions	Paying beta customers (or product development partners)
	Hire Director, Finance	
	Conduct product trials	
	Conduct manufacturing testing	
	Obtain 1–4 customers	
Series C	Hire Director functions	
	Hire Manager functions	Manufacturing and shipping of product to paying customers
	Release v1.0 of product	
	Obtain 5–10 customers	
Series D	Employee hiring ramp	
	Release v2.0 of product	Become cash flow positive; then become profitable
	New product development	
M&A/IPO	Expansion of product, team, geography, customers, partners, and vendors	

When Should I Start Approaching VCs?

Relative to each series of financing and the milestones that have been achieved, the process for raising money from a VC can take much longer than you expect, especially for a first time entrepreneur. Simply put, you should not approach VCs unless you are prepared with the right material, and you have achieved the milestones appropriate for the round you're raising. For example, at Series B, a software company should have working product and be ready to sell.

The timeline for fundraising from a VC varies on many factors, but generally looks something like this:

Fundraising Timetable

Step	*Activities*	*Duration*
PREPARE	Update operating/business plan	1 to 2 months
	Select investors to approach	
	Develop and practice pitch	
	Assemble due diligence material	
APPROACH	Approach investors	1 to 3 months
	Make pitches—multiple meetings	
	Due diligence starts	
NEGOTIATE	Negotiate term sheet	1 to 2 months
	Continued due diligence	
	Legal documents drawn	
	Close financing	
TOTAL TIME		3 to 7 months

You have the most control of this process, so take advantage of that and be well prepared. Doing so will make you appear more professional, and you'll find it easier to respond to issues. When timing your approach to a VC, consider the following.

When Will I Run Out of Cash at the Current Burn?

This question assumes you're operating on some level of seed funding. Clearly, the shorter your runway for continuing operations, the more desperate your situation becomes. Don't wait until two or three months of cash runs out before approaching VCs. Not only is it possible to run out of cash, but a short money leash gives VCs more leverage on negotiating terms. Time is on their side and they can wait you out until you submit to their terms. As the previous chart shows, it can take three to seven months to raise a round of financing. The stronger your early stage investors, the easier it is to get follow-on rounds of financing.

Do I Have an Operating Plan? How Much Money Do I Need to Reach My Next Milestone?

These two questions go hand-in-hand. What's needed here is a solid understanding of how you will move your business forward. Show how you will use the money, how and whom you will hire, how many customers you expect to get, and so on. Demonstrate that your plan is well devised and gets you to profitability. Also point out the strategies behind the plan such as margins and key ratios you're aiming to achieve.

Do I Have Other Financing Options?

Before you approach VCs, think about back-up plans in case the process goes too long or is unsuccessful. Not only can this enable you to continue operations, it also alleviates a lot of stress. Being prepared is better than being surprised.

Do I Have All My Due-Diligence Material Ready?

Having these materials ready allows you to respond quickly to questions and issues as they arise. If you can't respond quickly when asked for your operating plan or to set up a customer call, you will lose momentum.

What's the Fundraising Environment Like?

Lastly, while much of being prepared is about you, you also need to consider the investors. Specifically, you need to understand what the fundraising environment is like. If VCs are busy nursing their wounded companies in a down economy, it will be difficult to get their attention. That means the process of raising money will take longer and you should start sooner. It also means setting your own expectations with regard to the outcomes. In a difficult economy, raising money is tougher, as are terms and valuations. Remember, your ability to raise money is related to their ability to invest. That being said, no VC will pass up a good opportunity!

How Do I Get an Appointment?

A lot has already been written on this topic, but here is some (probably) obvious advice: Create a target list and manage the process like selling a product until you get a commitment and the check. That means you'll want to do the following:

- **Avoid mass mailings.** They are a complete waste of time. Spam is still spam, even if it's coming from an entrepreneur with a great idea. Not surprisingly, it will be treated as such: deleted without having been read. You need to know exactly who you want to contact and why, and you need to make sure that you've paved the way for the welcoming receipt of your message (for example, by having an introduction—even an e-mail introduction).

- **Look for a fit.** Study firms that do deals like yours. Put yourself in the investors' shoes and create a value proposition that will appeal to them. Look for something in the background that makes your targeted partner uniquely qualified to understand your company's value, technology/product, or target customer. Look to see if the VC firm or investor has complementary companies in their portfolio that would strengthen your—and their—business proposition, whether they have had a win in your space, and, certainly, whether they have a competitive company in their portfolio. (You don't want to present your plan to an investor who will only meet with you for the purpose of gathering competitive intelligence.)
- **Create a target list.** Based upon your due-diligence effort, develop a finite list of VC firms and rank them in order of fit. Identify which firm members you want to target and how you want to position your company relative to each person's background, and make a list of common acquaintances.
- **Get a warm introduction.** Successful entrepreneurs who were funded before by the firm you're targeting are a great source. They have lots of rope and goodwill. Other good sources are senior executives in big companies (Cisco, Siebel, and so on), because all VCs want to stay on their good side. Lawyers and accountants, especially good partners in brand-name firms, are also good because they see a lot of companies and VCs. That is certainly one advantage of going to a Wilson Sonsini, VLG, Brobeck, or any of the Big 4 accounting firms.

How Many Meetings Can I Expect?

The short answer is: many. The long answer is: many, many.

As mentioned earlier, the entrepreneur-VC relationship is a marriage; that means you should think of these meetings as dating. It's the time when you and the VC get to know each other. With each meeting, the VC will learn more and more about your killer technology, and how the market is ready to skyrocket. But with each meeting, the VC will also learn whether you're organized, how well you communicate, how you handle stress, and whether your team can deliver a compelling offering in a growing market.

This is also the time for you to similarly evaluate the VC. You've finally met the investors on your short list. Are they what you expected? Do they really have the right experience, judgment, and ability to help you the way you need? VC funding is very expensive; don't take dumb money.

What Happens in the First Investor Meeting? Who Will I Meet? Who Should I Bring? What's the Goal of this Meeting?

Your goal in the first meeting is very simple: to prove within 30 minutes that your team can deliver a dominating solution in a huge growth market.

In a first meeting, you will typically meet with one or two members of the VC firm. Although you may have an hour on their calendar, assume things are running late. The emphasis in the first meeting is the market opportunity and how your solution will address it, so bring with you someone who can cover these topics (usually the CEO and CTO/VP Engineering). Often, in more mature companies, the CFO is also involved in the first meeting to help explain the operating plan.

As with all meetings, come prepared. That means having a hard copy (paper slides) of your presentation in case the projector or laptop doesn't work. Hone your presentation skills. Have references and due-diligence material ready to deliver if asked. If the VC is interested enough to ask for more, you don't want to lose momentum by having to go back and put together that information.

What About Subsequent Meetings?

The goal of subsequent meetings is very simple: to prove within 60 minutes that your team can deliver a dominating solution in a huge growth market. If you're asked for additional meetings, the goal does not change. By this time, however, you've captured the VC's interest, and you will be allotted more time. Each meeting will explore in greater detail your team, the market opportunity, technology, and how you will execute. As the meetings progress, the VC will bring in other members of the firm to gather their opinions. This is also the VC's way of gaining consensus within the firm.

As an entrepreneur, try to get a sense of this momentum building within the VC firm. If you're having a lot of meetings with just the same one or two people, question whether there's real progress or whether they're just fishing for market information.

What if the Prospective Investor Wants Me to Meet with Potential Customer/Experts He/She Knows?

This is a great opportunity. Not only is it your chance to prove your product, but you can also get firsthand market data. However, unlike a regular sales call, you must be very deliberate about how you position your product, especially in relation to your roadmap. In other words, don't oversell what you don't have. Also, be cognizant of whether this customer is in your target market. If the customer doesn't fit your target customer profile, let the VC know that right away.

The goal of this meeting is to validate that the pain you've identified is one that a company will pay top dollar to heal. It is not necessary to close the customer, though it doesn't hurt to try.

If you're asked to speak with an expert, the goal is usually centered on proving the technology. Be ready for technical presentations, demos, code reviews, and so on.

What Happens in the All-Partners Meeting?

By the time you're invited to an all-partners meeting, you've cleared many hurdles. For example, you've probably met several, but not all, of the partners. At this point, the partner who is championing you is trying to get final consensus. The all-partners meeting does not always lead to a definitive decision to offer you a term sheet, but it is your chance to address in one place and time all the concerns the firm may have.

For this meeting, you should bring your full key management team, including those responsible for marketing, sales, business development, engineering, and finance. Note that although this may be the first time you meet some partners, your company will already have been discussed within the firm, and each partner will have specific questions for you. Listen to and address all the questions very carefully.

At What Point Does Due Diligence Start?

In a sense, due diligence starts after the very first meeting. That is why it's crucial to have your due-diligence material prepared *before* you approach investors. With every meeting, you will be asked to provide more information to validate your story, such as operating plan, customer references, and so on. Once you've signed a term sheet, a deeper form of due diligence will start. It will include reviews of legal documents, personal-reference checking, and more. With the exception of the legal-document review, you may be asked for some of this information before being offered a term sheet.

What Should I Do on a Site Visit?

At some point, the investors will want to visit you. This is also part of the due-diligence process. They want to see firsthand how you spend money and where and how you operate. Are you frugal with real estate, furniture, and equipment? Are there real engineering processes? What kind of employees do you hire? How do they interact with management? What's the overall working environment and mood of the company? During a site visit, it's important to demonstrate that you're a real company with real people who are dedicated. It's also important to show that you're not going to waste money.

What Should I Do If My Customers Get Annoyed with All the VC Calls?

A key part of due diligence is calling customer references. If your customer references start getting annoyed by many investor calls, that's a good sign. That means you've attracted a lot of attention from VCs. VCs have a driving need to speak with your customers; it's their most effective way to get market validation. It's also your most effective way to prove it. The best thing you can do is to prepare your customers well when you first ask them to be a reference. Let them know you're actively engaged in the fundraising process and they may be flooded with requests from VCs. They usually understand that if you get funding, it will also help them because then you'll be around to support them. Do try, however, to protect your customers until the final steps of the due diligence.

How Do I Maintain a Degree of Leverage Throughout This Process?

In the process, it is important to create *shortage value*. That means structuring your needs so there's only room for one more VC. Clearly, you're in a stronger negotiating position to accept the VC who offers you the best terms. The first rule is, don't show your full negotiating hand. Don't, for example, tell one group of VCs about other groups. Here are a few other points to consider:

- **Oversubscribe.** Set the amount you need to close as low as possible.
- **Insider pre-commitment.** Have insiders commit upfront, so a chunk of the round is already filled. (Sometimes, if there is enough inside money, you can set the minimum to close the amount the insiders have committed to.)
- **Exit.** Make sure you are working other options at the same time—for example, seeking corporate money or studying acquisition opportunities. Being able to say that you can choose whether to accept a financing or not (based on price, terms, and so on) provides you with powerful leverage.

What Does it Mean if the VC Says "Pass"?

If, after the presentation, the VC "calls you late" (a few days after your meeting), it usually means the firm is interested in continuing the process. If a week or more has passed after the presentation, however, the VC is likely signaling a pass without actually closing the door. If the VC specifically says the firm is not interested, try to understand why. It's often difficult to know the real reason, but here's a quick translation guide to common passes:

Pass Translator

What the VC says...	*What the VC could mean...*
Market too small	We don't think this will be a large enough market
	You've identified a niche solution applicable to only a small section of the market
	We don't like the team
Crowded market	We've seen better companies in this space
	You've identified a niche solution applicable to only a small section of the market
	You're late to the party; this space is over-funded and there are too many companies ahead of you
	We don't like the team
Technology isn't proven	Need some customers to kick the tires
	Show me a working prototype
	We don't like the team
Wrong business model	How can you make money selling used socks over the Internet?
	You're paying yourselves too much
	You've got the wrong distribution model
	You've got the wrong pricing model
	We don't like the team
Need customer validation	We'd be more interested if a customer agreed with what you've said
	We don't like the team
Out of focus for us	We have no interest investing in this industry, geography, or stage of a company
	We don't like the team

Although VCs look at teams very closely, it's rare that you'll get direct feedback of team disapproval after an initial meeting; it's just human nature to avoid telling a stranger you don't like them. (Yes, VCs are human, too.) Instead, you'll usually get other reasons for the pass, which may also be valid.

How Do I Know if it's a Hard Pass or a Soft Pass?

A *hard pass* is usually pretty clear: It says that there is no way the VC will invest in your company. *Out of focus* passes are usually hard passes. Maybe you pitched your optical networking company to a life sciences VC, or your Series D to an early-stage VC. Comments like "Market too small" or "too crowded" tend to be hard passes as well.

A *soft pass*, on the other hand, is not so clear. Very often, you will be told to come back when you have a customer. This is a soft pass. It usually means "We won't invest in you today, but under the right circumstances we'll consider it." In a soft pass, your job is to understand and address those circumstances.

What Can I Do About It?

Assuming you see some wiggle room in the pass, there are a number of ways to respond:

- **Overcome misperception.** If you discover the pass is due to a misperception, try to overcome that quickly. External validation is the best way to overcome misperception. For example, if the VC doesn't believe your technology is cutting edge and a competitive advantage, have your technical advisor vouch for you. Better yet, ask to speak to their technical advisor. If the misperception is market size, all the Gartner and IDC reports in the world will not help. Get customer validation. Prove that customers are willing to pay large dollars for your solution. Proof is always in action, not in PowerPoint slides.
- **Reposition the company/product.** Sometimes the VC will look at the market differently than you do. For example, where you may see a great idea that solves a real market pain, a VC may see only a point solution in a larger market. This is valuable feedback. If the VC is correct, then the longevity of your company will be limited. Your customers will migrate to more complete solutions. If the market space you've identified is real, then consider expanding your technology to encompass a broader solution set. You can still use what you have as a lead for sales opportunities. Don't be afraid to reposition the company when what the investor says makes sense.
- **Follow up with future developments/financings.** If you've been given a hard pass, there is little follow-up to do. If you've been given a soft pass, however, ask if it's alright to stay in touch with the VCs to keep them apprised of your progress. If so, you can alert them of customers you've acquired, key milestones such as the development of your beta product, executive hires, and so on. At the point when you've reached the milestones

identified in the soft pass, ask the VC to meet with you again so you can demonstrate your progress.

I Received a Term Sheet. Now What?

Until now, you and your VC champion have been dating. You've gotten to know and like each other and are ready for the next step. The term sheet is like planning the wedding, and it has all the ups and downs that go with it.

Now it's time to get down to business. A key person you must have on your side is a good lawyer who is experienced in fundraising. The lawyer should be well aware of the current market standards for term sheets. He or she should understand how to negotiate this round of financing and should also know how to set up for future rounds; the lawyer should know how to do this without requiring you to dilute yourself any more than necessary.

Chapter 3 provides more details on the specific elements of the term sheet and what investors are looking for in those terms. Be certain, however, that the VC is not just trying to buy time for further due diligence. Don't sign before the VC is ready to invest.

How Much Leverage Do I Have to Negotiate?

How much leverage you have depends on many factors. Do you have other term sheets from other VCs? How much cash do you have left? Do you have alternative financing methods? Do you have time to seek other financing? The least reliant you are on a single term sheet, the more leverage you have to negotiate terms.

What's Important to Negotiate and What's Not?

The key in these negotiations is to complete the current round with as little dilution as possible, while positioning the company to get to the next round of financing. This is where your lawyer and your CFO will earn their pay. This also means valuation by itself is not that important. For most entrepreneurs, valuation is an emotional issue.

Setting up for the next round means you should raise enough money to reach milestones appropriate for that round. For example, make sure you have enough money to complete the prototype or to hire a salesperson to get the first customer. Also be aware of terms with which future investors may have an issue, such as anti-dilution.

How Do I Decide Whether or Not to Walk Away?

As you negotiate, there will be times when you just want to walk away. Negotiations are always a challenge, but you have to keep the goal in mind. Your ability to walk away depends on how much leverage you have, as discussed previously: How much cash do you have left? Do you have other forms of finance? And so on. If you do have alternatives, and you are considering walking away, then think about *why* you are walking away.

Do I Disagree over Major Differences on the Term Sheet?

Major differences might include disagreements over the economic terms of the deal, like valuation and dilution, or disagreements over other term-sheet items. Market conditions and how much leverage you have will dictate whether you should walk.

If you decide that the investor is negotiating in bad faith and taking advantage of you far more than the market warrants, you should consider walking away—even if it means closing your business. Doing that is better than working like a slave for a reward that will never come. Likewise, if you decide the investor is not as good as you thought, you will be taking dumb money. Not only will that investor not be helpful, but that investor may become an obstacle. Such a deal may hinder your company operations and/or future rounds of financing. You should consider walking away from such an investor; otherwise, your company will not reach its full potential.

How Do I Handle the Close?

The signed term sheet is not the end, but it is the beginning of the end. You must manage the process until the money is in the bank. This involves a lot of legal work in which you and your lawyer must provide the VC and their lawyer with the actual legal documentation about your company. This includes articles of incorporation, stock option agreements, employment contracts, leases and other obligations, exceptions, and so on. If you've prepared ahead of time, this process will be smoother. You can also count on some more fine-tuning of the actual terms during this phase.

Understanding the Financial Issues

This section describes specific financial issues that arise during the negotiation of a term sheet. The actual terms are defined in the legal section of this book, and you should be familiar with them. What's covered here is how VCs use these terms to their advantage.

How Much Should I Raise? Should I Worry About Future Rounds Being Raised?

Raise no more than necessary to get you to the next round of funding with a quarter of cushion. This allows for schedule slips or negative fundraising conditions. Raising any more can unnecessarily dilute you. Be warned, however, that investors will try to get you to raise more. They will argue that it is always better to have extra cash in the bank, and there is validity in that argument. That said, you must remember that they also know that more money invested means more ownership. There's a fine balance here: If the price, valuation, and ownership terms are all fair, then raise as much as you can! A lot of companies fail because they run out of cash. You want to run a lean company and be very fiscally responsible, but you won't be able to do your best work if you are constantly worried about going broke!

How Many Investors Do I Need? Do I Have a Choice of Who and How Many?

Having only one investor is similar to putting all your eggs in one basket. Having a couple of investors is a good idea. You want to make sure your investors are capable of investing in future rounds. It also offers you a larger sounding board for advice. The other advantage of having multiple investors is that it spreads control over more people. Conversely, having too many investors means that no single investor has a large enough stake to want to help out in difficult times. You often find that when a VC leads with a term sheet, multiple other investors will follow. That means you'll normally have a lot of say in who the other investor is.

What Will Be My Valuation?

Valuation is expressed in terms of pre-money and post money. *Pre-money* is the valuation of your company before the VCs invest their dollars; *post money* is the valuation of your company after the VCs invest their dollars. So,

\$Post-money = \$Pre-money + \$VC investment

The amount of ownership the VC gets is simple math: it's their share of dollars as a percentage of post money.

note Generally, it's not a good idea to use public company comparables as the basis of valuation for a Series A private company.

Many factors determine your pre-money valuation, including how many milestones you've reached, the size of the market opportunity, and the fundraising environment. What *doesn't* always factor in are valuations from previous rounds. During 1999–2000, the market saw exuberant pre-money valuations for companies that didn't even have revenue. As the market corrected, valuations came down dramatically from prior rounds. So, if you are just starting a company, expect valuations no higher than the single-digit million-dollar range, whether or not you've raised money previously.

What Should Be My Percentage Ownership? How Do Terms Affect Ownership and Valuation?

Your ownership, how much control of the company you have, and how much money you receive upon an exit are not solely dependent on the preceding simple equations. Many terms affect your real ownership, control, and exit take. The best way to see their effect is to create a spreadsheet of a cap table. (The cap table lays out all the shareholders including founders, employees, investors, and unallocated shares.) Then, apply the terms on the cap table to see how your stake is affected. Again, a good lawyer is crucial to help you navigate.

To gain a better understanding of this, suppose a company raises three rounds of funding. The following chart shows a representative scenario for each new investor, their percentage of ownership, and the pro rata investment amount that early investors must make in order to keep their percentage of ownership when subsequent new investors come into follow-on rounds.

Investor	*Amount $ Raised*	*Pre $ Valuation*	*Ownership*
Series A	$3.0M	$7.0M	
Series A (New)	$3.0M		30%
Common	$0.0M		70%
			100%
Series B	$8.0M	$16M	
Series A (Prorata)	$2.6M		30%
Series B (New)	$5.6M		23%
Common	$0.0M		47%
			100%
Series C	$10M	$40M	
Series A (Prorata)	$3.0M		30%
Series B (Prorata)	$2.3M		23%
Series C (New)	$4.7M		9%
Common	$0.0M		38%
			100%

What Do All the Terms Mean?

The next sections take you through common terms and help you understand how they affect you.

Unallocated Options Pool

One way to increase investor control is to ask the company to increase the unallocated options pool before the funding round. There is a legitimate reason to increase the pool, including ensuring that options are available for future employees—especially executives.

Remember: Investors base ownership on a fully diluted basis. That means all shares are factored in, even unallocated ones. The larger the unallocated pool, the smaller your stake in the company. The size of the pool is simply a disguised valuation conversation. If you have any leverage, get the VC to increase the pool after funding. This way, the dilution affects everyone.

Vesting

If you're raising your first round, the investors may ask you and the employees to restart the vesting schedule (typically a four-year cycle with a one-year cliff, and monthly vesting thereafter). From the investors' point of view, they are putting money as much into the team as anything else. They want to give key members of the team incentives to stay. This is just one of the carrot-and-sticks in the term sheet. You should be able to negotiate some credit for the time you've put in since incorporation.

Liquidation Preferences

One of the reasons VCs buy preferred stock is for the preferential treatment during liquidation. *Liquidation* refers the sale or merger of the company, not just shutting it down. Having preferred stock means the VC will get their money before common shareholders (that is, the order is senior to common).

To continue from the previous example, in which a VC invests $4M in a company at $6M pre-money. Theoretically, the company is worth $10M after the round. Suppose, however, that a year later, the company is floundering and goes up for sale, and the best offer is $5M. In this situation, the preferred shareholders get their investment of $4M out first; the remaining $1M is then split among common shareholders.

Nowadays, it is not uncommon to see multipliers of the liquidation preference. For example, a 2× liquidation preference in the above scenario means the investor is entitled to receive two times the $4M that was invested. So the first $8M of a liquidation goes directly to the VC. This ensures the VC preference on the liquidation as well as up to 100-percent ROI if the sale is high enough. In the $5M sale scenario, then, all the money goes to the VC.

Entrepreneurs and investors want the company to be a home run. When that happens, everyone wins. Most companies, however, are not. And if a company is struggling, extreme liquidation preferences remove a company's incentive to make even a decent return, knowing that whatever little return exists goes directly to investors. It is crucial to understand current market conditions and recognize what is extreme.

Early-stage investors who insist on this are only doing themselves damage, as later-stage investors will make the same demand. As the entrepreneur, whenever possible, negotiate preferential treatment.

Participating Feature

Some liquidation preferences also have a participating feature that allows investors to get the return on their investment, but also participate in any remaining dollars on an as-converted basis (that is, their ownership share as if they converted to common). So for the company that raised $4M at $6M pre, if the company is sold for $5M, the investors receive the first $4M. The remaining $1M is then divided such that 40 percent ($400K) goes to the investors (40 percent represents their ownership) and $600K goes to common shareholders.

Warrants

Warrants are another means of adding ownership. A *warrant* is the right to purchase shares at a given price (called the *strike price*). For example, a warrant with a strike price of $1.00 is valuable only when the share price exceeds $1.00. If the stock price goes to $1.10, the warrant holder gets a capital gain of $0.10 for per share. Warrants are used in many ways, including as grants to employees, contractors, and service providers. They can also be tied to bridge loans and other debt financing.

Anti-Dilution

Investors use anti-dilution provisions for protection in case future shares are issued at a lower price than what they paid. Normally, preferred stock converts to common at a 1:1 ratio; however, anti-dilution clauses adjust this ratio in subsequent rounds that are priced lower (that is, a *down round*).

For example, suppose an investor buys Series A preferred at $1.00/share. Suppose also that a Series B is raised a year later at $0.50/share. If the Series A has anti-dilution protection, then the investor's conversion ratio is adjusted from 1:1

to something that gives the investor more than one share of common for every share of preferred Series A he or she owns. In this way, the investor keeps his or her ownership from being diluted by cheaper shares. The exact adjustment to the conversion ratio is called a *ratchet.*

Ratchet

Ratchets come in two flavors:

- **Full ratchet.** A *full-ratchet* is a harsh provision that allows investors to convert their series at the new price even if only a single new share is issued below their price. In the preceding example, the conversion ratio is adjusted to the (original price)/(new price) = $1/$0.50 = 2. That means the Series A investor converts to two shares of common for every share of preferred.
- **Weighted-average ratchet.** More common is the *weighted-average ratchet.* Under this clause, the new conversion ratio takes into account the number of shares raised at different prices. The actual formula will vary from deal to deal.

As a practical matter, in a down round, anti-dilution is usually debated between existing investors who have the protection and new investors who will refuse to invest unless the protection is waived or adjusted to a less harsh ratio.

Conversion

The actual conversion ratio is specified in the term sheet, and is subject to anti-dilution adjustments. Conversion clauses normally allow investors to convert to common at will. Other than during an IPO, preferred holders will convert to common as a means of controlling key board decisions.

Pay-to-Play

There are instances when existing investors are also the sole source of money in a subsequent round (specifically, a down round). Known as an *inside round*, it's a generally undesirable situation. Some investors may not want to participate. (They may not have the capital, they may feel the company is not worth the investment, or there may be other compelling or relevant circumstances.) Meanwhile, the investors, who are putting up the money, do not want the others to take a free ride. That is, they don't want the non-participants to keep their ownership while the rest of the investors put up the money. That's when a *pay-to-play* scenario comes in. The basic mechanism is to write a term sheet for a down round while at the same time using votes to waive anti-dilution rights. This combination greatly dilutes any existing investor who does not invest.

Registration Rights

This right allows investors to force the company to register for a public offering. The reality is that for a successful IPO, the company's management is involved in marketing the company to buyers of IPO shares. So for all practical purposes, companies do not file for IPO unless management agrees.

Board of Directors

Although investors don't want to run the company themselves, they do want certain management rights to ensure the company is delivering on its promises. They do this via the board of directors (BoD). The board's governance of the company includes setting executive compensation, approving financing, approving operating plans, and so on. Active investors will normally ask for a board seat, while inactive ones may ask for observer rights (that is, to be allowed access to board meetings but without authority to vote). In either case, investors will also ask the company for periodic reports showing status on revenues, expenses, hiring, and so on.

The CEO usually represents the company on the board. It's best for the CEO to be the only BoD member from the company, however. This allows, for example, for private conversations with the BoD about the management team. It also sends a clear message on the true company leadership. In practice, a founder with large ownership is often also on the BoD. Frequently, outside board members are also included for the impartial viewpoints they provide.

Voting Rights

Term sheets use voting rights to specify how the board is allowed to approve specific issues such as setting dividends, issuing securities, entering into a merger, and more. Often, approval requires a vote by class or even series. This happens because multiple series of investments tend to be raised at differing prices and terms. As a result, each series has an incentive to protect itself from activities that might adversely affect it. For example, suppose a Series A is raised without anti-dilution protection, and later a Series B is raised with anti-dilution protection. Series B will insist on having a separate series vote (rather than just preferred-class vote) for approval of future financing to ensure the anti-dilution right is not waived without approval.

Dividends

Dividends help investors extract additional returns beyond those based on pure percentage ownership. Most start-ups don't pay dividends on an ongoing basis.

Dividends are, however, usually payable at liquidation. In addition, if the dividends are cumulative, then upon a liquidation event, those accumulated dividends can add up over the years. In practice, these are never paid.

Redemption

Investors use the redemption clause to force the company to buy back the investors' shares. This comes into play most frequently when a company is somewhat successful, but not enough to have an IPO or to be sold at an attractive price. In other words, management might be content working for a small private company, but there is no real exit for investors. In that case, investors will force the company to repurchase investor shares. As an entrepreneur, you want the redemption clause to start being effective as far into the future as possible, typically five to seven years out. Sooner terms can jeopardize the company because during the early years, companies don't typically have the cash to pay back investors. Hence, a redemption call will force a sale of the company.

Right of First Offer/Pro Rata

This right enables investors to purchase enough shares in future financings to maintain their proportion of ownership, a.k.a., pro rata. When investors are eager to maintain pro rata, the marketplace sees this as a signal of confidence. The flip side is that it allows investors you don't want to maintain their position.

"Subject To" Clauses

As stated earlier, the term sheet is not the end, but the beginning of the end. Every term sheet will have a clause stipulating that the financing being offered is subject to certain conditions being met after the term sheet is signed. These conditions normally include a satisfactory completion of due-diligence. This due-diligence review is far more detailed than the one leading up to the term sheet. It always includes reviews of legal documents, financial documents, contract reviews, and anything else to understand and *prove* the state of the company.

Other than the legal review, these subject clauses can be bound to almost anything including technical reviews, inspections of remote offices, and even performance metrics. For example, the term sheet may provide half the financing immediately while the rest is subject to the company signing a key customer.

The term sheet will include a window of time in which the subject to clauses must be satisfied. Also, during this window, the VCs put in a no-shop provision prohibiting the company from soliciting other offers.

Although being subject to legal due diligence is a rather straightforward process, clauses around performance metrics are not always so. For one, measurement of metrics can be ambiguous. (For example, if the customer buys the product but pays only a nominal price, is the deal really signed?) Secondly, conditions out of your control may prevent you from hitting the target (for example, if your customer goes out of business). As an entrepreneur, you want the fewest subject to clauses and the shortest window possible.

I'm Ready to Sign the Term Sheet. Now What?

After you sign the term sheet, the legal due diligence begins. Keep the process moving. This is where good preparation really pays off. Having as much due-diligence material ready ahead of time ensures a smooth closing. Be warned: Legal bills can escalate in this process. Normally, the company pays legal fees of both the company and investor. As part of the term sheet, you should ask to cap the investor's legal fees. You should also try to cap your own legal fees, though this practice has not been in place for a while.

Once the VCs Check Is in the Bank, Is This the Only Money I Go After?

The answer is, it depends. The final answer centers on whether the start-up company has a capital-intensive business that requires expensive equipment purchases, needs to sign large licensing agreements, or would benefit from financing elements in their cash flow. If so, then pursuing institutional funding, or debt financing, would have the added benefit of stretching the equity dollars to meet product-development milestones and follow-on rounds of financing.

What Is the Difference Between Equity and Debt Financing?

Equity represents funding that is provided in exchange for a portion of an entrepreneur's ownership interest in a company. There is generally no set repayment schedule, and it is regarded as a residual claim (meaning that equity holders are repaid after debt holders). Equity holders expect to realize their return through long-term liquidity events, such as a merger, sale of their investments, or an initial public offering (IPO). Equity can be raised from founders, family, or friends; angels; venture capitalists; corporate investors; and private or public equity placements.

In comparison, *debt* does not require an ownership interest in a firm. It represents funds that have borrowed, and are repayable from the company's cash reserve or profitable operations according to a prearranged schedule. Unpaid debt is a liability of the firm and, if it is not paid, the creditors can claim the assets of the company. Sources of debt include bank loans, leasing, and private or public debt placements.

Do Financial Institutions Differ in Their Funding and Financing Services to Entrepreneurs?

It is important to understand that not all financial institutions focus on or cater to the technology entrepreneur. There are, however, some commercial banks that do have a definite focus on the entrepreneur and the growth potential of the technology company. These banks specialize in assisting the entrepreneur at every step of the life cycle—from idea to existence and beyond. Entrepreneurs require different types of financing options and business solutions as they grow from seed stage to later rounds of funding. Similarly, appropriate combinations of equity and debt capital are required.

It is important that entrepreneurs understand that every relationship they establish becomes a strategic component of their business. You need to consider all those with whom you work—from legal counsel to financing partners, banking, real estate, human resources, and your public-relations choices—as strategic partners. It's important to have a very clear view of the right players for each functional area of your company, and to link those players to the appropriate strategic partners. They have great potential in helping develop your business activities and in adding credibility to your start-up.

What Should an Entrepreneur Look for in a Bank Before Establishing a Relationship?

In light of today's economy and investment climate, you should be targeting smart capital, both in equity and debt. Smart capital means monies that will add value at every stage of your company's development.

Financial institutions will come looking for you. Typically, they are quick to call on technology companies that show three years of profit. (They are far less quick to call on companies that are in the seed or even first-round of institutional funding, however.) But whether banks come looking for you or you for them, there are some fundamental questions you'll need to have answered before choosing a banking partner:

- Does the bank truly understand the business of technology companies and their growth life cycle?
- Can the bank provide debt financing as necessary and business solutions as your company grows?

You need to do due diligence on the bank and require a demonstration of the bank's level of commitment to a start-up technology company (specifically yours).

The following criteria will help you make the right choice when selecting a bank:

- **Market leader.** How many years has the bank been in business? What has been the company's reputation in the technology community (get perspectives from other investors, as well as legal and accounting firms)? When did the bank start focusing on the emerging growth technology company? What market share does the bank have in banking the emerging-growth technology company?
- **Experience.** How many companies has the bank serviced in the technology sector to date? Does the bank understand the business model, challenges, and needs of emerging-growth technology companies?
- **Exposure.** What kind of exposure has the bank had with respect to the technology companies including industry and length of commitment? What is its willingness to lend to these companies? What has been the bank's exposure to the tech world in the dot-com and dot-bust periods? How has the bank weathered the storm?
- **Product and services.** What range of products and services is offered by the bank to assist the entrepreneur in growing his or her company? Does the bank specialize in its offerings depending on industry sectors?
- **Support.** What support has the bank demonstrated in the start-up technology community? (Typically, banks sponsor conferences and seminars and are a clear indication of the focus and target market.)
- **Value-add services.** What other non-credit services does the bank offer to the entrepreneur? Is the bank assisting the client in building partnerships and alliances with its other customers?
- **Financing and fundraising.** Does the bank have a program for direct equity investment? Most banks that see the value in investing in a start-up have benefited through their own direct investment into companies and taking warrants.
- **Network.** Is the entrepreneur able to leverage the bank's network of service providers, investors, and business contacts? Does the bank have the ability to provide introductions and references to the entrepreneur?

- **Trusted advisor.** Is the bank regarded as a trusted advisor in the raising of capital, loan structuring, due diligence conducted on behalf of VCs, and market intelligence for its clients? Again, what is the reputation of the bank in the technology community?

What Factors Are Taken into Consideration By a Bank When It Evaluates the Company's Source of Repayment?

When banks make loans to start-up companies, they examine the company's source of repayment as well as the following indicators:

- **Business relationships.** Who is in the deal—the management of the company and the equity partners.
- **Validity of the business plan.** Technology platform, market opportunity, competitive strategy, and any other sources of additional capital.
- **Performance to plan.** Financial covenants.
- **Collateral package.** Quality of assets, liquidity.

What Kind of Information Is Requested From Banks as Part of the Due-Diligence Process Before Loans Are Extended?

Banks will request the following as part of the due-diligence process:

- The company's business plan
- Monthly projections
- Historical financial statements (if available)
- Capitalization tables
- Accounts receivable/accounts payable agings (if available)
- Investor/service provider/customer references

What is the Bank's Process in Getting a Loan to the Technology Company?

After the bank has obtained all the necessary information from the company and the due diligence is completed, the process of business-point negotiations begins. These involve discussions with the entrepreneur on credit-facility amounts, pricing, advance rates, covenants, and collateral. When these have been agreed upon, the lender will obtain internal credit approval. Upon approval, legal documentation is completed and the credit facility is established.

How Can I Maintain a Good Relationship with My Banker?

It is important to note that your banker is your business partner and is willing to work through your company's up and down times. To ensure a healthy business-banking relationship, be proactive and provide your company's up-to-date information on a regular basis. Schedule frequent updates with your account officer at the bank and provide timely financial reports. Always try to anticipate credit needs with adequate notice. Finally, continue to provide your banker with specific supporting information to enable him or her to respond in a timely manner.

seven 7

CHAPTER

Finance and Accounting

Chair: John De Yonge - **Ernst & Young**
Mary Jane Bedegi - **Greenough Consulting Group**
Mark T. Curtis - **Salomon Smith Barney**
Harpreet Chadha - **New York Life**
Kalyani Chatterjee - **KPMG**
Gurjot S. Dhaliwal - **TiE**
Sanjeev Rao - **Ernst & Young**
Rod Werner - **Comerica Bank**
David Wright - **Nasdaq Insurance**

Introduction

Don't make the mistake of dismissing the bean counters in the back office. The finance function is one of the most critical areas of your enterprise. Because entrepreneurs are so often focused on value creation and because they are, by nature, risk takers, they often view finance as a non value-add or, worse, as an obstacle to getting business done. As you will see in this chapter, if you neglect the finance function, you do so at your peril, and you miss important opportunities to drive value.

By providing early warning, control, forecasting, regulatory compliance, and corporate housekeeping, a robust finance function minimizes the risk that any number of potentially fatal mishaps will befall you and your company. If you neglect the finance function you may well find that:

- VC funding becomes difficult or impossible to obtain.
- Credit becomes hard to get.
- Cash runs out unexpectedly.

- The M&A deal goes awry or occurs at a lower valuation.
- The IPO takes longer than it should and the window for an optimal valuation is missed.
- Forecasts are inaccurate and earnings must be restated, which results in a shareholder lawsuit, propelling the company into bankruptcy.
- Somebody goes to jail.

If you minimize risks like these, you will be able to accelerate value creation in several important ways. You too will able to focus on developing products and markets. Investors and lenders will be more comfortable placing significant bets on your company. Service providers will be more likely to invest time and resources in developing a relationship with you. This all adds up to realizing the full potential of your company faster.

This chapter provides an overview of what you need to know about finance and accounting as you set out on your value-creation journey. In this chapter you will find the following:

- The most common finance-related risks encountered by early-stage companies
- What you need to know and do now to set up your finance function
- The fundamental accounting policies you should be aware of as your company develops
- The essentials of banking, insurance, and personal-wealth planning
- Useful templates and checklists to help you get out of the starting blocks fast

AREAS OF RISK

The most immediate financial risks you face fall into three broad categories:

- **Assurance risk.** Your ability to assure investors that your financial statements and material information reflect the true state of your business.
- **Regulatory risk.** Your compliance with relevant laws and accounting practices.
- **Systems risk.** Your ability to collect and process financial data.

Assurance Risk: Failing Due Diligence

The growth of your company depends on completing a series of successful liquidity events—VC funding, debt financing, trade sale, or public offering. To complete these liquidity events, you must pass through increasingly rigorous financial due diligence conducted by or on behalf of potential investors. Without a strong finance function, you will find it difficult or impossible to do the following:

- **Secure financing.** If you cannot demonstrate that you have a control on the burn rate, that revenue claims are supported by signed contracts, and that your equity structure makes sense, you will not be able to secure equity or debt financing.
- **Go public.** In an IPO transaction, companies face underwriter due diligence and the SEC requirement to provide audited balance sheets as of the end of the previous two fiscal years, audited statements of operations, cash flows, and shareholders' equity for each of the previous three fiscal years plus five years of select historical financial information. Companies that have their housekeeping in order and maintain a financial infrastructure capable of meeting the demands of public-company status will enjoy a faster and cheaper IPO transaction. Those that don't have their financial house in order face costly accounting revisions, SEC comments, and sometimes a missed IPO window; they will also be unprepared to operate as a public company.
- **Sell your company.** You will be required to produce detailed financial, tax, compensation, IP, and operational data in a sales transaction (the information request list in M&A due diligence is usually upwards of 25 single-spaced pages). Maintaining robust financial systems and controls will contribute to a faster transaction—which usually means a higher valuation for you—because the necessary data is readily at hand and investors feel confident there are no hidden time bombs.

Finance Issues That Can Impede an M&A Transaction

- Performance versus budget (high cash-burn rate and/or the inability to account for burn rate in detail)
- Aggressive accounting policies (mainly revenue recognition)
- Excessive conservatism in accounting (mainly accounting for reserves)
- Spikes in revenues toward the end of each accounting period
- Inadequate accounting records—especially with respect to equity compensation
- Inexperienced finance professionals

Regulatory Risk: Breaking the Law

To operate a business legally you must meet all the laws for operating a business. In the United States, that means the laws of the federal government, and state governments of every state in which you do business. In addition, in many locales, even city and/or county laws govern business operation. As a public company or a company undergoing the IPO process, you will also need to meet the requirements of the Securities & Exchange Commission. Your finance function will be key in ensuring that you comply with relevant laws and regulations related to

- **Taxes.** Corporations are subject to, or responsible for, a host of local, state, federal, and often international taxes—income tax, sales and use tax, payroll taxes, VAT, and so on. Unexpected tax liabilities not only affect your bottom line but also can become an issue in due diligence
- **HR.** As your organization grows, increases in your head count will trigger a variety of federal laws relating to employees as certain thresholds are passed (one employee, 11 employees, 15 employees, 20 employees, 50 employees, 100+ employees).
- **SEC.** Companies that are unable to meet SEC accounting and reporting requirements pay a severe penalty at the hands of investors when quarterly estimates are missed or earnings are restated. SEC regulations do not apply to private companies, but if you hope to take your company public at some point, you should operate as though they do. Acting like a public company before becoming one allows you to avoid expensive and time-consuming regulatory pitfalls at the time of the IPO and also prepares you for the pressures of the public market. Because your IPO may be as few as three to five years away, now is the time to begin building a finance function that can manage the risk of public-company status.

Common SEC Problem Areas

- Revenue recognition
- Stock-based compensation
- Board structure (audit committees, compensation committees)
- Accounting for acquisitions
- Internal controls

Systems Risk: Not Keeping Up With Your Business

The ability of your finance infrastructure to keep pace with company growth and associated information demands represents another important area of risk. Companies that cannot close their books quickly at quarter's end, easily aggregate operational data, and connect with their supply chain, find themselves at a competitive disadvantage, often stumbling on regulatory and forecasting issues. The failure to maintain the financial systems, controls, and IT infrastructure needed to make accurate forecasts raises a number of risks:

- **Cost of the spreadsheet.** Time spent manually collecting and analyzing data.
- **Lost credibility with investors.** As your business grows, accurate forecasting will become increasingly important and difficult. Investors will expect you to set revenue and budget targets that you can meet consistently while your critical business planning—expansion, hiring, new-product development, facilities—will depend on gathering and analyzing data from increasingly disparate sources.

GETTING STARTED: ACCOUNTING BEST PRACTICES

Many people view the finance function as "bean-counters" in the back office, who add little value to the enterprise. This could not be farther from the truth. A robust accounting and finance structure provides the framework through which you manage and control your business, ensuring compliance with laws and regulations, fulfilling investor requirements, and assisting in the pursuit and achievement of your strategic objectives. The quality of the decisions you make as you bring your entrepreneurial vision to fruition will determine the ultimate success or failure of your enterprise. The finance function is critical in providing high-quality, reliable information to assist you in the decision-making process.

10 Most Important Finance Actions in the First Quarter of Operation

1. **Legal structure is set up.** Filings are complete and have received a certificate of incorporation from the Secretary of State and a federal tax ID number from the IRS.
2. **Bank accounts are opened.** Signature cards are complete and a deposit has been made. Consider longer-term banking arrangements.

3. **Payroll and benefits are started.** Select a payroll service and initiate discussions regarding employee benefits with a broker (you must have two people on payroll for a quarter before benefits can start).
4. **Accounting software installed.** Set up an accounting system with categories that capture your important expenditures; order computer check stock; back up system.
5. **Investor agreements and capitalization complete.** Complete all investor agreements and create a capitalization table showing all shares and options outstanding. Determine process for issuing shares and maintaining the capitalization table.
6. **Financial plan and financial reporting in place.** Create a detailed monthly budget for the first year that matches key milestones and shows cash availability; also have a long-term plan showing targeted results over at least two years. The monthly budget should be re-forecasted each month to reflect new information or plans. Prepare a consistent financial package for the board and internal management that covers actual financial results versus plan for key metrics as well as the new forecast.
7. **Financial accounting and reporting result versus plan.** Hire an accountant to establish basic accounting procedures and controls, close the financial books, and reconcile accounts to support. Establish process for approving expenditures and paying bills—including employee expenses—and for payroll. Organize files for vendors and for contracts.
8. **Compensation practices and stock administration in place.** Establish an equitable compensation and stock-option matrix for current and planned employees; create a process for hiring employees and for granting stock options. Organize files for each employee that contain offer letters, confidentiality agreements, and other information.
9. **Insurance.** Obtain appropriate insurance covering at least property and liability.
10. **Professional relationships.** Establish relationships with the expert professionals who can help you as your company grows, including legal, public accounting and tax, real estate, insurance, and banking.

The critical areas you will need to address are

- Financial information (what you need to prepare to get funding)
- Your alternatives for funding (the pros and cons)
- Preparing for due diligence
- Financial information (post-funding reporting and monitoring)
- People (who you need and when you need them)
- The implications of using stock to compensate employees and vendors
- Control procedures and processes
- IT systems

Preparing Financials For Potential Investors and Other Third Parties

The chances are good that soon after you form your company, you will begin to look for funding. Being able to provide accurate and reliable financial information to financiers before and after they commit their funds or make a loan to your company is vital. Strong financial capability will be required to prepare the information that you will have to present to third parties such as VCs and bankers.

What Financial Information Will I Need to Provide?

A well-thought-out business plan is key to securing funding. Although the financials of your business plan should be tailored to the details of your business, certain components are common to all good business plans:

- Profit and loss account
- Balance sheet
- Cash-flow statement
- Break-even analysis
- Key estimates and assumptions behind projections
- Key ratios

Estimates will have to be made for items such as sales, cost of sales, administrative, and research-and-development expenses. Assumptions are the foundation of your plan and should be specified. For instance:

- Levels of projected sales and increases in volumes or price
- Gross-margin expectations
- Expected capital expenditures and timing
- Inventory turnover
- Receivables collection period
- Creditors' payment period

Following are some do's and don'ts to consider with respect to business-plan financials:

- **DO** be realistic in setting your assumptions. It is tempting to be overly optimistic.
- **DO** take into account any seasonal fluctuations that could affect the business.

- **DO** allow for some cushion in your estimate of cash requirements. You don't want to have to go back to the lender for additional funding because your assumptions were too optimistic.
- **DO** include some sensitivity analysis indicating the impact on your cash requirements of changes in some of your key assumptions.
- **DON'T** underestimate the time it will take to get out of R&D mode to generate revenue.

Alternatives For Funding Operations:

Your decision whether to finance operational requirements through equity, debt, or some other source of funds is important and will be a function of a number of factors, including

- Availability of equity, debt, or asset financing
- Cost of that source of funds
- Use to which the funds are to be put (working capital or long-term financing)

Some pros and cons of each source are considered below:

- **Equity.** This is the longest-term and most expensive source of funding for a start-up. It ties up capital for an indefinite period for the initial investor, whose return is realized either though a liquidity event such as an IPO, the acquisition of the company, or dividends. Initial investors are likely to require preferred stock, which have a higher priority in liquidation than the common stock of the company.
- **Long-term debt.** This should generally be used to finance long-term projects (for example, fixed-asset purchases). Loans are generally secured against the assets acquired.
- **Working capital finance.** Creditors are you cheapest source of working capital finance. Once you have established your credit-worthiness, you may be able to negotiate favorable payments terms of 30 days. It is unlikely that you will be able to obtain credit from this source when you first establish your business, however.
- **Bank overdrafts.** As a source of short-term funding, overdrafts are more expensive than a bank loan. The benefit of overdraft funding, however, is that you can alter your financing requirements from day to day, according to your cash flow. Interest is charged on a daily outstanding balance based on the rate negotiated between you and your bank manager. This source of funding is short term and, generally, the bank can call for repayment at any time, if it believes that the business is not being properly run.

Preparing For Due Diligence

Due diligence is an iterative, fact-finding process, conducted by prospective investors and lenders. You should develop a routine practice of preparing yourself for a due-diligence investigation. Too often, emerging companies fall into the trap of delaying major housekeeping until there is a financing on the table and investors want to know all the details of patent filings, operational plans, and those contractual deals hidden in the closet. Resolving these nasty issues at the last minute is costly, untimely, and sometimes impossible. The due diligence process can kill a company that is not prepared! Entrepreneurs should pay attention to these critical financial and legal matters from the day a company is born and thereafter religiously follow a continuous process of quality control.

What Are the Areas I Should Focus On to Have the Most Positive Impact On Due Diligence and Investor Reporting?

These due-diligence "stitches" are a simple quality-control program that, when "done in time," can add market value and even save a company:

- **Protecting intellectual property.** Patent attorneys say that dollars spent on defending a company's intellectual-property rights in court almost always could have been saved by spending a tiny fraction up front on simple protective contracts and filings. All possibilities of other parties, especially independent contractors, laying claim to your company's IP should be eliminated. Thoroughly research trademark names before use. Negotiate licensing terms that protect the downside risk such as fixed-payment amounts and termination rights.
- **Financial check.** Run all important operational decisions, such as pricing plans, volume and returns assumptions, and staffing plans through a financial check to ensure they line up with the financial goals. Involving a financial and operational expert up front in the details of implementation plans will accelerate the release and decrease chances of rework. Watch out for non-cash deals that can affect earnings and valuations, such as software-recognition rules and issuance of warrants.
- **Contract review.** Negotiate favorable terms for every contract and avoid contingencies such as guaranteed payments or non-cancellation clauses. Have legal experts review key agreements—especially those related to commitments. Keep a complete database of all contracts and terms.
- **Stock records.** Keep meticulous records of all stock and option transactions that you update regularly. Investing in a stock-tracking software program can more than pay for itself.
- **Process efficiencies.** Organize and document everything you do, especially in the financial area. Experiencing a first-time audit without having done

this is painful, expensive, and could hold up the closing of a financing. Redirect financial resources to those tasks that are important to resolving issues and staying efficient.

- **Human resources.** Develop a written plan for equitable pay and incentive programs. Document company policies and follow them consistently. Thoughtful actions can help you avoid many wrongful-termination and compensation claims.

Post-Funding: Measuring and Reporting Performance

A company should measure and react to key financial indicators for three basic reasons:

- To measure performance against a goal
- As a baseline for future performance
- As a comparison to the performance of other relevant companies

Most companies develop an annual financial plan before the start of their fiscal year. More frequent forecasts of financial results are created as needed. Both plans are used to measure performance in comparison to actual results.

After I Secure Funding, What Financial Information Will I Need to Provide to Investors?

Investors are a critical group, so you must keep them happy and informed. Significant investors are likely to have negotiated a board seat in order to keep a close eye on their investment, and they will receive pertinent company information that way. In any case, stock-closing agreements will clearly outline the type of information that investors require. Typically, quarterly or monthly financials are required to be provided to investors who have invested over a certain amount. Sometimes, financial operating plans and forecasts will also be required; the same goes for annual audits. Investors, who are not on the board appreciate receiving regular status reports about the company.

What Performance Measures Are Other Parties Such As Financiers, Banks and Lessors Likely to Require?

Banks and other third parties that provide the company with financing will require financial information prior to providing a loan. Typically, they will want to see

- A business plan
- Financial statements (historical)

- Cash-flow, balance-sheet, and income-statement projections for at least the next twelve months
- Schedules of capital expenditures

Following funding, lenders will want to maintain a close relationship with the company, getting regular updates on financial results and revised projections so they can monitor the financial health of the company and the security of their loan.

Typically, for early-stage companies, loans may be secured on certain assets of the company, in which case there may be restrictions on the company's ability to dispose of those assets. Banks and other lenders may also include financial covenants within their lending agreements, which the company will have to monitor and report on to the lender on a regular basis.

What Are the Key Financial Elements That an Early-Stage Company Should Measure and Monitor?

Although each industry and company size will dictate many of the key factors that should be measured, there are many basics for any company. Commonly used measurements in the early stage are

- **Cash-burn rate versus plan.** This covers not only expenditures for expenses but also equipment purchases and the timing of other receipts and bill payments
- **Trended expenses.** Sorted by department and by expense category. A detailed comparison to the financial budget and operating milestones is critical. The most expensive expenditures should be monitored closely. These could include contractors, prototype expenditures, outside design, network costs, and so on.
- **Head count versus plan.** This maps your actual personnel needs and HR expenditures to anticipated needs based on milestones in your business plan.
- **Capital expenditures versus plan.** This includes computer equipment and software, licenses, and facilities.

Likewise, the prototype stage features its own set of commonly used measurements, which you will have to add to your monitoring regimen. They include the following:

- Costs of building a prototype/developing beta product and projected future costs
- Delays in development projects, which often mask costs
- Revenue from beta or real customers

- Backlog

In the early-revenue stage, you'll also want to apply the following additional measurements:

- Revenue by customer
- Installed base
- Revenue per sales representative
- Costs of service or product
- Gross margins on sales
- Revenue per employee
- Costs per employee
- Utilization/billable hours versus actual hours

In the early stages, it is difficult to compare yourself to other companies because little or no information is available for private companies. Your investors, accountants, or trade publications may be able to provide you with benchmarks, however. Also, examining the financials of larger public companies can be useful; their financial information for the past five years is available, and you can get a sense of how fast these companies have grown and what their overall financial performance has been.

People: Staffing Your Finance Department

A start-up needs experienced financial management, but usually does not require these resources full-time at the beginning. Indeed, a CEO may find it advantageous to outsource the CFO or other higher-level financial professionals until the organization requires a full-time position. The same can be true for the accounting staff. Most companies with fewer than 60 employees, or that are going through some type of transition, are good candidates for outsourcing. In fact, it is sometimes more cost-effective to outsource this function even if the cost per hour may be higher than the salary for a regular employee. A major advantage is that, with the right resources, the CEO does not have to be concerned about the operation of the finance function and can devote his or her precious time to other important matters.

What Are the Roles of Individuals in the Finance Function?

The finance function requires a delicate balance. It must lead the company in strategic business planning, yet be responsible for protecting company assets and business controls. A good CFO is able to play both these roles at the same time.

The key responsibilities of the CFO include the following:

- Capital structure and financing
- Investor relationships
- Accounting and reporting of financials results
- Budgeting and forecasting
- Cash and asset management
- Internal control
- Financial system development for the enterprise
- Risk management
- Other administrative functions

Often, the CFO is the CEO's right-hand person because the CFO is responsible for the overall well-being of the entire organization, and both share visibility in all aspects of the company. In the later stage of the company, skills related to managing investors and the public markets and leadership in developing and closing strategic relationships become critical.

The CFO's finance group can be structured in several ways, depending on the size and talents of the group and the importance of certain transitions within the organization. Typically, these functions are controllership, business planning, human resources, and information services. (Some companies may decide to have human resources and information services report directly to the CEO. Later-stage companies will have a separate reporting function for investor relations and internal audit.)

- **Controller.** The controller is responsible for the integrity of the financial statements and all financial transactions, as well as for analyzing and communicating financial trends and deviations from plan targets. It is also critical to establish and enforce a sound control environment, including segregation of duties, physical inventories of assets, and company safeguards.
- **Business-planning manager or financial analyst.** The business-planning manager's primary responsibility is to create financial plans and forecasts that reflect the operations of the executive team. The plan must be realistic and able to change based upon changing variables. The manager must work with operating units to integrate sales targets, pricing, and manufacturing plans into the master plan.

Implications of Using Stock to Compensate Employees and Vendors

Start-up companies need to attract and retain the best available talent, but often they cannot afford to pay significant cash salaries. The culture of the technology sector, moreover, places an emphasis on company ownership by all employees. This means that many start-ups provide stock options as an important part of employee compensation. If you plan to make stock options part of your compensation package, be sure to keep meticulous capitalization tables (see Appendix III in this chapter) and understand the associated accounting implications.

The compensation costs of stock options granted to employees are generally accounted for using the *intrinsic* value of the stock. This is the difference between the exercise price at the date of grant and the quoted market price at that date. If a quoted market price is unavailable, the best estimate of the market value of the stock should be used to measure compensation. Accordingly, in applying the accounting rules, a privately held company must make its best estimate of the market value of its common stock on the option grant date.

In reality, estimating the market value of the common stock of a private company is difficult in the absence of recent sales of that stock to third parties. In some cases, the sale of convertible preferred stock to investors occurs in close proximity to the option grant date; therefore, the estimate of the fair value of their common stock can be based on recent sales prices for their convertible preferred stock. Companies have also historically applied *rule of thumb* discounts of up to 90% of the preferred stock value to value the common stock; the Financial Accounting Standards Board, however, no longer considers this acceptable.

Any compensation cost associated with the options will be expensed over the service period (usually the vesting period of the options). Although these are non-cash charges, the impact of these items on earnings may be considerable.

tip This is a complex area of accounting and you should seek guidance from your financial advisor on the appropriate accounting for such transactions.

Pros and Cons of Stock Compensation

Pros	*Cons*
Non-cash compensation expense, conserves scarce cash resources.	Can result in considerable *cheap stock charges* if issued at less-than-fair value. This can become a significant issue close to the date of a liquidation event such as an IPO.

Pros and Cons of Stock Compensation

Pros	Cons
Vesting period helps employee retention.	Dilutes generally accepted accounting policy (GAAP) earnings per share although companies often present "pro forma" earnings information, which does not include the effect of such non-cash items for investors.
Gives employees a sense of ownership and added incentive to contribute to the success of the company.	

I Have Heard That It Is Possible to Obtain Services from Vendors in Return for Equity. What Are the Consequences of Doing This?

In today's marketplace many companies, particularly in the early stages when cash is limited, use their equity as currency, issuing equity instruments to non-employees in exchange for goods and services. These transactions do not require the company to make a cash outlay, but they do have an inherent cost, which must be measured and reported in the company's financial statements. The accounting standards in this area are extremely complex. To avoid unexpected volatility in future income statements, you should understand and consider the rules when negotiating agreements that involve issuing equity instruments to your vendors or customers.

Leaving aside considerations of diluting the ownership equity of the company, you will have to account for the equity you give them at fair value. Accordingly, you need to understand the following:

- How the cost is measured for accounting purposes
- When the cost is recorded
- How that cost is reported in the financial statements

The cost is the fair value of the consideration received or the fair value of the equity instruments issued, whichever is more readily determinable. Generally, companies use the fair value of the equity instruments they issue because this is easier to determine. For a private company, the alternatives are an option pricing model or other valuation technique, because there is no publicly traded price for the instruments.

Unlike payments in cash, the ultimate cost of issuing equity to vendors (or non-employees) may not be known until the vendor's performance is complete. Under accounting rules, the cost of the equity provided in payment is measured and recorded either on the date on which the vendor completes performance or on the date on which a performance commitment is reached, whichever is earlier. But unless a contract contains a performance commitment, the company is required to recalculate the cost of the equity and account for the portion of the services rendered in interim reporting periods. This requirement often results in earnings volatility because increases or decreases in the stock price result in changes in the fair value of equity provided to vendors and to the corresponding expense. This effect may be of particular concern to a company that completes an initial public offering before the equity instruments vest and ends up paying far more than anticipated for a good or service.

To attempt to fix the cost of goods and services acquired in exchange for equity, it is possible to grant equity awards that are fully vested, non-forfeitable, and exercisable at the commencement of the contract. If non-forfeitable equity instruments vest on the date they are issued without further condition, the company records the fair value on that date and the expense over the expected period of benefit.

The expense associated with equity issued for goods and services is recorded as if the company had paid cash or used cash rebates as a sales incentive. Companies need to consider the nature of what they have received in the transaction to determine the appropriate period in which to recognize the cost and the appropriate line item in which to report it in its financial statements. For example, suppose a company issues equity instruments to a software vendor for a license to an ERP system to be used internally by the company. The company should capitalize the internal-use software at the fair value of the equity instruments that it issued, and should amortize the amount capitalized over the expected useful life of the software.

tip As with equity instruments issued to employees, this is a complex area of accounting. You should seek guidance from your financial advisor on the appropriate accounting for such transactions.

Pros and Cons of Paying for Services with Equity

Pros	*Cons*
As a non-cash transaction, it saves valuable cash resources.	Accounting consequences can be complex.
	Valuation can be difficult to determine.
	Accounting can result in significant volatility in the reported results of the company
	Potentially dilutes ownership of the company
	Ability to issue may be restricted by investor agreements

Control Procedures and Processes

Although internal controls cannot eliminate risk, they are the first line of defense against mishaps such as financial inaccuracies, unexpected loss, theft, fraud, and uncontrolled burn rate. There is generally a relationship between the objectives of internal control, risk assessment, and control activities, and a cost/benefit assessment that must be made. You will need to make an informed assessment of the most significant threats that you see to the achievement of your business objectives. Once you have identified these, within the constraints of your available resources, you will need to develop control procedures to help mitigate those risks. The finance function of a company is usually expected to create an internal control structure that provides reasonable assurance of the following:

- Reliability of financial information
- Compliance with applicable laws and regulations
- Effectiveness and efficiency of operations

In the early stages of development, the policies and procedures in the finance organization will probably be relatively simple and will focus on the following key areas:

- Controlling cash receipt and disbursements
- Ensuring adequate safeguarding of tangible physical assets
- Ensuring that contractual arrangements entered into with vendors, suppliers, landlords, and other third parties are properly controlled
- Ensuring a system of basic accounting procedures and controls

In order to do this, you will need the following:

- Appropriate segregation of duties between those individuals responsible for the custody of assets and the recording of transactions
- Adequate control procedures to ensure protection of key assets (cash, tangible and movable fixed assets), including physical safeguards as well as accounting controls, such as reconciliation procedures
- Set authority limits for committing the company to expenditures, entering into contractual arrangements, and making cash payments
- Limited access to financial records and accounting systems
- Established monitoring mechanisms, such as budget-to-actual-variance analysis
- Established budgetary/expense responsibility

Is Setting Up a Proper Control Environment Expensive/Time-Consuming? Does It Require Formal Documentation? Will It Be a Drain on Limited Management Resources?

In a word, no. The various components of the control environment in a small organization can exist without a lot of formalized policies and procedures. The communication process may be informal. Because there are fewer people and levels of management within the entity, the management style is likely to be hands-on; formalized reporting may be limited. Business activities are generally less complex, and there is generally less need to summarize and interpret data. In addition, because management is likely to be closely involved in operations, inaccuracies in operating or financial data or variances in expected results are easily detected.

The most important aspect of the system of controls is the control environment. In a small enterprise, there is less documentation and more face-to-face communication both inside and outside the entity. This makes management's demonstrated commitment to integrity, ethical behavior, and good business practices essential.

How Do I Determine the Minimum Controls That Should Be Implemented from the Outset?

The answer to this question depends on your appetite for risk and the stage of development of your organization, because there is generally a time and monetary cost associated with setting up and operating controls.

In the Beginning

As you start your business, you are likely to have very few employees and few tangible assets other than cash. Accordingly, your focus will likely be on ensuring that there are adequate controls over your bank accounts and expenditure. For instance, it is vital to ensure that you have the following:

- Check signatory authority levels
- Dual signatures for expenditures over a certain amount
- Approval procedures for all cash payments and proper supporting documentation (supplier invoices and expense reports)
- Physical safeguards over the corporate checkbook and access only to authorized personnel
- Regular reconciliation of your bank-statement balance with the cash balance in your accounting ledger and review of the reconciliation by someone other than the preparer
- Segregation of duties between those individuals who handle cash receipts, banking, and cash-payments functions

As Business Starts to Take Off

You will find that more controls are needed as you grow as a result of having more employees (payroll), capital assets (computer equipment, furniture, and fixtures), and expenses.

Payroll

Payroll is time-consuming to administer in-house, and calculations are prone to error. For these reasons, it is often advantageous to use an external payroll agency to prepare your payroll reports, deduct withholdings from employees' gross wages, generate payroll checks (or direct deposit) for your employees, and calculate and remit federal, FICA, FUTA, state income, and state unemployment taxes to the relevant agencies. Although the payroll agency will relieve much of the administrative burden, you will still need to have processes and controls to ensure the following:

- Payroll checks can be made out only to genuine employees.
- If employees are paid hourly, the hours worked are properly authorized, prior to being approved for payment.
- The payroll report and actual checks generated by the payroll agency are reconciled to the time-card information or timesheets.
- Checks are distributed to employees by someone outside the payroll/personnel function.
- The payroll payment is properly recorded in the financial books and records.

Capital Assets

As you grow and invest in infrastructure, it will be important to take some basic steps to safeguard your assets:

- Maintain a capital-asset log to record assets as they are acquired. (Include information such as description and serial number, date of acquisition, check number, location or person to whom the asset has been issued, depreciation method, and useful life.)
- Assign each asset a unique identifying number, which is included in the log and is also fixed to the asset.
- Perform periodic physical inventories of your assets to ensure they are still on your premises or can be otherwise accounted for.
- Ensure that terminating employees return all company property (including laptops or other computer equipment issued for their use) prior to receiving their final paycheck.

Expenses

In the early stages of operation, it will not be difficult to personally manage and control expenses, because the ability to commit the company to expenditures and authorize payments will be limited to one or two individuals. As your business grows, however, and the number of vendors with whom you deal and the range of expenses increases, you will need to delegate more of these responsibilities. Steps you can take to ensure you continue to control and manage these costs include the following:

- Setting an approved budget for expenses by department (or by individual with responsibility for different functions) and monitoring actual costs against that budget
- Establishing purchase requisition–approval procedures
- Creating a list of approved vendors with whom you deal (so that you can negotiate volume discounts and credit)
- Shopping around for the best price for significant purchases (the additional effort can save you a lot of money)
- Ensuring you don't enter into purchase commitments that will be expensive to terminate (for example, locking in a low price on inventory purchases through a high-volume commitment)

What Controls Do I Need to Establish Over the Accounting System?

The accounting books and records of the company will be maintained in the general ledger (G/L). The general ledger should accurately reflect the accounting activity for any given period, and is used to compile financial statements. Accordingly, controls are necessary over information being entered into the G/L, such as the following:

- Establishment of a chart of accounts that make up the G/L and controls over changes/additions to that chart of accounts
- Approval of journal entries prior to posting
- Reconciliation of the various sub-ledgers in the accounting system (such as the detailed accounts-receivable, fixed-assets, and accounts-payable ledgers) to the G/L on a timely basis

Accounting Software

An accounting software package robust enough to meet your company's immediate and anticipated medium-term needs is an essential risk-reducing tool (plus, it makes life much easier). Many companies fall into the trap of using Microsoft Excel or some other basic spreadsheet software to keep their books at the outset, then sticking with it long after their company's accounting needs have surpassed the software's capabilities. They face a number of risks as a result: late reporting, insufficient controls, inaccurate forecasting, increased audit costs, and time wasted on manual processes. Make sure that the accounting software you use can accommodate the requirements of your projected growth over the next few years.

What Alternatives Do I Have When It Comes to Selecting an Accounting Software Package for My Business?

Your choices vary depending on your budget and your requirements. When you first start operations, you can probably operate satisfactorily with a basic off-the-shelf package such as QuickBooks. As the volume of transactions and complexity of operations grows, however, you will probably need to migrate to a more robust package such as Great Plains. The top accounting software solutions for a newly formed business are

- Business Vision (Business Vision 32)
- Peachtree (ePeachtree and Peachtree Complete Accounting)
- Oracle Small Business (NetLedger)
- Intuit (QuickBooks Pro 2002)
- ACCPAC International (Simply Accounting)

As you shop, consider your company's expected growth requirements over the next three-year period and whether they will include reporting as a public entity. Triggers for more robust systems include the complexity of a company's transactions, reporting requirements, head-count growth, and the expected timeframe for recording revenue. Pay attention to security and access controls, including Internet and remote dial-up access. Most of the top accounting software solutions are available through application service providers (ASPs), which offer an alternative to hosting and maintaining the system in-house.

ACCOUNTING ESSENTIALS

Accurate and reliable financial information is critical to a company at all stages of its life cycle. The role of a finance function includes compilation of historical information, forecasting and budgeting, and consideration of the accounting consequences of proposed operational decisions. Informed management decision making depends on the availability of timely and accurate financial information. The following discussion surveys some of the critical areas of accounting that you should be aware of as you expand your business and build your finance function.

A System of Controls

Risks are ever-present in the business world. Companies set for themselves strategic and business objectives, and then manage risks that threaten the attainment of those objectives. Sound internal control and risk management supplement entrepreneurship rather than smothering it.

note See Appendix I later in this chapter for a checklist of some of the controls that should be considered within different functions of the organization.

Control activities include the following:

- **Risk assessment.** Company management will want to monitor and mitigate the business risks that could threaten the achievement of its objectives. It does so by evaluating which risks it considers to be the greatest and developing a system of internal controls to mitigate those risks.
- **Information and communication.** A company's information system is comprised of the resources (people, expertise, facilities, processes, computer systems, and data) designed to provide information to accomplish business objectives. The financial-information system is a part of the entity's larger information system. The information system should provide reports that enable management to operate and control the business and make informed business decisions.
- **Monitoring and control activities.** *Monitoring* refers to the assessment of the performance of the internal control system over a period of time. Ongoing monitoring occurs in the course of operations and includes regular management and supervisory activities. *Control activities* are the policies and procedures put in place by management to mitigate the business risks it has identified as the most significant to the achievement of the company's objectives. These kinds of controls are implemented at all levels of the organization to provide reasonable assurance that management's objectives are being carried out.
- **Creating a good control environment.** These are the factors that set the tone for how the organization is run and managed. Not limited to just the finance function, they include
  - Integrity and ethical values
  - Management philosophy and operating style
  - Organizational structure
  - Assignment of authority and responsibility
  - Human resources (policies and practices)

Managing Cash and Capital Resources

The secret to managing cash is to establish a financial plan and make the management team accountable for its elements. This means developing a detailed budget that contains all the material elements of the financial plan, so managers can easily tell whether a given expenditure is within budget. Use a system of approvals to ensure that the budget is adhered to, that senior management is aware of what is actually being spent, and as a way of slowing or stopping expenditures before the purchase is made if plans or conditions change. You might, for example, decide that managers can approve expenditures up to $1,000, while department managers can approve expenditures up to $10,000. Purchases above $10,000 might require approval by the CFO and the CEO. These amounts should reflect the degree of control over spending that the CEO desires and the experience of the management team.

What Areas Should I Watch for Excess Cash Expenditures?

Anything that must be done at the last minute will cost a premium. These expenditures typically include travel, tradeshow production and attendance, Fed-Ex bills, expediting prototype development or design, and various consulting projects. Planning is a key to cost control. Travel premiums can be avoided by booking flights in advance, requiring coach travel, or canceling travel plans altogether. Often, huge amounts are paid to expedite design projects just a few days or a week. Ask yourself, is this reduction of time worth the extra cost, or is it just a way of saving face for missing a deadline?

On the revenue side, shortening payment terms from customers will increase cash availability and chances of collection. Whenever possible, attempt to receive deposits in advance of product or service delivery. Add a fee for late payment. Do not assume your customers will pay in a reasonable time frame. Follow up on collections the minute an account is overdue.

What Opportunities Are There for Alternative Financing to Conserve Cash? How Do I Evaluate Them?

Financing large expenditures, such as equipment purchases, is one of the easiest ways to stretch out your cash. You must make a decision about the cost of borrowing—which can include interest rates and equity warrants provided to the lender—versus the value of stretching your dollars (often referred to as the *cost of capital*). It is often difficult for a small venture to receive lease financing unless it has strong investor backing and a year's cash requirements in the bank, or unless the owners personally guarantee the debt. Personal guarantees are a very risky choice for entrepreneurs, and are usually not done.

Once the revenue stream is open, obtaining a receivables line of credit is very practicable. This will protect the business from a temporary cash shortage due to a lag in receivables collections.

I Can Save Cash by Exchanging My Software Products with Those of Other Vendors. Are There Accounting Implications in Doing This?

The simple answer is, yes. It has become common for companies, particularly those that are cash constrained, to exchange software products (also referred to as a *barter transaction*). The accounting for software barter transactions is complex and, depending on the circumstances, could result in *no* revenue being recognized for sale of your product. If you plan to enter into barter transactions, you should consult your financial advisor regarding the accounting implications.

Setting Accounting Policies and Procedures

As your company grows, acquires assets, and begins selling a product or service, it will be important to establish accounting policies and procedures that conform to generally accepted accounting principles (GAAP) for its business model and industry. The way you account for aspects of your operations such as accounts receivable, inventory, intangibles, and revenue recognition can have a significant impact on your financial statements; improper accounting can lead to a financial picture that is too rosy or too bleak and could ultimately result in a credibility-busting restatement.

Each industry tends to have its own "hot button" accounting issues. Revenue recognition, for example, is a particularly thorny issue in the software industry as well as in many others. Be sure to consult your accountants on what the key accounting issues are for your industry and business model and which policies to implement to get started on the right track.

Once the right accounting policies have been identified, it will be important to ensure that your business units understand the implications for their operations and how to track and report data. How your sales department structures contracts and reports sales, for example, directly affects revenue recognition.

Revenue Will Be a Key Metric on Which My Company Is Measured. What Are the Alternative Methods of Revenue Recognition, and How Do I Select the Appropriate One for My Business?

This is potentially the most complex area of accounting. In addition, depending on the industry in which you operate, the rules will differ. Simply stated, revenue is recognized when the earnings process is complete (that is, goods or services have been delivered) and collectibility of the receivable is probable.

This is, however, a gross over-simplification; you should discuss your revenue model with your financial advisor early in your development, because the structure of your sales contracts can have a significant impact on the timing of how you will be permitted to recognize revenue. This applies particularly for those companies providing software and services, or services in combination with a tangible product. The following table summarizes the revenue-recognition policy.

Revenue-Recognition Policy Summary

Type of Revenue	*Revenue Recognition*
Shipment of product—FOB origin	Revenue is recognized at point of shipment, unless there are other contractual clauses that preclude revenue recognition.
Shipment of product—FOB destination	Revenue is recognized when goods reach their destination point.
Shipment of product combined with services (such as installation)	If services are not essential to functionality of the product and there is adequate evidence of relative fair values of each element of the deal (product and service), revenue on product sale is recognized when product is delivered. Revenue on the service element is recognized when the services have been provided.
Sale of software license and support services	Software-revenue recognition is governed by very complex accounting literature. At its most simplistic, license revenue may be recognized on delivery of the software, provided there is vendor-specific objective evidence (VSOE) of the fair value of the license element of the arrangement. Fees for support services (PCS) are recognized over the PCS term. Where VSOE does not exist for undelivered elements of the arrangement, revenue is deferred and recognized ratably over the license term.
Sale of professional services—fixed fee	If the company is able to reliably estimate its expected costs, revenue may be recognized on a *percentage of completion* basis. In the absence of reliable information on which to estimate progress to completion, revenue is deferred until the contract is complete.
Sale of professional services—time and materials	Revenue is recognized as services are performed.

Internal and External Reporting

In the financial information that a company compiles for its use, a distinction can be drawn between the type of information that is provided principally for the use of third parties (external reporting) and that which is generated for the management of the business. Information for external reporting is usually prepared using accounting conventions known as *generally accepted accounting principles* (GAAP), while financial information prepared for internal reporting may, but does not have to, follow these rules.

One of the key differences between GAAP and management financial statements may be the use of the accruals basis versus the cash basis of accounting. The *accruals basis* (also known as the *matching principle*) of accounting is used in GAAP financial statements. It requires that companies record income and expenses as they occur, regardless of whether cash has exchanged hands. The *cash* method records transactions in the financial books, and records are based on the actual cash flows in and out of the business.

Pros and Cons of Cash-Basis Financial Statements

Pros	*Cons*
Simple to maintain, because transactions are recorded	Not a true reflection of the assets, liabilities, income, and expenses of the company based on actual cash flows
Income is taxable when received and expenses are incurred	Cannot be used if you have inventory or if you have revenues in excess of $10M deductible when paid

How Should I Prepare for External Reporting?

The external financial reporting requirements for a private company are likely to be financial statements and information prepared for the use of investors and lenders or in support of tax returns. The form and content of these statements will therefore vary depending on the specific requirements of the third party. You should be set up to prepare periodic historical information (income statements, balance sheets, and cash flows), debt covenant compliance schedules (specific ratios that are required to be maintained, based on your individual debt agreement), and updated forecasts. Keep the following in mind:

- **DO** ensure the statements are internally consistent.
- **DO** ensure that you can speak knowledgeably about the key items in each statement.
- **DO** ensure that the statements you present are consistent from period to period (that is, you have a standard chart of accounts from which the income-statement and balance-sheet captions are derived).
- **DO** ensure the information has been prepared in accordance with GAAP.

What Internal Financial Information Should I Prepare?

On a monthly basis, most companies develop and produce a fairly standard financial package. Comparison to financial plans and budgets is critical to establishing management ownership for performance. The CEO must make it clear who is responsible for each element of the financial plan and reinforce the importance of operating within the plan guidelines. A summarized version of this reporting system is typically provided to the board of directors.

More frequent reporting systems must be developed so that managers can access the basic information they need to stay on track with their budgets. This is typically accomplished by obtaining detailed reports from the accounting system on a real-time, daily, or weekly cycle. The internal financial information prepared by the organization should be tailored to its needs but typically will include information that management needs to accomplish the overall goals of the company and also manage its day-to-day objectives.

Here are some golden rules for preparing internal financial information:

- **Budgets**
    - Ensure that the budget is realistic and that each budget item has an *owner* (somebody who is responsible for it).
    - Ensure that actual results are monitored against budget, and that variances are followed up.
    - Keep your business milestones in mind and try and align the financial budget to operating milestones.
- **Cash-flow reporting (historical and projected)**
    - Manage this closely (probably weekly or even daily) to identify possible shortfalls so that you can address them early, before they become a crisis.
    - Ensure that you are not tying up working capital (in inventory or receivables) so that you run out of cash to meet your current liabilities.
    - Remember that profits do not equal cash, and that an increase in assets reduces cash while an increase in liabilities increases cash.
    - Update your projections regularly for actual results and changes in assumptions in your operating plan.
- **Ratios**
    - Use financial operating ratios to establish goals, measure performance, and communicate results.

- Monitoring key ratios can help managers of the business monitor the factors that affect the company's performance.
- Select the right ratios to evaluate performance, based on the company's goals.
- Liquidity (current and quick ratios) and interest cover are always important. As the business matures, additional working-capital ratios such as accounts-receivable turnover, inventory turnover and gross margin, revenue per employee, utilization, and other measures can be key indicators of performance.

Stock Administration

Stock administration incorporates aspects of legal, HR, administration, and finance. For companies following the Silicon Valley model of providing stock options to many of their employees, tracking the number of options and administering them can be burdensome and expensive. Besides setting up the official written stock-options plans, companies must have the options approved by the board of directors and issue letters to the option recipients. Actual physical stock certificates must also be issued. Most plans require employees to exercise their vested options within 30 days of leaving the company; option information must therefore be kept up to date. Additionally, there are very complicated requirements for reporting stock-options data, which can become time consuming to calculate once the company reaches over 50 employees.

Some companies ask their legal counsel to administer all the details of stock transactions. If the appropriate resources can be found within the company, however, it would usually be more cost effective to maintain this administration in house. Stock and stock option–tracking software are real time savers and are usually priced at a lower fee before a company goes public.

note Granting options to non-employees, granting options below the fair market value of the stock, and repricing options can create real accounting headaches, and can result in a huge non-cash expense. Consulting with your accountant on the impact of these is critical, especially when you are planning to take your company public.

Information Systems and Security

The ability to perform essential finance functions in a timely manner depends on adequate information systems. Many companies have run into trouble because their financial information systems were not able to meet internal needs or the demand of investors (for example, reporting financial results as scheduled).

Because the finance function is the custodian of sensitive personnel and company data, its information systems must be secure as well as robust.

How Do I Minimize the Risk That My Business Infrastructure Either Outpaces or Fails to Keep Up with Its Rate of Growth?

To minimize these risks, consider the following:

- Align the infrastructure to the size of your organization and resources.
- Incorporate anticipated IT needs into your business plan.
- Balance simplicity of process with adequate controls over processing of transactions.
- Consider whether alternatives to purchasing are available and would be appropriate for your needs. There are a number of application service providers (ASPs) that can provide outsourced accounting systems.

What Are Other Things I Should Consider When Thinking About Information Security?

When considering information security, you'll want to think about the following:

- **Password control and confidentiality.** Passwords and menu access levels should be assigned to personnel based on job requirements. Standards should be adopted to ensure that passwords are unique, kept confidential, and changed periodically (at least once a year).
- **Access control.** At the beginning, when your company is small, your employees will wear many different hats and will need access to a wide variety of data. As your company matures, however, duties will become segregated and access to information should be granted on an as-needed basis.
- **Filtering/blocking.** How much of your IP or financial data can be sent to a competitor with a single e-mail? Look into filtering and blocking technologies.
- **Hacking.** Your company's IT system should be tested periodically for its ability to withstand external attempts to obtain IP or competitive information.
- **Disaster control.** Are you backing up your data? A comprehensive disaster-recovery plan is necessary to ensure the continued ability of your company to provide information-systems support in the event of a disaster.

Selecting An Independent Auditor

The word *auditor* comes from the Latin *audire*, to listen. Translated to modern day, the auditor reviews the financial statements produced by the company's management in order to issue an opinion, or attestation, that the statements have been prepared in accordance with GAAP. The auditor's opinion provides assurance to the company's board of directors and investors that the financial statements are accurate. Although the auditor does advise clients on accounting policies and procedures, the auditor cannot prepare its clients' financial statements because doing so would impair the independence of its opinion.

The selection of an independent auditor represents an important milestone in the life of a start-up company. The need for an independent auditor means that the company has achieved sufficient growth or investment for its stakeholders to require a third-party review of its financial statements. The independent auditor becomes one of the company's key long-term business advisors, assisting the company to identify areas of risk, evaluate financial systems and controls, and provide assurance to investors and stakeholders.

When Do I Need to Hire an Independent Auditor?

A large venture-capital or bank financing typically first triggers the need for an independent audit. Investors and bankers generally will accept unaudited quarterly financials, but want to see audited annual statements. If you are planning to go public at some point, keep in mind that you will have to provide three years of audited financial statements in your Form S-1 registration statement submitted to the SEC.

Should I Wait until I Need an Auditor before Talking to an Accounting Firm?

Absolutely not. It is never too early to begin seeking advice from an accounting firm. Most accounting firms are happy to maintain a casual "cup of coffee" relationship with early-stage entrepreneurs, and will offer general advice on the financial and tax implications of the corporate structure and business model. Take advantage of this free advice before entering into significant revenue-generating contracts that could cause accounting and regulatory headaches down the road.

Do I Need a Big 4 Accounting Firm as My Auditor? Or Can I Use a Regional or Boutique Firm?

Big 4 refers to the four largest accounting firms: Deloitte & Touche, Ernst & Young, KPMG, and PricewaterhouseCoopers. All four have yearly revenues in the billions of dollars, maintain offices in nearly every country on the globe, and offer almost every kind of accounting and tax service.

There are also a number of accounting firms in each market, which operate only on a regional basis or perhaps focus on serving a boutique niche, such as early-stage technology companies. Regional firms will occasionally do SEC registrant work; boutique firms hardly ever do. Most of these smaller firms maintain a referral relationship with one or more of the Big 4 accounting firms so that they can pass on clients who have outgrown their service capabilities.

The answer to the question of whether you need a Big 4 accounting firm depends on the kind of company you plan to establish. If you are planning to develop a niche technology or service with the intent of being acquired by a larger company, you probably do not need a Big 4 accounting firm. Ditto if you plan to remain a privately held regional player. But if you plan to ramp quickly, go public, and roll out global operations, you should strongly consider bringing in one of the Big 4, whose services can quickly scale to meet your needs. Indeed, many VC firms require that their portfolio companies engage a Big 4 auditor.

What Are the Factors on Which I Should Base My Auditor Selection?

In hiring an auditor, you will be hiring a business counsel whose advice and activities will touch nearly every aspect of your business. You need to ask both your auditor and yourself a number of questions before making this decision:

- **Do I have a good business relationship with the partner leading the service team?** You need to have confidence that your accountant will be able to work well with you in all situations and will be accessible when you need help most.
- **How deep is the partner's and the firm's experience in my industry?** Your accountant should understand your business model and be able to share knowledge and insights gained while working with other firms in your space.
- **What are the qualifications of the rest of the service team?** You are buying the expertise not of just one audit partner, but of a team of senior managers and managers who will be performing important elements of the audit with staff under their direction. Know the bench strength of the firm you hire.
- **What do other entrepreneurs and my other service providers say about the firm and the partner who would be leading the service team?** Like any hire you make, references are important. Your lawyers and bankers, who have typically worked with a number of accounting firms and partners,

can be particularly helpful in providing insight into the accountants you are considering engaging.

- **What is the firm's audit approach and how will it add value?** The firm should be able to clearly articulate how it plans to work with you and the company resources it will require during the audit. Moreover, it should be able to tell you how it will align the audit process with your business goals and share the insights it gains into your organization during the audit.
- **What are the estimated fees, the basis for determining them, and how will differences between the actual and estimated fees be handled?** Even though most accounting firms provide early-stage companies with discounted services, work performed by your auditors outside of the agreed-upon scope of services can quickly add up. Be sure to understand the deliverables you can expect from your auditor as well as what the auditor expects from you in terms of company resources and information—and when. This will avoid potentially costly delays and uncomfortable misunderstandings later.

What Process Should I Use to Select an Auditor?

Although the board of directors is responsible for appointing an independent auditor, the management team works most closely with the auditors and is routinely asked by the board to evaluate the level and quality of services provided. Some managers select their auditor on the basis of one meeting, while others subject their auditor candidates to a lengthy "bake-off." How you select your auditor really depends on your management style and corporate culture. Most companies will meet with several accounting firms—usually on the recommendation of board members, service providers, and other contacts—to evaluate them on the criteria described previously. Based on these meetings, management will make a recommendation to its board of directors for approval.

How Can My Small Company Afford an Audit?

Although the true cost of even the simplest audit is upwards of $100,000, most accounting firms discount their fees for promising start-up companies. The discount is typically greatest in the first year, and then declines in subsequent years as the company grows and faces more complex issues and becomes better able to afford independent auditor services. The price of an audit varies according to the market, the company's investment in finanace resources and infrastructure, and the specific circumstances of the company being audited.

If I Hire an Auditor, Does That Mean I Need to Form an Audit Committee?

Audit committees are recognized as an important best practice in corporate governance—both as a means of preventing fraudulent financial reporting and as a way of demonstrating a company's commitment to strong internal controls. Although private companies are not required to form an audit committee on the board of directors, they should establish one if they anticipate becoming a publicly held entity. The SEC and most stock exchanges require an audit committee comprised of outside directors. The sooner an audit committee is in place, the easier it will be to make the transition to public- company status.

Tax Planning

Benjamin Franklin remarked famously that "...nothing is certain but death and taxes." Nonetheless, many start-up entrepreneurs, because their company does not yet have revenues or is cash-flow negative, put off tax planning and miss an opportunity to position their company for the lowest-possible effective tax rate. It is perhaps counterintuitive that the best time to put tax-effective structures in place is well before you are actually making any money. Effective tax planning can serve as an accelerator, however, by increasing retained revenues and providing a competitive edge, ultimately increasing shareholder value. This section examines some of the common misperceptions, requirements, strategies, and pitfalls related to tax for start-up companies.

My Company Isn't Making Any Money. I Can Worry About Taxes Later, Right?

Wrong. Proper tax planning at the early stages of a company's life can cost very little, but yields great long-term benefits. Many tax strategies that you can put in place right now will not be allowed later when your company is making lots of money. If you plan to sell your products or services in more than one state or country, believe that your IP is going to appreciate significantly, and intend to expand your head count with a view to turning a profit, you should be thinking about taxes now.

At Least I Don't Have to Pay Any Taxes Right Now, Correct?

Wrong again. There is a host of transaction taxes that companies pay even while they are burning VC dollars faster than they are receiving payments from customers. Transactions taxes include sales & use tax, property tax, payroll tax, environmental tax, and customs & duties. These taxes represent "above-the-line" costs, which can drain precious cash from your company. Managing these taxes can significantly help your cash flow.

What Are Some of the Filing Requirements I Should Be Aware of?

What and when you must file depends on your company's revenues, number of employees, headquarters, and offices. Be sure to consult a tax professional to chart out your filing requirements; this is not a do-it-yourself endeavor. Here are some of the typical filings companies make, depending on their particular situation:

- **Annually**
  - Federal corporate tax return
  - State income tax return
  - State franchise tax return
  - Property tax return
  - Excise tax return
  - Unclaimed property (escheat) return
  - Local business licenses
  - Statement of officers (usually filed in state where incorporated)
  - State sales/use tax returns*
  - Annual federal employment tax returns
  - Annual state employment tax returns
  - W-2s (federal and some states)
  - 1099 (federal and some states)
- **Quarterly**
  - Federal corporate estimated tax payments
  - State corporate estimated tax payments
  - Federal employment tax returns
  - State employment tax returns*
- **Other frequency**
  - New hire reporting every 20 days

How Should I Approach Tax Planning?

To be effective, your tax plan should take into account and support the key elements of your business plan, reflecting your company's objectives and envisioned

**Frequency of filing may differ for some states and some taxpayers.*

future state. A number of factors derived from your business strategy will drive your tax strategy, such as:

- Where the product will be developed and/or manufactured
- The supply chain and method of distribution
- IT infrastructure needs
- How the customer will be "touched" (sales and post-sales, service, or support)
- How the business will be grown (organically or through acquisition)
- Support functions needed and their location (marketing, G&A, and so on)

The goal of tax planning is to create shareholder value through the permanent or temporary deferment of taxes. The contribution of your tax strategy to financial performance should therefore be measurable (for example, earnings per share) and balanced against costs and tax risk. Implementation and maintenance costs for certain tax strategies can be significant and need to be factored into the cost-benefit analysis. It is also important to understand a particular strategy's place on the continuum between conservative and aggressive (where an aggressive strategy might be one more subject to regulatory change and review) and whether its place is consistent with your company's appetite for risk.

What Are Some of the Common Tax-Planning Strategies I Should Be Aware of?

Following are several tax-planning strategies of which you should be aware:

- **Net operating losses (NOLs).** Net operating losses may generally be carried back or carried forward for a certain period of time to offset taxable income in other years depending on current federal and state laws in your jurisdiction. Federal legislation enacted in 2002 extends the carry-back period for losses incurred in 2001 and 2002, and provides alternative minimum tax relief. Some of the states may or may not decide to follow the newly enacted federal legislation.

  note A limitation on the future use of NOLs may exist if the company has experienced a significant change in its equity structure, either through various rounds of financing or as a result of an acquisition greater than 50% during a three year period. The rules related to the NOL limitation are very complex, and companies should consult their tax advisor to determine whether an ownership change has occurred.

- **Incentives.** Too many entrepreneurs overlook the incentives that cities, states, counties, and special enterprise zones offer to companies to build facilities and hire workers in their jurisdictions. Even loss-generating companies may benefit from these incentives, because many incentives will save the outlay of cash. Incentives often take the form of

- Temporary or permanent property-tax deferral
- Special NOL treatment
- Allowing capital expenditures to be excluded from the property-tax basis
- Hiring and training credits
- State R&D credits
- Sales and use tax credits and exemptions
- State income tax credits
- Free-trade or development zones
- Employment tax reductions and /or credits

- **R&D tax credit.** The annual expense related to certain R&D activities can be deducted from federal taxes, providing a tax refund for past open years, an annuitized cash flow for successive years, and a reduction in the client's effective tax rate.
- **International structuring.** Many companies realize tax savings by transferring all or part of their income-producing activities to a lower-taxed foreign-based entity.
- **Foreign tax incentives.** To attract foreign investment, numerous countries offer tax incentives, which should be considered as part of any foreign expansion. Examples of some of the foreign tax incentives available include:
    - Tax holidays, in which the host country offers a reduced rate or tax-free status for a negotiated term
    - Tax incentives, such as R&D credits
    - Government grants and/or loan programs to finance infrastructure needs (these can be offered through statutory programs or on a negotiated basis)

What Are Some of the Common Tax Pitfalls I Should Avoid?

Common tax pitfalls include the following:

- **Waiting until there is a problem to get tax advice.** Believe it or not, tax can be a value driver if properly integrated with your business plan. The sooner you have tax strategies in place, the greater the long-term benefits.

- **Not filing tax returns.** The "I am not a taxpayer" mentality will get you into a lot of regulatory-compliance trouble, which could lead to lawsuits, problems with investors, and loss of employee morale.
- **Missing out on state and local tax incentives.** Collect all the tax breaks you can.
- **Failing to manage transaction taxes.** Sales & use, property, payroll, and customs & duties add up fast; manage them appropriately.
- **Expanding into other states or countries without thinking of the tax implications.** Just opening a one-person sales office in a neighboring state can create new tax obligations. Sometimes companies can end up paying foreign taxes while incurring a U.S. loss.
- **Not knowing the tax implications of an ownership change.** Depending on your jurisdiction, an ownership change could result in the inability to use 100% of your NOL carry-forwards in the year in which you have taxable income.
- **Failing to implement a personal tax strategy.** Most entrepreneurs fail to implement a personal tax strategy to preserve the wealth they have created (see the section "Personal-Wealth Management" later in this chapter).

Banking for Entrepreneurial Start-Ups

Establishing the right financial foundation will properly position your company for growth. A business banker is a key business partner who can help you in times of growth as well as in times of economic difficulty. The right bank and a solid banking relationship are important aspects of a company's financial plan.

Selecting the right commercial bank for your emerging-technology company is important because very few banks focus on the start-up segment of the market. Using the bank where you have your personal checking account is usually a mistake because the skills and capabilities you need in a personal banker are very different from the ones you need in a business banker. A business banker will provide an array of customized services that will be appropriate at various stages of your company's growth rather than the standard structures provided by consumer banks.

Here are a few tips on choosing a business banker:

- Choose a bank that has an emerging technology–company practice that provides a full range of banking services to start-ups, including credit.

Traditional commercial banks want to work with established companies, and will provide only depository services to start-up companies.

- Look for a bank that offers products and services tailored to emerging-market companies, that is financially strong, that is FDIC insured, and that has a reputation of working with its clients in difficult times.
- Your bank should demonstrate an understanding of your business and the stages of growth that you will experience throughout your company's life cycle.
- Get a business banker who will listen to you, understand your business, and make the relationship work for you; the customization of terms in business banking makes communication between the entrepreneur and the banker critical.

What Are Some of the Tools That Commercial Banks Can Offer to Help Manage Risk?

Many people are not aware that banks offer many products that can provide a company with timely information to reduce its risk of fraud and theft. Banks offer an array of treasury management products from basics like accounts and online banking to more advanced options like check imaging and positive pay—which allow a company to visually identify and verify an electronic copy of its check before it is paid. Further, account reconcilement allows a company to determine whether a check has been duplicated or if a batch or a check out of sequence has been stolen.

It is also important that you choose a bank that continually enhances its products with new technology and has a reputation for collaborative development with its customers to meet their needs. One of the biggest risks an early-stage company faces is not having the right banking software products in place when it starts to experience rapid growth.

When Is the Right Time to Start a Business-Banking Relationship?

You should develop a business-banking relationship as soon as you form your company. Take advantage of the fact that bankers do not charge you hourly for financial advice. A banker can offer much more than a place to deposit your cash and provide a loan. A banker who understands your business and is focused on the emerging-technology market can provide referrals to venture capitalists, venture leasing, potential customers and suppliers, conferences, workshops, and much more.

What Do I Need to Provide to the Bank to Open a Checking Account? What Do I Need to Provide for the Bank to Consider Providing a Loan Proposal?

You will need to provide the bank with the following information:

- Articles of incorporation
- Certificate of good standing from the state in which the company is doing business
- Tax ID number
- Executive summary of a business plan
- Current interim financial statements
- Last fiscal year-end CPA audited financial statement, if applicable
- 18 to 24 months of income-statement and balance-sheet projections
- Capitalization table

What Are Some of the Main Items That a Bank Considers When Performing its Due Diligence?

Most banks do not provide debt financing to early-stage companies because of the risks associated with their dependency on investors, lack of revenues, the need to raise more cash in the very near future, and so on. Banks willing to take the risk will focus on the following:

- Quality of the management team, investors, and financials (including projections)
- Relationship with the management team and investors
- Product-development and customer-adoption risk
- Competition and market opportunity
- Sufficient liquidity to achieve milestones necessary to raise additional capital or to reach break-even
- Market conditions for raising capital for a particular industry segment

Why Should I Get Debt Financing?

Cash is the lifeblood of an early-stage company, and debt can help extend its life. Debt rather than equity financing is cheaper when, for example, you're financing equipment and software purchases; it also conserves cash for better uses such as product development and/or marketing.

Debt financing, moreover, can extend an equity round or even reduce the total amount of equity financing needed. Remember: Equity is more expensive than debt, and that's a major consideration for entrepreneurs when they think about getting equity financing from outside investors.

You will need to manage cash flows, judiciously use debt capacity, and optimize your firm's capital structure at all stages of its life cycle. By financing long-term assets over time, you can smooth out the cash demands of your operations. Bank loans and leases can help with these financial challenges.

Four Reasons to Obtain Debt Financing

- Leverages the initial and follow-on rounds of equity.
- Extends remaining months of cash to maximize the follow-on valuation.
- Trade creditors consider a good banking relationship when setting credit limits, which enhances negotiations with suppliers, OEMs, and prospective customers.
- Experienced technology bankers can provide quality service and advice, and understand your needs.

What Debt-Financing Options Are Available?

When choosing the type of debt that will benefit your company, it is important to understand the general purpose of each type of debt option. Debt can be obtained in many forms and structures, but it is prudent for an entrepreneur to match the debt with its appropriate use; otherwise, a company could limit its debt options at a future date. One of the biggest mistakes you could make is to think that debt is "one size fits all."

You should consider not only the type of debt that is appropriate for your company today, but also what you may need in the near future. Many companies prepare balance sheet projections on a cash basis rather than on an actual basis. This creates a potential cash-flow problem for a company that expects strong revenue growth and payment within 30 days. Good balance-sheet projections that use realistic averages for accounts receivable, accounts payable, and inventory turnover can allow you to plan your working-capital needs accordingly and enable you to look at other debt-financing options to help with a possible cash-flow problem.

Listed next are some brief examples of different types of debt options:

- **Equipment financing.** Debt provided to start-ups to purchase equipment and soft assets that are not traditionally financed through traditional commercial banks and leasing companies. Equipment-financing loans typically range between $250,000 and $5,000,000; offer an advance period called *tranches* of six to 12 months; and are typically amortized between 24 and 36 months from the first advance.
- **Bridge loan.** Aptly named, this loan *bridges* the time until the next round is expected to close or a major event like an acquisition is to occur.
- **Accounts receivable line of credit.** The best time to get A/R financing in place is three to six months before revenue. A typical line of credit to an early-stage company is between $250,000 and $2,500,000; has a one-year maturity; and requires a full blanket lien on all assets. An early-stage company, either negotiating with its first customers or with new ones to increase revenues, will often find it necessary to provide discounts (which reduce gross margins) or extended terms (which affect cash flow). Banks and asset-based lenders typically provide A/R financing to help a company better manage its working capital needs, which can help it make better business decisions.

A/R Financing Pitfalls

Companies often miscalculate A/R turnover on their balance-sheet projections when taking into account revenue growth. It is important to use the industry average to make adjustments for the company's revenue size when calculating how often it expects to collect A/R (i.e., be paid).

It is also very important that a company not give a blanket lien on all its assets to anyone unless it can provide an A/R line of credit. A blanket lien would include A/R, inventory, equipment, deposit accounts, and general intangibles, including intellectual property. Venture-leasing companies recently have been taking blanket liens on all assets, and it is very important that you either require a sufficient carve-out for bank debt or fully understand the potential cost and risk

- **Letter of credit.** A financial institution backs a letter of credit (also referred to as an *L/C*) as a way for a company to provide a guarantee to another company for a future obligation. Start-ups commonly use standby L/Cs because most landlords, manufacturers, and suppliers are not willing to risk not being paid. Standby L/Cs are typically used to support a lease on a building, for a supplier, and for the manufacturing or assembly of products. A performance L/C is typically used for the manufacturing or assembly of products, and sometimes for suppliers.

- **Acquisition financing.** This financing is typically for later-stage companies that have revenues and a balance sheet that can support the acquisition of another company to enhance growth prospects.

What Are Some Typical Debt Structures?

There are many ways to structure debt; the best way is to customize it to your needs while at the same time meeting the desired risk level of the bank. Banks use covenants and controls to monitor a company's performance and to mitigate risk. Entrepreneurs often expect banks to take equity risk, but banks are regulated and must meet certain credit requirements imposed by either the federal or state regulatory agencies. Further, debts provided by banks are priced at roughly a 90–95% discount to equity.

What Is the Difference Between Bank Debt Versus Venture Leasing?

Both leases and bank equipment loans achieve the same benefit of smoothing out cash requirements, but there are some important differences. Generally, leases are better if you want to manage/maximize cash, while bank loans are better for lowering overall borrowing costs. For early-stage companies, the depreciation and ownership issues will be similar. The advantages of leases, such as tax-advantaged leases and unique structuring, are reserved for mature companies and specialized assets. Historically, leasing companies are focused on the quality of the asset financed, while banks are focused on the overall quality of the company and a comprehensive banking relationship. Some typical characteristics of banks versus leasing companies are outlined next:

- **Pricing**
  - **Banks:** Prime rate (floating) plus 0–2%, fees up to 1%. For early-stage companies, there may be a warrant option, typically 3–6% of the loan amount. Deposit balances and the overall banking relationship can affect pricing.
  - **Leasing companies:** More expensive than bank financing, with the goal of achieving an "all in" internal rate of return of 15% or more. This is broken down into prime + 2.50% and up (usually at a fixed rate), fees of 1–2%, and warrants of at least 5%. There may be lower monthly payments, but there is usually a buy-back clause at maturity of a 10% residual value of equipment; there may also be other exit charges. Non-warrant deals usually are relegated to later-stage and public companies, and are thus priced higher (unless large volumes are involved).

- **Covenants**
  - **Banks (start-ups):** Combination of liquidity, equity milestones, revenue, and/or loss covenants.
  - **Bank (later stage/public):** Liquidity, leverage, net worth, profitability, or debt-coverage ratio.
  - **Leasing companies:** As a rule, no set financial covenants.
- **Collateral**
  - **Banks:** Typically UCC-1 (refers to a provision in the Uniform Commercial Code) blanket lien covering all assets, with the bank allowing for additional lease debt. The UCC-1 blanket lien allows the bank to liquidate the assets covered by the lien if it is unable to collect the funds in the normal course of business.
  - **Leasing companies:** Typically, UCC-1 filing on specific equipment, which allows the borrower the option to work with any bank or leasing company in the future.

In addition, leasing companies are characterized by the following:

- Most banks are not good at equipment-only lending; leasing companies are much better if that is what is needed. Larger leasing companies have a remarketing department and know the value of used equipment.
- Certain leasing companies offer a small working capital line in addition to the lease in order to obtain a general lien on the company's assets. This limits the company's future borrowing options, because it shuts off borrowing from banks until the leasing debt is restructured, repaid, or refinanced.
- Certain leasing companies will attempt to get the right of set-off against deposit accounts from the borrower by having a control agreement signed by the borrower's bank.

Pros and Cons of Working with Banks

Pros	*Cons*
Lower pricing and warrants.	Possibility of more financial covenants; and a blanket lien on all assets.
Access to other services, which can mitigate pricing and help during bad times.	
In troubled times, banks often work with the company's venture capital investors.	
There are no pre-payment penalties on floating-rate loans.	

Pros and Cons of Working with Leasing Companies

Pros	Cons
No covenants.	Higher cost.
Potentially, a lower monthly payment.	
A lien is typically taken only on the assets financed, rather than a general lien on corporate assets.	A lessor may be more aggressive in recovering money and equipment during a default situation.
Lessors make their money on the utilization of the debt facility and the potential for warrant income as there are no other sources of income in the relationship as a bank would have.	Leases often have exit penalties, prepayment structures, back-end payments, and so on
A good lessor will work with venture-capital investors in difficult times.	Some leasing structures have a blanket lien, causing them to be very inflexible for the borrower. This makes additional financing difficult because these structures and liens shut out additional secured lenders.

Case Study: Lease Line Versus Bank Term Loan

Following is an example of the differences between a lease loan and bank term loan that you will likely have to consider in your banking activities. This case study will help you compare the total cost of the two loan types and consider the benefit of paying higher fees and rates with no covenant structure in a lease loan versus lower fees and rates with covenant structures in a bank loan. You should consider the benefit of either credit facility based upon your specific financial needs.

This analysis provides a financial summary, which includes the differences and effects of monthly payment amounts, up-front charges (typically, these are one time administration fees charged at the time of closing the credit facility), total interest charges, total payments, and potential after tax savings. The following table summarizes the assumptions made in the analysis.

Lease Line Versus Bank Term Loans

	Lease	Term Start Date:
Term	01/01/2002	01/01/2002
Loan amount	$2,500,000	$2,500,000
Number of payments	30	30
Interest rate	9.75%*	6.75%**
Interest compounding	Monthly	Monthly
Upfront fee	0.50%	0.50%
Lease buyout fee	7.5%***	NA

**Prime + 5.00% (lease loans are typically priced at the prime rate plus 4.00–7.00%).*

***Prime + 2.00% (term loans are typically priced at the bank's prime rate plus 1.00–2.00%).*

****Lease buyout fees generally fall between 5% and 10%.*

Financial Summary

	Lease	*Term*	*Difference*
Payment amount	$94,238	$90,795	$3,443
Upfront Fees	$12,500	$12,500	$0
Lease buyout fee	$187,500	NA	$187,500
Total interest charge	$327,146	$223,875	$103,271
Total payments	$3,027,146	$2,736,375	$290,771

What Is the Right Amount of Debt? Can You Have Too Much Debt?

The proper balance of debt and equity changes as a company moves from start-up to maturity. Early on, a company builds on a foundation of equity financing and adds debt as other business risks are reduced. Equity financing is long-term risk capital that has an expected future liquidity event but has no near term repayment requirement. Debt is structured with regularly scheduled payments of principal and interest, and these payments must be rigorously adhered to. Taking on debt means that the payments that are associated with this debt must be carefully planned for. Maintaining an excellent credit history is as important to a company as it is to an individual. Bank and lease debt will affect trade credit, which is critical to a company's daily operations.

Like ingredients in a good recipe, debt needs to be used in the proper proportion to equity or you will not achieve your desired result. A common problem for many companies is not too much equity financing but too much debt. An excess amount of debt will inhibit future equity investments and limit the company's options in the future.

What is the Typical Cost of Debt Financing?

Banks and venture leasing companies typically require warrants in connection with lending money to start-ups. Warrants are typically priced as a percentage of the loan amount and the share price of the current or upcoming equity round. An example would be a $1,000,000 term loan with 5% warrant coverage at the Series A share price of $1.00. The 5% is multiplied by the $1,000,000 loan amount and then divided by the per-share price of $1.00, which means it would cost the company 50,000 shares at a $1.00 per share.

How Can a Bank Help My Company in Today's Global Economy?

International issues are complex, and you may need help or services in each country where you plan to do business. A bank with full international service capabilities can help you mitigate many types of risk, including

- **Foreign-currency swings.** Many large companies experienced severe losses during the "Asia Flu" by not properly hedging on customer sales or supplier purchases that were made weeks or months prior to payment. These can be avoided through proper hedging of the currency that will be traded at a future date. You may want to consider hedging foreign currency in countries that have unstable governments or economic issues, or when dealing with large supplier purchases.
- **International transaction problems.** International suppliers often require a letter of credit securing their payment before shipping to a start-up. A bank with a good international department will help you with the common business practices and letter of credit terms of the country with which you are doing business.
- **A/R risk.** International customers not only typically pay slowly, but their accounts receivable may not be eligible to secure an A/R line of credit because a lien on foreign A/R cannot be perfected with a standard UCC-1 filing. Your bank can help you manage that risk through foreign credit insurance, a letter of credit, or ExIm Bank insurance, which could be used to increase the your ability to borrow on your line of credit.

Cash Management

Once your company receives a round of funding, the management of your corporation's cash becomes a very important responsibility. Using an expert in handling your cash management is essential to ensure that your cash management is consistent with shareholder expectations. Your cash-management structure must also be consistent with your company's needs and risk tolerance.

The role of cash management is a complex issue. The corporation has a responsibility to its shareholders to manage cash in the most effective and safest way possible. Using an outsource capability is not only an easy way to handle this issue, but it is the prudent thing to do on behalf of your shareholders. Choosing the right partner is essential. Remember these simple concepts when choosing your partner:

- Safety
- Liquidity
- Value-added returns
- Simplicity
- Optional fee structure

How Do I Start?

The first thing you need to do is select a partner to work with you on your cash management. Usually after a round of funding, you can expect to get several calls from different banks and brokerages offering to handle your company's cash-management needs. Keep in mind that size does matter in this case. A lot of regional banks or smaller firms will have good cash-management departments, but the majority of them are not dealers in the marketplace. Economies of scale play a big role in the safety and liquidity of your cash management, so use a large reputable partner. Also check with your VC, accountant, or other companies that they use. Interview several firms and select a partner that is scalable and can assist your company from now through IPO.

What Is the Process?

You will first need to formulate an *investment-policy* statement (see Appendix IV later in this chapter) with your financial advisor. After devising a strategy that is in line with your investment policy, you must execute and monitor your cash management very carefully. Most large Wall Street firms and large banks have groups dedicated to serving cash-management needs.

Now That I Have an Investment Policy Statement, How Do I Develop and Implement a Strategy to Invest the Company's Money?

The management of a cash portfolio can be very complex, especially when you consider the detailed investment guidelines set forth by the investment-policy statement. Work with your partners to design a strategy that is consistent with your corporate goals and objectives. This is an ongoing process that should change as your corporation changes.

There are two types of approaches to managing your cash portfolio:

- **Traditional cash management.** This approach involves buying and holding to maturity. The goals of this strategy are to meet current cash-flow needs, meet future cash requirements, and minimize portfolio risks. It does not consider yield curve changes, swap opportunities, or reinvestment risk.

- **Active cash management.** This approach centers on market timing. The goals of this strategy are to maintain the portfolio's liquidity and stability with shorter maturities (normally from one day to one year), take advantage of market opportunities (normally from nine months to three years), and seize opportunities for higher overall return due to interest income minus realized gains minus losses, with an emphasis on high-quality securities with potential for selling opportunity.

Can I See an Example of What an Asset Manager Goes Through With This Process and How it Adds Value to What I'm Trying to Accomplish?

Let's take a look at an enhanced–cash management model (ECM)to see how active management can add value to company cash management. ECM uses an underlying interest rate–anticipation methodology as its foundation. This four-step methodology has been in place for over 15 years:

1. Analyze interest-rate environment.
2. Determine average maturity position.
3. Identify value and structure portfolio.
4. Monitor portfolio and reposition as appropriate.

Step 1: Analyze the Interest-Rate Environment

During this step, consider the following:

- Real economic activity determines interest-rate trends.
- Monitor key fundamental data to gauge economic activity.
- The analysis of these key fundamentals determines the appropriate portfolio position:
  - **Duration analysis.** The portfolio duration is based on economic and market analysis. A series of timely indicators is used to help judge the strength of the economy and its position within the economic cycle. Market demand/supply factors and Federal Reserve Board (Fed) outlook are critical inputs to this decision.
  - **Yield curve analysis.** Historical relationships between different maturities are analyzed. This analysis is interfaced with economic indicators and expectations of Fed activity, and takes into account

political as well as fundamental realities. By comparing the interest-rate outlook with the derived forward rate curve, the optimal maturity structure can be chosen.

Step 2: Determine Optimal Maturity Position and Structure

There are three portfolio positions:

- **Defensive.** In a rising interest-rate environment, ECM will structure the portfolio to be defensive in nature and may have a portion of the portfolio in floating-rate securities, which reset monthly or quarterly. Because the coupon resets periodically, the prices of these securities fluctuate less than longer-term fixed-rate bonds and annual/semiannual reset floaters—something that is especially important in a rapidly changing interest-rate environment.
- **Neutral.** When market conditions appear uncertain, ECM will maintain a neutral posture. The portfolio may have a mix of fixed and floating-rate assets depending upon the relative value of the various asset classes.
- **Positive.** When interest rates are falling, ECM will have a positive stance. In this environment, ECM will own a larger percentage of fixed-rate bonds, thereby allowing you to lock in the prevailing interest rate and seek capital gains.

Step 3: Identify Value and Structure Portfolio

This step involves the following:

- **Sector allocation.** Seek to maximize total return by searching for the best relative value investments across a variety of asset classes. Both internal and external analytics are used to evaluate relative value, pre-payment characteristics, and sensitivity to shifts in interest rates.
- **Security selection.** Individual security selection is executed carefully with an emphasis on price. In the corporate sector, the quantitative credit-analysis models allow a manager to focus on those issues with a high probability of being upgraded. Research shows that this emphasis on credits can contribute to achieving substantial excess performance. In the mortgage- and asset-backed sectors, highly sophisticated quantitative tools are used to model cash flows over different market scenarios. This helps sift through a wide array of securities to identify truly cheap issues.

Step 4: Monitor Portfolio and Reposition as Appropriate

Specifically, you should

- Change sector allocation dependent upon relative value.
- Analyze markets and review securities.
- Capitalize on temporary price discrepancies.

Insurance

As soon as you start your company, it will face an array of risks, such as property damage, theft, personal injury, and lawsuits. Insurance provides an essential risk-management tool by transferring the risk of monetary damages resulting from events such as these from your company and its officers to the insurer. Even in early stages, appropriate insurance coverage is key to protecting both the value your company builds and the personal assets of its management.

You company's risk profile will change—and, therefore, so will its insurance needs—as it receives funding, grows, builds value, and makes the transformation from a private entity to a public entity. The following flow chart illustrates some of the major risk-management issues associated with different stages of financing and development:

What Insurance Coverage Should I Consider as I Start Out?

Your insurance coverage should be based on an analysis of your business and the probability and magnitude of the risks it faces, balanced against the cost of covering those risks. A qualified insurance broker can assist you to develop an insurance program that is appropriate for your risk profile and budget. Some of the coverage options you should discuss with your broker include

- General liability
- Property
- Non-owned and hired automobile liability
- Umbrella liability
- Fiduciary liability
- Employee dishonesty (crime coverage)
- Workers compensation
- Foreign exposures
- Professional/cyber/Internet liability

Financing/Risk Management Service Cycle for an Emerging Technology Company

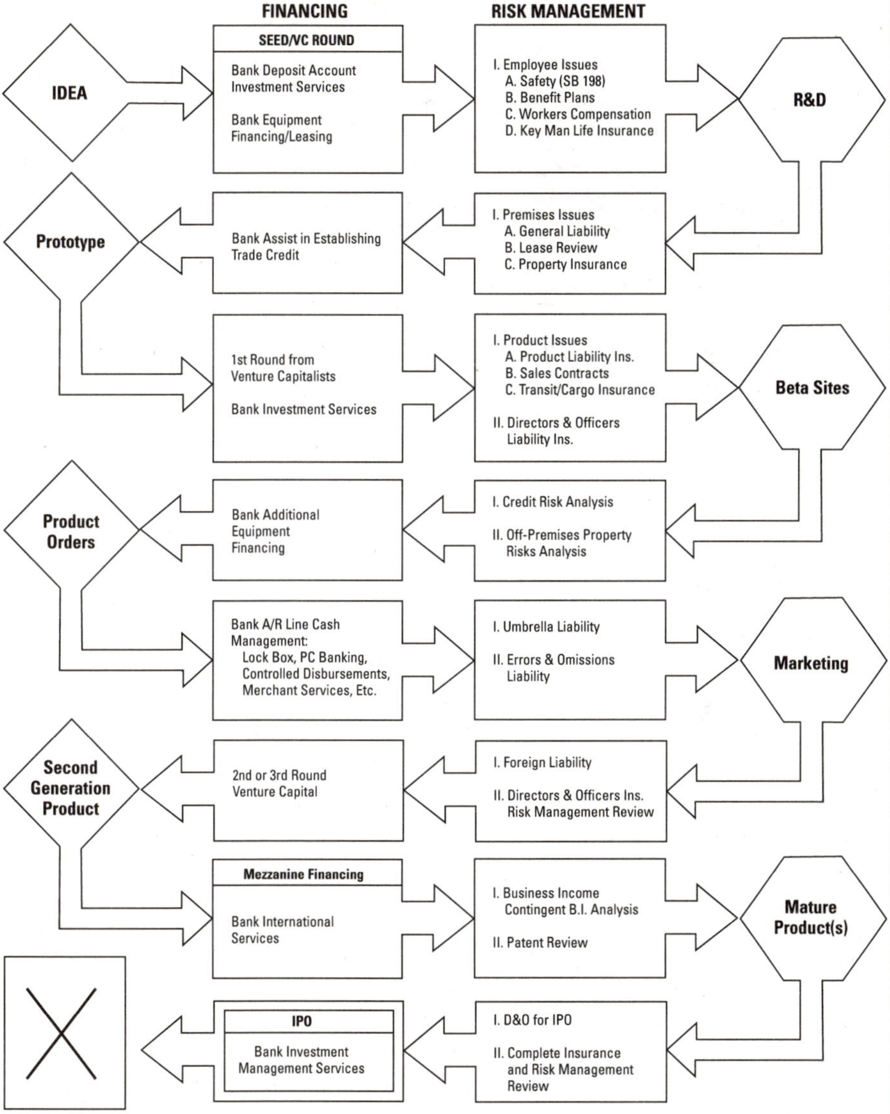

Source: NASDAQ Insurance

- Clinical trials liability (life sciences/biotechnology companies)
- Key person life
- Employment practices liability
- Directors' and officers' liability

General Liability

General liability provides coverage for bodily injury, property damage, personal injury, and medical payments. Some aspects of general liability insurance include

- **Fire legal liability.** Covers damages from a fire to the building where the leased premises are located.
- **Host liquor liability.** Provides protection against damages related to a lawsuit resulting from serving alcoholic beverages to clients, guests, and employees if, as a result of their drinking, they later injure other people.
- **Advertising injury.** Provides coverage against injury caused through your company's advertising activities, such as libel, slander, defamation, piracy, unfair competition, copyright infringement, and so on. Internet/e-commerce and software technology often are unable to secure advertising injury coverage because of the high amount of litigation in this area.

Property

This policy provides coverage for damage resulting from events such as natural disasters, fire, theft, or accidents to three basic types of property: buildings, business personal property, and personal property of others. Some of the possible elements of property insurance are

- **Earthquake sprinkler leakage coverage.** This coverage should be considered whenever property is located in earthquake-prone area but is not insured for damage by earthquake. A sprinkler system could go off during an earthquake, destroying all the business property; this coverage would protect against such a loss.
- **Agreed amount coverage.** Under the terms of this coverage, the insurance company agrees that adequate amounts of insurance have been purchased and that policy coinsurance requirements are waived.
- **Business income and extra expense.** In the event of a property loss that discontinues business operations, a business-income policy would cover the net income that would have been earned and continuing normal operating expense (including payroll) incurred during the time required to repair, rebuild, or replace damaged property. An extra-expense policy would cover other-than-normal operating expenses incurred to avoid or minimize the suspension of business operations.

Non-Owned and Hired Automobile Liability

Most start-up companies do not own vehicles. Therefore, you should purchase non-owned and hired automobile liability if your employees are using their own vehicles or renting them. Possible policy elements include

- **Hired auto physical damage.** This coverage should be considered when employees are renting vehicles and collision-damage waivers are not purchased.
- **Fellow employee coverage.** This provides employee coverage for bodily injury to other employees injured in the course of their employment. For example, suppose two employees are in the same car traveling to a sales meeting, the car is involved in accident in which the passenger is injured, and the employee sitting on the passenger seat sues the employee driving the car. The employee driver named in the suit would have no coverage unless this policy is in place.

Umbrella Liability

The primary function of this policy is to supplement the underlying policies such as general liability, employee-benefits liability, automobile liability, and employer liability by providing additional limits to protect against large or catastrophic losses. Possible elements include

- **Drop down coverage.** This enhancement enables the umbrella policy to "drop down" to provide additional coverage in the event that the underlying policies limits are exhausted. This can enable the umbrella policy to become primary if needed.
- **Personal-injury definition.** The policy definition of "personal injury" should include bodily injury (including intentional bodily injury to protect life or property), false arrest, malicious prosecution, wrongful entry or eviction, libel or slander, advertising injury, humiliation, and mental injury.

Fiduciary Liability

This insurance coverage protects the fiduciaries of subject company benefit plans against legal-liability exposures arising out of the Employee Retirement Income Security Act of 1974 (ERISA). A *fiduciary* is defined as someone who exercises discretionary control or authority over a company's benefit-plan management; who has discretionary authority or responsibility in the administration of a plan; or who provides investment advice to a plan for compensation. It is important to note that fiduciaries are personally liable for any losses sustained by a plan as a result of an error, omission, or other breach of fiduciary duty. The definition of *insured* in this case should include all company plans subject to ERISA, the employer sponsoring the plans, trustees of the plans, directors, officers, and employees.

Employee Dishonesty (Crime Coverage)

This policy covers a variety of theft, burglary, and fraud situations. The policy should include blanket employee dishonesty coverage for employee benefit/welfare plans. The purchase of fiduciary liability protects against liability arising out of the ERISA, but it does not satisfy the act's fidelity-insurance (crime or employee dishonesty) requirements. ERISA stipulates that subject plans must be protected by dishonesty insurance in amounts equal to at least 10% of plan assets.

Workers' Compensation

This insurance policy pays for the medical and compensation benefits (injuries occurring at work) specifically required by the workers'-compensation statutes of the state or states in which operations exist. The policy also affords protection for employers' liability. Employers' liability coverage responds if an employee rejects workers' compensation benefits and brings suit for damages under common law.

Foreign Exposures

When a company has operations in foreign countries or has employees traveling into foreign countries, the following policies should be considered to provide adequate coverage:

- Foreign general liability
- Foreign automobile liability
- Foreign voluntary workers compensation
- Travel accident
- Local property policy

note Some countries require that the company purchase coverage with a local insurance company.

Professional/Cyber/Internet Liability

This type of policy protects the company against claims for breach of duty, neglect, error, misstatement, misleading statement, or omission in performing or failing to perform professional services for clients for a fee. The opportunities of e-business present many new and complex risks. The open nature of Internet technologies increases vulnerability to network disruptions, security breaches, introduction of computer viruses, electronic espionage, and information theft. Additional exposures to loss include infringement of copyright, trademark, trade dress service mark, trade secrets, privacy violations, libel and slander, and so on. Other risks of loss are Internet and network wrongful acts including security breaches, errors or omissions that can cause financial damage to third parties, and software-code infringement. Anyone with a Web site or conducting business on the Internet needs to be aware of the risks and address these exposures.

Clinical Trials Liability (Life Sciences/Biotechnology Companies)

This type of policy covers losses arising from the liability of performing clinical trials in the U.S. or internationally. It usually includes Phase 1, Phase 2, and Phase 3 clinical trials.

Key Person Life

This coverage provides funding to offset the loss of a key employee. Because the probability of losing a key employee is relatively high compared to other exposures, this coverage can be expensive depending on the underwriting profile of the key employee. The policy provides guaranteed cash when needed, policy cash values (which are a business asset), affordable protection, and improved credit standing.

Employment Practices Liability

This policy provides coverage for claims arising out of alleged wrongful termination, sexual termination, sexual harassment, and discrimination (to the extent permitted by law).

Directors' and Officers' Liability

This policy is becoming crucial for start-ups because it protects board members, executives, directors, officers, and outside board members. Many venture capitalists require this type of coverage prior to any funding. This type of coverage is so important it deserves a lengthy discussion all its own (see below).

Directors' and Officers' Liability Insurance

Often, directors' and officers' (D&O) liability insurance is explained and valued solely in terms of its worth to the individuals it protects, but you must also understand how it functions to protect the assets of the enterprise itself.

As the ultimate guardians of shareholder value, your directors and officers face personal liability for their acts, errors, and omissions in managing the enterprise. For the directors and officers of newly public companies in particular, the risk of shareholder lawsuits is high. Management teams not used to the demands of public-company reporting and operating often make missteps in the first few quarters after going public; unfortunately, a legal industry has been built up around filing class-action lawsuits against young public companies.

Private companies also face significant D&O liability risk, especially related to claims by employees, competitor litigation, and regulatory investigation. Investors in private placements also frequently bring suits related to disclosures made in financial statements.

The first line of defense is *indemnification* (a contractual promise to reimburse expenses incurred/damages paid as a result of activities undertaken on behalf of the company) made by the enterprise to these key individuals. Indemnification, however, may not be permissible in all circumstances, and any funds paid to indemnify individuals cannot be used for the capital needs of the enterprise. Where indemnification is appropriate, determining how to fund this significant obligation remains an issue.

Although established companies may have options to fund this obligation, such as the creation of trust funds or establishing a letter of credit, start-ups will most likely find that risk transfer is the correct choice when faced with the potential of enormous defense costs and severity of loss in claims brought against management. We conclude with a few key considerations when evaluating this insurance.

At What Stage Should the Purchase of D&O Be Considered?

Although the evaluation of D&O is often prompted by later rounds of funding and the expansion of the board, you should consider the risk from the moment the internal indemnification provision is active (through the bylaws or certificate of incorporation). If you have identified the main risks around key shareholder value drivers and begun to put in place the controls, processes, and technology outlined elsewhere in this guide, you will probably find favorable treatment from D&O underwriters.

What Coverage Elements Should the D&O Policy Contain?

Unlike other insurance contracts, which take on a set form regardless of the stage of the enterprise, D&O can be negotiated to encompass a changing set of risks as the enterprise grows. A few common coverages are

Top Ten Reasons Why Private Company Directors and Officers Need D&O Insurance

1. Involvement in day-to-day operations makes private company directors and officers particularly vulnerable to claims brought by employees.
2. Third-party discrimination claims brought by customers and clients are increasingly common.
3. D&O insurance from a quality insurer can take private companies through their IPO and into public ownership well-protected.
4. Complex claims brought by competitors, such as anti-trust and unfair-competition claims, can generate sky-high defense and settlement costs.
5. Investigations by government and regulatory agencies can generate enormous defense costs—even if no wrongdoing is found.
6. Company assets can be closely tied to the personal wealth of directors and officers, making protection for claims solely against the company vital.
7. When the company cannot indemnify its directors and officers in D&O claims, insurance can step in instead.
8. Shareholders of private companies frequently sue for inadequate or inaccurate disclosure in financial reports and statements made in private place materials.
9. D&O insurance can protect the personal assets of a director's or officer's spouse, as well as the assets of a deceased director's or officer's estate.
10. With D&O insurance in place, management can focus on managing the company rather than managing protracted litigation.

- **Employment practices liability.** Risk surveys have shown that employees bring the majority of D&O claims. Although it is often cost-effective to package this coverage with the D&O, you should make sure that members of the board realize that their individual risk in this case is aggregated with the company's limit on compensation from the insurer. Therefore, separating the board's liability limit from the company's limit should be considered so that a settlement made on behalf of the company does not exhaust the directors' individual coverage.
- **Securities claims.** Because these types of claims can be the most damaging, this coverage needs to be carefully modulated as the enterprise raises capital. The level of coverage ranges from none to full coverage for prospectus liability in your IPO.
- **Entity coverage.** Most contemporary policies for the privately held enterprise will include the entity as an insured. The policy exclusions need to be reviewed carefully, however, because major areas of enterprise risk will be retained by the insured, including intellectual property, breach of contract, and claims brought by clients arising out of professional services provided.

Personal-Wealth Management[1]

You will have a lot on your mind as you approach any major business event such as an IPO or M&A, but don't overlook your personal-wealth management. It's a sad fact that most CEOs do not have a personal financial plan in place at the time of IPO[2], but putting a proper financial plan in place prior to a liquidity event can provide significant savings in future estate and gifting taxes.

The communication between your key advisors (estate-planning attorney, CPA, and financial consultant) is important to the success of your financial plan. Most major financial institutions and service providers have specialty groups designed to help entrepreneurs and executives with both their pre–wealth creation planning and post–wealth created planning. The plans are designed to effectively transfer wealth for estate purposes, tax-efficient sales of concentrated positions, charitable giving, or to leave a legacy. Once the planning is finished, you need to focus on preservation of capital, growth of capital, and asset management with acceptable risk.

What Do I Need to Do to Start This Process?

A major barrier to setting up an organized financial plan is inertia. You just can't get going. People often procrastinate when they don't know where to begin or what to do. A financial planner helps you overcome inertia by organizing the details for you that ensure that you take the right next steps. A financial planner will assist you in implementing your strategies and coordinating the efforts of your attorney, insurance agent, CPA, and investment advisor to make sure all the planning is taken care of.

Now That I Have Found the Time, What Are the First Steps?

The smartest move you can make is to hire a reliable, objective financial planner who can help you devise and carry out your financial plan. To begin this process, do the following:

- Interview several financial planners.
- Ask the financial planners you are considering for references and to describe their experience in dealing with a situation like yours.

---

1 CitiGroup Asset Management and the Private Portfolio Group, Salomon Smith Barney. "Enhanced Cash Management." 2002.

2 Blowers, Stephen C.; Griffith, Peter H.; Milan, Thomas L. Ernst & Young Guide to the IPO Value Journey. John Wiley & Sons, Inc. 2001.

- Ask for recommendations from your peers or friends.
- Understand the capabilities of the financial planner's firm before you commit to the relationship.
- Choose the financial planner with whom you are most comfortable. You should have a strong sense of confidence that your financial planner will do all the due diligence to ensure that your—and your family's—needs are understood and met. Having that kind of confidence (or level of comfort) will provide you with great peace of mind.
- Ask your financial planner for referrals to other professionals who will become the other core members on your personal wealth–planning team (attorney, CPA, and insurance specialist).
- Make sure that the members of your wealth-planning team have specialists within their respective coverage areas to deal with unusual issues.

How Should the Process Go Once the Team is Selected?

After selecting the team consisting of a financial planner, attorney, and CPA, it is your job to make sure that they all work together in designing the financial plan for you. The first thing they should do is interview you to find out all important information regarding your financial picture, including what you have done to date and what you want to achieve in the future. The understanding needs to extend to potential beneficiaries such as your spouse, children, grandchildren, or anyone else you may be gifting to or who is listed as beneficiary on any of your accounts. Your team will use this information to create a comprehensive plan that meets you goals and objectives.

Financial plans are very specific and detail-oriented, and should change as your life changes. Prior to implementing the plan, make sure that you understand what it will accomplish for you and the consequences of its implementation. If you feel comfortable, have the plan put in place. If you do not feel comfortable, ask questions and make changes as needed.

Here are a few things to keep in mind about the process of personal financial planning:

- Provide the information; it will be kept confidential.
- Don't just go through the process, *drive it.*
- Don't be afraid to ask questions.
- All life changes that can affect the integrity of your plan need to be passed on to your team immediately.

- Remember: You are the boss, and this is your wealth. Expect the best from your team.
- Sleep well knowing you did the right thing.

What Should My Plan Accomplish Pre-liquidity Event?

Now that the plan has been implemented and your company has either moved into an M&A agreement or completed an IPO, you need to understand what your plan accomplishes for you. Because the value of the asset is not realized until a liquidity event, the majority of pre–liquidity event financial planning deals with wealth transfer of assets and gifting of assets at a low-cost basis. By gifting stock early, before it has the opportunity to appreciate substantially, you will significantly decrease estate and gift taxes. Wealth transfer and gifting will be the major accomplishments of the pre–liquidity event portion of your financial plan.

Following are several wealth-transfer strategies that may be used to accomplish your goals:

- Outright gifts
- Grantor retained annuity trusts
- Family limited partnerships
- Installment sales to defective trusts
- Leveraged gifting programs
- Estate freeze techniques
- Gifts of nonqualified stock options
- Charitable remainder trusts

Use the following checklist to ensure that you've taken the proper steps in financial planning.

Personal Financial Plan Checklist

Pre-Liquidity	*Post-Liquidity*
❑ Create a core financial consulting team.	❑ Protect your new wealth.
❑ Consider gifting shares to family members through trusts or partnerships.	❑ Utilize trusts and foundations to minimize taxes.
❑ Consider exercising your stock options (consult your advisors).	❑ Utilize a properly allocated and diversified portfolio to preserve and grow your wealth.
❑ Establish basic estate-planning documents such as wills, revocable trusts, living wills, and so on.	❑ Implement additional corporate benefit plans.

Pre-Liquidity	Post-Liquidity
❑ Review/adjust your asset allocation.	❑ Review on a quarterly basis all plans in place with your team.
❑ Review/adjust your insurance policies.	❑ Educate your employees on the above.
❑ Educate your employees on the above.	❑ Have fun—you have earned that right!

After Executing the Plan and Completing the Liquidity Event, What Should I Think About Next?

Now that you have gone through your liquidity event and have realized the wealth created from your company, you have several new problems. Specifically, most of your net wealth is concentrated in one position; your liquidity needs do not match up with the lock-up period required by the SEC; and you face a potential tax liability if you exercise your options. The team you have established should be aware of these issues and will consult with you on the best ways to diversify your assets, limit taxes, and provide a credit facility so you can access your money. Through your team, you should be able to design a portfolio and use trusts, personal foundations, and charitable giving to limit the taxes on the sale of your position. After the sale, the proceeds you receive need to be managed effectively. Your team will help you create a portfolio that preserves and grows your assets at an acceptable risk rate for you. Your plan should be reviewed every three months, and should change as your life changes.

Case Study: The Value of a Smart Financial Plan

Charlie, the CEO, Chairman, and co-founder of XYZ Corporation, was in an enviable position. He held incentive stock options (ISOs) entitling him to buy 2,000,000 shares of his company stock at $1 a share. Charlie exercised his ISOs just as his company was going public, at which point the stock was trading at $120, giving him a paper profit of $238 million.

Assuming that the stock of his hot technology start-up would continue to appreciate, Charlie developed a simple plan: He would hold the shares for a year before selling any because the profit on the sale would then qualify for capital-gains treatment. Six months after going public, however, the stock markets crashed and the company's share price dropped to $20, making Charlie's stock worth only $40 million. The problem: Charlie was now faced with an alternative minimum tax (AMT) of $67 million. Charlie had to sell his shares at the higher tax rate to avoid AMT because he did not have a financial plan in place with provisions to protect his wealth if the stock price fell. *Sorry Charlie, you should have planned better!*

Shanti, the CTO and co-founder of XYZ Corporation, was in the same enviable situation as Charlie—but Shanti was wise enough to realize that she had very limited experience dealing with sudden wealth and needed proper strategies to handle her financial success. She contacted several firms and, after interviewing the consultants, chose the consultant in whom she had the most confidence to handle her financial planning.

Shanti and her financial consultant put together her core team of advisors. Prior to the IPO, Shanti's team advised her to use gifting strategies that would allow her to gain significant savings on future estate and gift taxes. After the company went public, Shanti and her team worked carefully to protect her new wealth. They designed a hedging strategy that protected the downside stock movement. They used trusts and foundations to make any sale of her stock tax efficient. After the stock peaked and started moving back down, Shanti's strategies went into action, and she sold her position at a $100 a share. Shanti and her team had already created a plan for the management of the proceeds in the event of a sale, using a proper asset-allocation and -diversification strategy that was in line with her risk tolerance. Shanti currently has a large portfolio built around ongoing active management of her assets, which is specifically tailored to her needs and changes as her life changes. *Shanti is currently engaged to a Hollywood film star and plans to get married at the end of the year in Hawaii on an island that she has leased for the week.*

What About My Employees?

It is important to implement a well-constructed benefit plan for your employees. An employee-benefit plan is essential to a company's ongoing health. It allows you to hire and retain talented personnel and to motivate them to make decisions consistent with being a shareholder. The employees in a pre–liquidity event situation will experience many of the same problems as the entrepreneur. Educating your employees is very important to help ensure their financial success and to maintain morale.

What Are the Key Elements of a Corporate Benefit Program?

A good benefit program should deliver the intended benefit and be easy to manage. To achieve "best of class" management of the benefit plans while avoiding multiple time-consuming decisions, select your benefit partner as though the company is already public. All good corporate client groups will be completely scalable and will grow as you grow. All major Wall Street firms have a dedicated corporate client group. When establishing a corporate benefit program, consider the following:

- Do not forget that you are also an employee.
- Good benefit programs enhance you personal wealth–management strategies.
- Having happy, financially secure, and educated employees increases retention rate (executives have specialized benefit plans, which are important in attracting and retaining key employees) and indirectly maximizes shareholder value.

The type of benefits you offer depends on what stage your company is in:

- **Pre-IPO benefit absolutes**
  - 401k plan
  - Stock Option plan
- **Before you go public, but after you file**
  - Stock purchase plan
  - Directed shares program (often referred to as *friends and family*)
- **Post IPO choices**
  - 529 college-savings plan
  - Deferred-compensation plan for executives and key employees
  - 10(b)5-1 plan (systematic sales plan for 144 employees)

APPENDIX I: Controls Checklist

Purchasing

Vendor Selection

- ❑ Establish procedures (and ensure they are followed) to qualify and evaluate vendors prior to their becoming approved vendors.
- ❑ Ensure that competitive bids are obtained for large or unusual purchases. Establish a threshold for obtaining competitive bids.

Vendor Setup and Management

- ❑ Maintain a master file or listing of approved suppliers.
- ❑ Establish procedures to control changes and update information included on the master file or listing of approved suppliers. Assign responsibility for approving any additions/deletions to the list.
- ❑ Ensure that individuals who can add vendors cannot make disbursements without a review by an approver/check signer.
- ❑ Make sure procedures are in place to ensure that relevant vendor information is recorded completely and accurately; and that the information is consistent and not duplicated; and to delete names of vendors no longer used.

POs/Purchase Requisitions

- ❑ Create purchase orders or contracts for all purchases. Limit access to purchasing data files, programs, and related records.
- ❑ Establish procedures for initiating a purchase.
- ❑ Use standardized purchase requisitions or purchase orders.
- ❑ Establish a threshold for approvals. Establish approval hierarchy for purchases and multiple approvals for purchases over a certain threshold amount.
- ❑ Create an authorized approvers list and make it available to personnel responsible for purchasing.
- ❑ Ensure that the persons who perform the purchasing function are independent of requisitioning purchases, preparing vouchers for payment, receiving, and disbursements.
- ❑ Ensure timely follow-up of missing and open purchase orders.
- ❑ Establish a process to ensure that purchasing data is processed completely and accurately in the proper accounting period (for example, that all goods

and services received are accrued for at the end of each month), and that rejected entries are followed up on a timely basis.

Receiving/Return to Suppliers

- ❑ Limit the access to receiving data files, programs, and related records.
- ❑ Ensure that goods received are counted, inspected, and matched to approved purchase orders or other ordering documentation.
- ❑ Establish a procedure to prevent payment (or recover payment, if made) for rejected goods, over or short deliveries, price differences, and returned goods.
- ❑ Establish a process to ensure that accounts payable is debited in a timely manner for returned goods.

Processing of Vendor Invoices

- ❑ Limit access to supplier invoice data files, programs, and related records.
- ❑ Ensure that the finance department receives invoices.
- ❑ Create system controls where possible to recognize whether the same vendor invoice has been entered twice for payment.
- ❑ Ensure that suppliers' invoices are matched with approved purchase orders (or other ordering documentation) and receiving reports prior to approval for payment. Ensure that the individual authorizing payment is independent of the purchasing, receiving, and check-signing functions.
- ❑ Ensure that differences followed up on a timely basis.
- ❑ Ensure that suppliers' invoices are checked for accuracy (for example, mathematical extension, proper freight charges, discounts, and proper tax charges) prior to payment.
- ❑ Ensure that GL coding of invoices is reviewed.

Processing of Employee Reimbursements

Reimbursements for Business Purposes

- ❑ Establish written policies and procedures for reimbursement of business expenses.
- ❑ Institute a process to ensure that corporate procurement cards are used for business purposes only.
- ❑ Establish authorization for individual corporate procurement cards.

- ❑ Establish approval thresholds for procurement card transactions.
- ❑ Ensure that HR notifies accounts payable in the event of card cancellations for terminated employees.
- ❑ Ensure that all reimbursements are reviewed for appropriate support, business purpose, and compliance with company policy.
- ❑ Establish a policy for receipted and non-receipted expenses.

Moving or Relocation

- ❑ Ensure that there is a process for approving moving/relocation expenses.
- ❑ Ensure that supporting documentation and approval for all expenses is obtained.
- ❑ Ensure that invoices are approved by someone other than the person being relocated.
- ❑ Ensure that relocation expense is reconciled to billing detail.

Disbursement Process

- ❑ Establish a process to ensure that only valid invoices are paid in accordance with management's payment and discount policies. Perform a three-way match (vendor invoices should be matched to POs and receiving documentation).
- ❑ Limit access to cash-disbursement data files, programs, and related data.
- ❑ Consolidate multiple checks to the same vendor.
- ❑ Establish a process for making payments (for example, after invoice matching/invoice due date/30 days after receipt of invoice/30 days after invoice due date). Ensure that the policy maximizes cash flow.
- ❑ If there is a check-signing machine, ensure that the individual who operates it and maintains custody of the keys and plate is independent of the voucher and check-preparation functions.
- ❑ Establish a process and controls over the check-signing process and who has signing authority. Establish dollar thresholds for signing and dual signatures for checks in excess of a certain amount.
- ❑ Ensure that there is a bank-authorized signer form on file and that that form is updated periodically.
- ❑ Ensure that check signatories are independent of those responsible for preparing vouchers for payment, purchasing, and receiving functions.

- Ensure that persons who sign checks are presented with approved supporting vouchers for comparison and inspection.
- Ensure that secondary approvals are obtained on checks that are authorized by the individual signing the check.
- Ensure that checks are not signed by persons involved in the preparation of vouchers for payment. (A more appropriate signatory would be the controller or CFO].)
- Ensure that supporting documents for cash disbursements are properly canceled under the control of the check signer [i.e. indicated (that is, noted as "paid" to avoid duplicate payment)].
- Ensure that checks are mailed directly after being signed by persons independent of preparing vouchers for payment, purchasing, receiving, shipping, cash receipts, and accounting functions.
- If petty-cash accounts are used, ensure that receipts are reviewed for reasonableness and balanced by an independent party prior to reimbursement of account.
- Ensure that petty cash is being used properly for emergency purposes, not employee reimbursement (that is, not for mileage and parking).

Check Security

- Ensure that access to un-issued checks is limited, and that those with access are independent of the check-signing function and the preparation of vouchers.
- Ensure that blank-check stocks are secured at all times.
- Have an independent party periodically inventory the check stock.
- Ensure that check-usage logs are maintained and kept secure separately from check stock. Ensure that a supervisor periodically reviews these logs.
- Ensure that spoiled checks are properly voided and defaced to prevent use.
- If manual checks are used, ensure that manual check–usage logs are maintained and reviewed periodically by a supervisor to ensure that all checks are accounted for and entered into the system in a timely fashion.

Investment Management

- Ensure that the board of directors defines authority limits for the types and size of investments that can be acquired and those individuals authorized to carry out investment transactions.

- ❑ Establish regular monitoring procedures for investment performance relative to objectives and to ensure that investment activities are being conducted in accordance with company policy.
- ❑ Ensure that physical instruments are held for safekeeping at banks.

Accounts payable and Accrued Expenses

- ❑ Undertake reconciliations of unpaid vouchers or accounts-payable subsidiary ledgers to the general ledger on a monthly basis. Have these reconciliations reviewed by someone other than the person who prepared them.
- ❑ Establish a process for ensuring that all significant liabilities have been recorded at the balance sheet date (that is, to ensure all vendor invoices received have been recorded and that goods and services received but not yet invoiced are accrued). Ensure that accrual balances are reviewed each month for adequacy and reasonableness.
- ❑ Review the payables detail record for obvious omissions, large debit balances, or other unusual items.

Bank Reconciliations

- ❑ Prepare monthly reconciliations between bank statements and the general ledger. Ensure that the individual responsible is independent of access to cash and the ability to create a check without supervisory review.
- ❑ Ensure that the reconciliation is reviewed and that performance of the review is documented.
- ❑ Ensure that stale checks are followed up on periodically, and that stop-payment notices are issued and recorded if appropriate.

Fixed-Asset Management

- ❑ Establish approval thresholds for fixed asset purchases. Limit authority to approve fixed-asset purchases.
- ❑ Ensure all fixed-asset purchases are supported by approved requisitions.
- ❑ Limit access to fixed-asset records.
- ❑ Ensure that fixed assets are appropriately identified and assigned (that is, classification, dollar value, life, depreciation method, and so on).

- ❑ Establish controls to safeguard fixed assets. (Perform periodic inventory of fixed assets.)
- ❑ Establish a process to reconcile differences between physical inventory and the fixed-asset sub ledger, and make adjustments in a timely manner.
- ❑ Establish a capitalization threshold.
- ❑ Determine the method of depreciation used.
- ❑ Establish a fixed-assets tracking system (tagging, detailed register, and so on).
- ❑ Establish a procedure for recording additions, disposals, or transfers. Assign authority for such transactions.
- ❑ Ensure that the responsibility of recording gains or losses from disposal of an asset is segregated from the responsibility for disposing of such assets.
- ❑ Ensure that reconciliations are performed between all separate fixed-asset accounts and their corresponding accumulated depreciation accounts and the general ledger.
- ❑ Ensure that fixed-asset registers are reconciled to the general ledger periodically.

Processing of Payroll

- ❑ Limit access to payroll data files, programs, and related records.
- ❑ Ensure that payroll files and documentation are properly secured at all times.
- ❑ Ensure that original source documents for "sign-on" bonuses are reviewed to ensure accuracy of bonus.
- ❑ Obtain written authorizations from employees for withholding exemptions and voluntary payroll deductions.
- ❑ Establish procedures to control changes and update information included on the master file or listing of employee data used to prepare payroll.
- ❑ Assign authority for initiating monetary payroll changes (pay rate/status changes/changes to benefits/other deductions/changes to vacation or PTO accruals) for existing employees and new hires.
- ❑ Ensure that variable data used to calculate gross pay (for example, hours worked, overtime, and bonuses) is approved by departmental heads.
- ❑ Ensure that reasonableness of payroll computations for a particular period is reviewed prior to payment.

Payroll Disbursements

- ❑ Where possible, use automatic deposits rather than checks.
- ❑ Maintain a separate bank account used for payroll disbursements.
- ❑ Ensure that recipient of payroll checks and register is independent of payroll data-entry function.
- ❑ Balance the payroll account prior to distribution of checks.
- ❑ Ensure segregation of duties between the following functions:
  - ❑ Hiring and setting pay rates
  - ❑ Maintaining employee personnel records
  - ❑ Timekeeping
  - ❑ Preparing payroll
  - ❑ Signing checks and distributing payroll
- ❑ Reconcile payroll register to the general ledger.
- ❑ Reconcile payroll bank accounts to the general ledger.

Debt Financing

- ❑ Set approval thresholds for financing arrangements, covenants, and obligations.
- ❑ Establish thresholds for decisions requiring board approval.
- ❑ Ensure that borrowings have written agreements and have been reconciled to bank statements.
- ❑ Ensure that journal entries relating to the financing activity are approved and reviewed.

Compliance with Covenants

- ❑ Ensure that covenants are documented, compliance tracked, and reported to management on a regular basis.
- ❑ On failure to comply with covenants, ensure that corrective actions are taken or releases are negotiated with lenders.
- ❑ Ensure that reports are available for managers to track compliance with covenants.
- ❑ Establish authority for actions to retire debt outside of normal repayment schedules.

Equity Financing

- ❑ Establish authorization and documentation procedures around the issue of equity instruments.
- ❑ Ensure that stock certificates are controlled (uniquely numbered) for identification.
- ❑ Maintain records to track shareholders of record. Include information such as name, address, number of shares, and date of transfer of ownership.
- ❑ Limit the number of individuals with authority to record equity issues, share ownership, and changes in share ownership.

Manage and Invest Cash

Banking Arrangements

- ❑ Establish controls over opening new bank accounts.
- ❑ Ensure that banks are informed about who is authorized to draw on particular accounts. Provide signature cards, which are regularly updated for changes in authorized personnel.
- ❑ Ensure that the responsibility for reconciling bank statements is segregated from authorization to draw on accounts.
- ❑ Ensure there is an approval process for non-routine transfers of cash.
- ❑ Ensure that separate transactions exist for creating transfers and wire transfers and for approving such transfers. Ensure that individuals performing these two functions are segregated.

Establish and Maintain Account Structure

Chart of Accounts

- ❑ Define and document a chart of accounts.
- ❑ Ensure that additions or changes to the chart of accounts are properly approved and updated in the system and are communicated.
- ❑ Ensure that system logic requires the use of valid accounts for all journal entries.

Period-End Procedures

- ❑ Document all period-end procedures using checklists where needed to ensure that all necessary procedures are performed in the time and manner required.

- ❑ Standardize procedures to ensure consistency.
- ❑ Ensure that individuals with access to transactions to define, initiate, or modify period-end activity reports are segregated from those who have authority to approve the same transactions.
- ❑ Review and follow up on any exception reports generated.

Cycle Independent Accounting

Approve and Post Manual General Ledger Entries

- ❑ Ensure that logs are maintained for all required recurring manual entries.
- ❑ Use standardized forms to ensure that recurring entries are made in a consistent manner.
- ❑ Ensure that all manual entries are approved and supported by appropriate documentation.
- ❑ Limit authority to access and post manual entries.
- ❑ Where possible, establish system controls that prevent posting of entries that do not balance and that enforce the use of valid account numbers.
- ❑ Use system-generated reports to identify differences between general and subsidiary ledgers, and follow up on reasons for discrepancies.

APPENDIX II: Key Metrics

Creating reliable financial information for your own decision-making purposes and for reporting to your investors is critical to your survival. The extent and type of information that you compile will depend on your company's stage of development. In the early stages, you will be focused on expenditures and on your ability to meet your obligations from your existing assets. As you start generating cash inflows from sales, however, other metrics and reports will become relevant. The metrics detailed in the following table are a small selection of the items that may be relevant at each stage of your company's development.

Key Metrics

Key Metric	*Rationale*	*Start-up*	*Prototype/ Revenue*	*Mature*
Burn rate	Monitors rate of cash expenditure.	*	*	*
Details of budget to actual expenditure	Enables analysis of significant variances from expectation.	*	*	*
Forecast information	Helps monitor and manage cash requirements.	*	*	*
Days accounts-payable outstanding	Helps you make the most of taking credit from suppliers.	*	*	*
Current ratio	Tests liquidity.	*	*	*
Quick ratio	Tests immediate liquidity.	*	*	*
Accounts-receivable aging	Ensures that collections are keeping pace with revenue and that there are no indicators that customers may fail to pay for goods and services received.		*	*
Days sales outstanding	Another metric to evaluate collection risk.		*	*
Sales pipeline/backlog	How much revenue for the immediate future is "guaranteed" because you have signed orders from customers, and how much still has to be found.		*	*
Gross margin analysis	Analyzes your product profitability before overheads.		*	*
Inventory turnover	Helps ensure you have enough but not too much inventory on hand.		*	*
Return on assets	Measures how the company uses its assets to generate profits. A measure of profitability and asset management.		*	*
Cash flows—analyzed by type of inflow/outflow	The importance of cash flows from operations increases.		*	*
Key metrics relative to competitors	Helps identify areas where you beat or need to catch up with competitors.			*

APPENDIX III: Board-Reporting Toolkit

Waterfall Analysis

SAMPLE COMPANY, INC.

Waterfall Analysis
As of April 30, 2002

	January 2002	February 2002	March 2002	April 2002	May 2002	June 2002	July 2002
CASH (on hand)							
Budget	7,000	6,600	6,050	5,575	5,075	4,625	4,125
February 2002	7,050	6,550	6,200	5,850	5,500	5,150	4,800
March 2002			5,850	5,550	5,250	4,950	4,650
April 2002				5,150	4,750	4,350	3,950
CASH BURN RATE (Monthly)							
Budget	400	400	550	475	500	450	500
February 2002	350	500	350	350	350	350	350
March 2002			700	300	300	300	300
April 2002				700	400	400	400
REVENUE (Monthly)							
Budget	300	300	350	500	500	600	600
February 2002	300	250	350	400	500	550	600
March 2002			200	350	400	500	500
April 2002				400	400	500	500
TOTAL EXPENSES (monthly)							
Budget	600	625	800	850	900	950	1,000
February 2002	550	600	700	800	800	900	900
March 2002			800	800	800	900	900
April 2002				900	700	750	800

Cash, Burn Rate, Revenue & Expenses Table

SAMPLE COMPANY

Income Statement and Variance Analysis
April 30, 2002
(In thousands)

	MONTH			YEAR TO DATE		
	Actual	Budget	Variance	Actual	Budget	Variance
Revenues	$ 400	$ 500	$ (100)	$ 1,150	$ 1,450	$ (300)
Net Revenue	**400**	**500**	**(100)**	**1,150**	**1,450**	**(300)**
Cost of Goods Sold	200	200	-	950	950	-
Gross Margin	**200**	**300**	**(100)**	**200**	**500**	**(300)**
Operating Expenses						
Sales & Marketing	-	100	100	-	125	125
Research & Development	500	400	(100)	1,400	1,200	(200)
General & Adminstration	200	150	(50)	500	600	100
Operating Expenses	700	650	(50)	1,900	1,925	25
Operating Income	**(500)**	**(350)**	**(150)**	**(1,700)**	**(1,425)**	**(275)**
Interest Income/(Expense)	(20)	(25)	5	(100)	(150)	50
Net Income/(Loss)	**$ (520)**	**$ (375)**	**$ (145)**	**$ (1,800)**	**$ (1,575)**	**$ (225)**
Employee Headcount	**40**	**35**	**(5)**	**40**	**35**	**(5)**
Revenue per Employee (Annualized)	**$ 120**	**$ 171**	**$ (51)**	**$ 86**	**$ 124**	**$ (38)**
Number of Customers (Cumulative)	**5**	**8**	**(3)**	**20**	**30**	**(10)**
Revenue per Customer (Annualized)	**$ 960**	**$ 750**	**$ 210**	**$ 173**	**$ 48**	**$ 124**
Cash	**$ 5,150**	**$ 5,575**	**$ (425)**	**$ 5,150**	**$ 5,575**	**$ (425)**
Change In Cash	**$ (700)**	**$ (475)**	**$ (225)**	**$ (2,250)**	**$ (1,825)**	**$ (425)**

Cash, Burn Rate, Revenue & Expenses

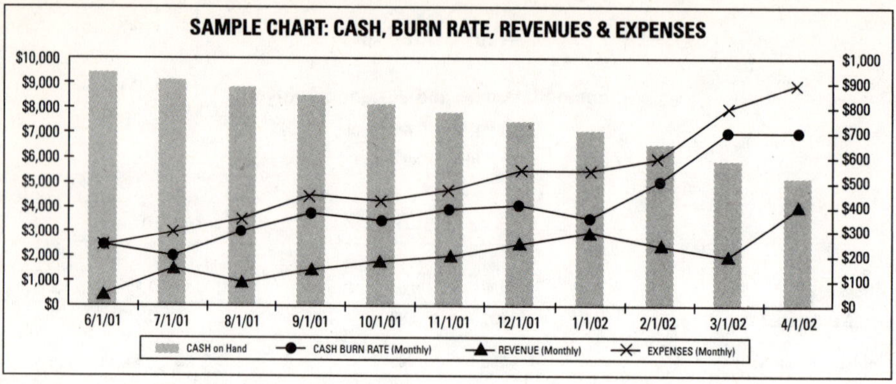

Capitalization Table

SAMPLE COMPANY
Capitalization Table
April 30, 2002

	Common	Price	Series A	Series A Price	Warrants	Price	SeriesB	Options	Price	Total	%
Employee 1	2,000	$0.01	-		-		-	-		2,000	7.1%
Employee 2	2,000	$0.01	-		-		-	-		2,000	7.1%
Employee 3	600	$0.01	-		-		-	-		600	2.1%
Employee 4	300	$0.01	-		-		-	-		300	1.1%
Employee 5	200	$0.01	-		-		-	-		200	0.7%
Employee 6	100	$0.01	-		-		-	-		100	0.4%
Employee Options Outstanding	50	$0.01	-		-		-	2,000	$0.30	2,050	7.3%
Other Options Outstanding	-		-		-		-	100	$0.30	100	0.4%
Total Employees/Consultants	**5,250**		**-**		**-**		**-**	**2,100**		**7,350**	**26.0%**
Investors											
Investor 1	-		10,000	$1.00	2,000	$0.20	-	-		2,000	42.5%
Investor 2	-		4,000	$1.00	800	$0.20	-	-		4,800	17.0%
Investor 3	-		2,000	$1.00	400	$0.20	-	-		2,400	8.5%
Investor 4	-		1,000	$1.00	200	$0.20	-	-		1,200	4.2%
Investor 5	-		100	$1.00	-		-	-		100	0.4%
Investor 6	-		100	$1.00	-		-	-		100	0.4%
Investor 7	-		100	$1.00	-		-	-		100	0.4%
Investor 8	-		100	$1.00	-		-	-		100	0.4%
Investor 9	-		100	$1.00	-		-	-		100	0.4%
Total Investors	**-**		**17,500**		**3,400**		**-**	**-**		**20,900**	**74.0%**
Total	**5,250**		**17,500**	**$1.00**	**3,400**	**$0.20**	**-**	**2,100**	**$0.30**	**28,250**	**100.0%**
Authorized	**20,000**		**30,000**							**50,000**	
Paid in Capital		**$53**		**17,500**						**17,553**	

APPENDIX IV: Sample Investment-Policy Statement

Included here is a standard investment policy as a guide. The policy will place emphasis on

- Preservation of capital
- Liquidity
- Tax deferment
- Simplicity

Corporate Investment Policy

Purpose

To establish corporate guidelines and responsibilities regarding the investment of surplus cash balances.

Objectives

To utilize cash not immediately required by operations with the objective of

- Preserving capital
- Maintaining liquidity
- Maximizing return
- Reducing tax liability

Administration

Corporate cash investments can be made by the CFO, Vice President of Finance, Controller, Treasurer, or other individuals approved by the Chief Financial Officer.

Policy

Permissible instruments:

- Treasury bills, notes, bonds, or other obligations of the U.S. Government or agency securities guaranteed by the U.S. Government
- Repurchase agreements (backed by instruments stated in the preceding bullet) of any approved bank of financial institution
- Money market–fund shares of an approved institution with assets in excess of one billion dollars

- Corporate and bank debt including, but not limited to, commercial paper, Eurodollar, Yankee and Cayman Island deposits, corporate bonds, medium-term notes, bankers' acceptances, certificates of deposit, master notes, floating-rate notes, and auction-rate securities
- Municipal notes, bonds, tax-exempt commercial paper, municipal auction-rate securities, and municipal preferred stock
- Auction-rate preferred stock

Constraints

- **Ratings.** Minimum ratings for all permissible must fall under the following guidelines:
    - Short-term ratings must be A1 or P1 or equivalent.
    - Long-term ratings must be A or equivalent.
    - Approved rating agencies include Standard & Poors (S&P), Moody's, Duff and Phelps, Fitch, and Bank Watch.
- **Maturity.** The maximum maturity for the portfolio will be no longer than two years. The average maturity of the portfolio may not exceed 12 months.
- **Sovereign risks.** Not more than 25% of the portfolio can be invested in any one country outside the United States.
- **Weighting.** At the time of purchase, no security can represent the greater of $1,000,000 or more than 10% of the portfolio, with the exception of treasuries and government agencies, which can be 100% of the portfolio.
- **Custodians.** Investments will be held in a custodial account, or safe-kept in a broker's segregated account.
- **Insurance.** Brokerage accounts must carry a minimum of $2,500,000 in insurance.

APPENDIX V: 12 Strategies for Estate Planning[1]

1. Annual Exclusion Gifts

Individuals can gift $11,000 per year indexed for inflation to an unlimited number of beneficiaries—$22,000 per year if married and a couple elects to "gift split." Annual exclusion gifts are not subject to the generation-skipping transfer tax. Gifts paid directly to educational institutions for tuition payments and gifts made to cover medical costs are not subject to gift tax.

2. Minority Interest Gifts

A lifetime gift of a minority interest in a closely held corporation or family limited partnership is effective because of the leveraging available. A married couple can make a gift to their child of a 10% interest in their business, worth $300,000. This gift should qualify for a minority interest valuation discount (assume 33 1/3%)[3], which would lower the value of the gift to $20,000. By applying their annual exclusions, they may be able to avoid any taxable gift.

3. Estate Tax Applicable Exemption Amount

The current applicable exemption amount of $675,000 increases to $1,000,000 in 2002 and is then subject to the following schedule:

2002–2003	$1,000,000
2004–2005	$1,500,000
2006, 2007, 2008	$2,000,000
2009	$3,500,000
2010	$0 and
2011	$1,000,000

Beginning in 2002 and thereafter, the applicable exemption amount for the gift tax will be $1,000,000 ($675,000 in 2001). A lifetime gift transfers not only the principal, but also all the appreciation between the time of the gift and the time the person dies. Unlimited gifts can be made between U.S. citizen spouses without incurring a gift tax.

1 "12 Strategies for Estate Planning," New York Life Insurance Company, August 2001.

2 These strategies are for informational purposes only and do not guarantee or predict the results of any particular case.

3 Determining the appropriate valuation discount is the responsibility of an individual's own tax and legal advisors.

4. Unlimited Marital Deduction

A husband or wife can leave everything outright or in a qualifying marital deduction trust without incurring any estate tax on the first death. Non-citizen spouses must use a QDOT (Qualified Domestic Trust) to take advantage of the unlimited marital deduction.

5. Gifts to Grandchildren—GSTT Exemption

The GSTT is a complicated transfer tax that involves gifts to a so-called "skip" generation, such as grandchildren. Individuals have a $1,000,000 GSTT exemption indexed for inflation (currently $1,060,000).[4] If that $1,000,000 is allocated to gifts placed in trust for grandchildren, and these gifts are then used to buy insurance on a second-to-die basis on the grandparents, the amount that can be transferred without incurring a GSTT is magnified.[5]

6. Irrevocable Life Insurance Trust (ILIT)

The insured may create an ILIT specifically designed to be the owner and the beneficiary of life-insurance policies outside the insured's taxable estate. The trust can be funded with single and/or survivorship life policies. On the death of the insured(s), the trustee, using discretionary powers, can buy appreciated assets from the estate of the surviving spouse, so the appreciation will be in the trust and pass estate-tax free. The cash in the estate can be used to provide income or general liquidity as it is needed.

7. Charitable Gifts of Life Insurance

Life insurance can be an appropriate vehicle for gifting. The following are some of the ways it can be used as part of a charitable giving program:

- **Making a gift of a current policy.** The donor names the charity as the irrevocable beneficiary of the policy and assigns the ownership rights, including the ability to surrender the policy for cash or to create loans. The income-tax deduction is either the fair-market value of the policy or its cost basis, whichever is less.

---

4 Note: For estates of decedents dying and generation-skipping transfers after 12/31/2003, the GSTT exemption will equal the increased unified credit exemption equivalent amount against estate tax.

5 Under the 2001 Tax Act, the GSTT is scheduled for repeal after 2009.

- **Make the charity the beneficiary of a policy.** A donor can name a charity as the beneficiary of a policy while maintaining all ownership rights, including access to the cash value. On the insured's death, an estate-tax deduction is available to the estate for the amount of the proceeds.
- **Charity purchases a new policy.** Here the charity is the owner and beneficiary of the policy (subject to state insurable interest requirements). The donor is the insured and makes annual cash contributions to the charity equal to or greater than the amount of the premium. An income-tax deduction and a gift-tax deduction are available for the amount of the premium paid.

8. Charitable Remainder Annuity or Unitrust

A donor generally gifts a highly appreciated asset to a charitable remainder trust (CRT). A percentage of the income goes to the donor for his or her lifetime or a term of years up to 20. At the donor's death, the remainder interest is transferred to the charity. Because an asset has been transferred to the charity, insurance is used to replace the asset that's been gifted to the charity.

9. Charitable Lead Trust

In a charitable lead trust (CLT), an interest is paid to the charity for the term of the trust. At the end of the trust term, the principal is paid out to a named beneficiary. The CLT can provide a federal estate-tax deduction that can reduce or in some cases zero out the estate tax on the transfer to an heir.

10. Personal Residence Trust

An individual can place his or her primary residence (or vacation home) in trust and retain the use of the house for a term of years with the house passing to the children at the end of the trust term. The value of the parent's interest is subtracted from the value of the house in determining the gift amount. This gifting technique can reduce the transfer taxes on a house given to children.

11. Grantor Retained Annuity Trust (GRAT)

A GRAT may be useful with stock in a growing business concern (especially S corporations and partnerships). The IRS has developed valuation tables to place a value on a person's ownership interest in property or trust. These tables assume that a business will grow at a rate that is based on existing interest rates. Through the use of a GRAT, the growth of the stock of a closely held business or any other asset, that exceeds the IRS rate, can be transferred with minimal or no transfer costs to children. The donor must survive the term of the trust and the asset transferred must produce a return over the rate selected by the donor.

12. Disclaimers

Planned Disclaimer Will

In spite of the potential estate taxes saved by the unified credit, some married couples want to be able to leave everything to each other outright, usually when the size of combined estates is moderate and the surviving spouse wants control of the inheritance. A planned disclaimer will leave everything to the surviving spouse outright, but allows any disclaimed amount to pass to a *by-pass* (unified credit) trust that gives the spouse a lifetime income interest. This gives the surviving spouse the flexibility to take the inheritance outright or choose the savings generated by a credit-shelter trust while being assured of a lifetime income.

Qualified Disclaimer

Although many estate-planning tools are used primarily during an individual's lifetime, a qualified disclaimer is one of the so-called post-mortem estate-planning tools. With a qualified disclaimer, an individual, often the surviving spouse, can effectively shift wealth to the children by using the deceased spouse's estate tax unified credit even though his or her will didn't take advantage of this estate-planning tool. A beneficiary may disclaim life insurance or annuity proceeds subject to the rules with regard to qualified disclaimers.

BIBLIOGRAPHY

Bagley, Constance E. (Stanford Business School) and Dauchy, Craig E. (Cooley Godward LLP). *The Entrepreneurs Guide to Business Law.* South-Western Pub. August 2002

Ernst & Young. *Audit Committees: Providing Oversight in Challenging Times*, Ernst & Young. 2002

Ernst & Young. *Ernst & Young's Doing Business in the United States*. 2002.

Ernst & Young. *The Ernst & Young Financial Planning Guide: Take Control of Your Money for a Lifetime of Wealth*. October 2001.

Ernst & Young. *The Ernst & Young Guide to Financing for Growth*. March 2001.

Ernst & Young. *The Ernst & Young Guide to Mergers and Acquisitions, 2nd Edition*. Mar 2001.

Ernst & Young. *The Ernst & Young Guide to Taking Your Company Public*. February 1995.

Ernst & Young. *The Ernst & Young LLP Guide to the IPO Value Journey*. June 2001.

Ernst & Young. *The Ernst & Young Tax Guide*. January 2002.

Ernst & Young. *The Ernst & Young Tax Savers Guide*. October 2001.

KPMG LLP. *Defining the Digital Future—Business and Accounting Issues*. 2001.

KPMG LLP. *Software Revenue Recognition—An Analysis of SOP 97-2*. 2000.

KPMG LLP. *Starting and Running Your Own Business*. 2001

KPMG LLP. *Stock Compensation Handbook*. 2001

eight 8

CHAPTER

Marketing and Sales

Chair: Vijay Bobba, Partner - **The McKenna Group**
Co-Chair: Venktesh Shukla - **Everypath Inc.**
Lokesh Jindal - **The McKenna Group**
Jayaram Bhat - **Jayaram Bhat & Associates**
Kelly Breslin Wright - **AT HOC**

Introduction

The words *passion* and *entrepreneur* go hand-in-hand. Even so, passion alone will not turn an entrepreneur's dream into reality. Witness the numbers that John Nesheim cites in "High Tech Start Up"[1]: He says that most start-up companies don't even get to the funding stage, and of those that do, 60% go bankrupt. Another reality check: 40% of new businesses fail within the first five years of operation.

There are two major reasons for these failures:

- Most entrepreneurs don't figure out the right way to take their technology to market; too often, they show lack of focus, poor differentiation, and improper execution.
- Potential investors never get to a comfort factor about the company; clear business propositions are lacking or time-to-revenue projections are unrealistic.

As an entrepreneur, in order to attract customers and reassure investors you must have—and you must be *seen* to have—a razor-sharp marketing strategy. Indeed, this may be the biggest bugaboo you face; in a recent TiE meeting on storage

1 Nesheim, John. High Tech Start Up. Simon & Schuster. 2000.

solutions, fully 90% of the entrepreneurs in the audience said their biggest problem was in marketing their solutions.

Fortunately, you can learn from the mistakes of others. Strategic-marketing problems tend to fall into three buckets, related to focus, differentiation, and execution.

Focus

Too many entrepreneurs are highly opportunistic. They're so hungry for customers that they go after every lead and every possible opportunity. Doing this will keep you busy, but it's not likely to win you a lot of business. You're more likely to be successful if you focus on a few customers and market segments that you have clearly identified as your best possible targets. Remember: If you bite off more than you can chew, you'll end up with indigestion.

At the other end of the food chain, some entrepreneurs are far too narrowly focused. If you start out in a niche market without a clear view of how you can leverage that space later to expand into other target markets, then you will be stuck with a limited business market. "Starvation" is the result.

note Oddly, in the world of business, starvation isn't considered as bad as indigestion. That's because if you recognize your problem early enough, you will still have the opportunity to re-position your company—whereas in the indigestion scenario, you waste so much time and energy chasing every lead that, as a result, you may have no resources left when you finally realize your mistake.

Differentiation

Having a product with "me too" positioning, or a product that is "nice-to-have" rather than one that solves a significant problem for the user, won't cut it. Your solution must be a "have-to-have," and you must be able to clearly explain why.

Too often, entrepreneurs come up with an idea for a product or a service whose benefits to the target market are only incremental. As a newcomer, you must have a solution or a service that is a quantum leap over existing competitive offerings. It's also important that the benefits of your solution—what sets it apart—rise above the pure technology level. Unless your product or service also provides (or at least addresses) a whole solution to your customers' needs, they will have trouble understanding where they'll get their ROI—and you'll face problems trying to position your company with the right messaging and business model.

Execution

High praise for a preschooler (and an indication of future academic success) is "Plays well with others"; you should make that your goal too. Every market and every company is part of an ecosystem, consisting of channels, technology partners, system integrators, and so on. Members of the ecosystem work together to fulfill the needs of the customer. By joining an existing ecosystem, you will benefit from the resources, access to customers, and leverage opportunities that already exist. A reactive and non-leverageable approach and/or lack of an appropriate business model will only hurt your chances for success.

Take the storage industry, for example. It has at the least three established ecosystems around the major companies Veritas, EMC, and Brocade. These large companies own access to the customer, and also work with a number of other industry partners. If you're a storage start-up, you should pick the ecosystem where your value proposition resonates the most, and align yourself accordingly. This will enable you to leverage all the market relationships that are already in place as part of the ecosystem!

CAUTION: You can't just announce that you're playing with the other kids and expect them to welcome you with open arms. First, you must observe how they play together, and figure out where you'll fit in. In the business world, this means thinking through the appropriate business model—at the solution, application, platform, module, or tool level. For example, some firms attempt to market services and products and eventually fail miserably in both because the business model for marketing services is fundamentally different from that of marketing products and vice versa. The CEO of an IT-services firm gives this example: "IT service providers address the customer problem by *owning* the customer pain, while product providers address the customer problem by *solving* the customer pain point."

Marketing Versus Sales

Marketing is the process of identifying the customer segments and their pain points, defining sustainable differentiation, and positioning the solution. The ultimate responsibility of marketing is to create a winning product. *Sales*, on the other hand, is the actual act of delivering the product to the customer in return for money (or something else of value). Sales requires deep investigation of specific and individual customer situations, and includes the decision-making process, assessing specific needs, and tailoring the solution to create maximum value. The ultimate responsibility of sales is to create win-win relationships.

Marketing Versus Sales

Marketing	*Sales*
Focus on customer segments.	Focus on individual customers.
Strategic.	Transactional.
Product tailored to average customer demand.	Product matched to specific customer demand.
Creates a winning product.	Creates win-win relationships.

Business Marketing and Sales

To be successful in business marketing and sales, you must have clear strategies in each of the following areas:

- Company marketing
- Product marketing
- Marketing communications
- Strategic sales

Your broader marketing strategy will address issues ranging from the type of business opportunity that you're targeting to the differentiated position that your company has in the market. A well-defined marketing strategy will minimize the focus, differentiation, and execution risks described previously.

In order to develop a robust product marketing plan, you must figure out how you will define your whole product, develop a compelling value proposition and optimal pricing plan, and identify various routes to market. In addition, you must define compelling messages, identify the audience to deliver the messages to, and develop an implementation plan. Finally, you must win your first few customers and ensure that they, in turn, will provide you with the kind of references you need to help you scale your business. All these topics are discussed for the remainder of the chapter.

Strategic Marketing

Getting customers to try, never mind accept, a new product or a service is extremely challenging. Because your resources, starting out, are likely to be limited, you need to clearly define your business goal with your customers in mind. Your goal has to coincide with what makes sense for your target customers.

To have a realistic chance of customers accepting your new product or service, you have to choose the right customers. They must demonstrate a need for what you're offering, be able to justify the cost, and have the money to pay you for it! In return, you must be able to clearly articulate what pain point you are healing for your customers, and why your solution is superior to and different from those of your competitors. Strategic marketing is fundamentally about positioning the company in a way that these criteria are met.

Defining Your Business

The first step to creating a successful company is being able to define what business it is in. To define your business, you must drill down from the big picture to the specifics. Are you building a product or providing a service? Are you going to make middleware or an end application? Will you have an application-development platform or a toolset? What is your business model?

Suppose, for example, that you have developed some technology that can be used as a tool to streamline IT operations, something that can be embedded in certain IT devices, or that can be leveraged to create a full-fledged piece of application software. In all three instances, although the basic technology is the same, the customer and the associated market infrastructure are very different. Money spent pursuing one opportunity cannot be leveraged for any of the other opportunities, especially when you are new to the market. That's why, right from the beginning, it is extremely important that you decide which one of the three opportunities you want to pursue, and put all your resources behind that goal. After you are successfully entrenched in the space you have targeted, you can decide whether you want to pursue the other businesses.

Choosing which strategy to pursue depends on a number of factors:

- **Your goal as an entrepreneur.** What business do you want to be in? What drives you?
- **Size and growth.** Is the business benefit related to a problem that has a significant market? Or if the market is small today, is it likely to grow fast?
- **Uniqueness of your solution.** Is the business benefit that your solution provides significantly different from that of the competition? How established is competition in that sector? (This is the "It's better to be different than to be better" school of thought.)
- **Your ability to enter an existing ecosystem.** It is almost impossible to break into new markets without becoming a part of an existing ecosystem. Choose a domain in which there is a realistic chance of establishing the necessary relationships to enter the ecosystem.
- **The sustainability of your ability to differentiate.** Can you create barriers to entry after you have established yourself in the segment? Does scale give you any benefit over later entrants?

What Is a Business Benefit? How Do I Define It?

Although your goal is to be able to state the business benefits of your technology or service, start from where you are most comfortable—that is, articulating the technology characteristics or features.

- List the characteristics or the key features of your technology or service.
- State the business benefits that are derived from the characteristics that you've articulated.

Let's use the storage-industry start-up discussed earlier as an example:

- **Technology characteristics:**
  - Allows bi-directional flow of information
  - Has all standard protocols (i.e. CORBA, SNMP, etc.)
  - Has pre-built interfaces with all types of storage elements including SANs, NAS etc.
  - Enables multi-vendor interoperability in a storage environment
  - Allows both monitoring and control of heterogeneous devices
- **Business benefit:** Reduces cost (TCO) of storage by enabling the entire storage to be treated as a single pool rather than silos dedicated to specific applications

What If My Technology Is Much More Generic and Thus There Are Numerous Business Benefits?

An astonishing number of young entrepreneurs are too opportunistic, pursuing every prospect afforded by the marketplace. In trying to gobble up everything on the menu, they lose focus, and thus hurt their chances of success.

Resources are always limited for start-ups—and not just monetary resources! You will also face limits on your human resources (and risk stretching the tech wizard too thin) and time (your window of opportunity). Your strategy must have three key components: Focus, focus, and focus!

Identifying Your Customer

A technology idea without customers should stay in the research labs of the government or universities. As a small start-up, even before you start developing your technology, you should have a very clear view of who your customers will be. To figure out who your customers will be, do the following:

- List the pain points that are solved by the defined business benefits.

- List the characteristics of companies likely to have those pain points.
- Define a segmentation for those companies.

Let's continue with the storage example, whose business benefit reduces the cost of storage by enabling the entire storage to be treated as a single pool rather than silos dedicated to specific applications:

- **Pain points:**
  - Extremely high cost of managing storage
  - Increasing storage costs due to rapidly increasing storage requirements
  - Unable to lower cost by optimizing capacity across applications/ storage systems
  - High cost due to over-specification of system for transient requirements
- **Customer segment characteristics:**
  - Companies that use multiple applications requiring large amounts of storage
  - Companies that have multiple standards in storage systems either due to M&A activities or non-centralized organic growth
  - Companies with significant transient storage requirements
- **Potential customer segments:** Broadly speaking, large enterprises. Transient requirement would be in sectors like retail, where holiday shopping generates spikes; in media companies; and so on.

How Do I Choose My Target Customer Segments?

Now that you have a list of potential customers, you need to further narrow the segments. Consider the following:

- **Level of pain.** Does your offering resolve the primary needs of the target segment? Does it solve 80% of the problem, or only 20% of the problem?
- **Length of sales cycle.** Is the sales cycle in a particular segment(s) likely to be much larger or shorter than in other segments?
- **Ease of access.** Is there a segment in which you have better access through management-team contacts or board-level contacts?
- **Geographical proximity.** Is a significant percentage of the segment concentrated in your region?

What If My Initial Chosen Market Segment Is Too Narrow? How Do I Grow Beyond That?

The "beachhead approach" is a proven method for accelerating market adoption, reducing costs of sales, and building the base of customer references that you will need to expand into the broader market.

If you have outgrown your initial market, you should evaluate all the segments within the market, and then determine which are experiencing the most pain points that your solution can address. With this knowledge, you can prioritize potential beachheads according to their attractiveness and your ability to reach and serve them effectively.

note Interestingly, the market segment that needs your solution the most is not necessarily the ideal candidate. The best beachhead is the one that gives you the most influence over the other segments in the market, and gives you a realistic point of entry.

To expand beyond the initial beachhead, you must leverage your market influence by delving deeper into the customer base of the same market in which you have established relationships. You need to leverage product influence by introducing the same product to different markets, which will be influenced by the success of the product in other markets.

Defining the Problem That You Solve

Starting with your technology or service and reaching the relevant customer segment gives you a good "inside-out" perspective. The next step is to take the "outside-in" perspective. Start with the customer, and determine whether he really feels the pain in your chosen field. Is the pain a minor headache? Or is it a migraine? This will tell you whether he is willing to pay for curing the pain, and if so, how much.

Staying with the previously mentioned storage example, it is essential to talk to "suspect" target customers to find out what pain they are feeling in the area of storage. If the "migraine" is that the cost of managing existing storage is very high, while the prospect of buying more storage is only a "headache," then the customer is unlikely to pay for your solution if positioned in the way described here. That's because your solution works to avoid incurring more cost on storage hardware, but does not necessarily reduce the cost of managing existing storage.

What If the Target Customers Do Not Have a Strong Need for My Product?

Although some customers may exhibit interest in your product, they may only provide you a false sense of demand. When it comes to opening their purse strings, you may well hit a roadblock. In that case, you need to ask the following:

- **Is it possible to leverage my technology to ease the migraine rather than the headache?** Use primary research and in-depth customer interviews to really identify the migraine. Then, evaluate whether you can architect a solution to solve the migraine. This will involve some costs and may force you to consider some solution partnerships, but your overall value proposition will then resonate with the customer.
- **Have I missed other customer segments in which the problem that my solution solves *is* the migraine?** Consider the possibility that you are targeting the wrong customer segment. Re-evaluate your segmentation and, if necessary, broaden the scope of the primary research and customer interviews to identify the right segment.
- **Is this market so nascent that this issue will become a strong need in, say, two years?** If you are convinced that the problem is a growing one and will definitely become a migraine in a couple years, then you must address what you can do to sustain yourself in the interim.

Last but not the least, there is always the possibility that your technology just doesn't cut it. Your goal should be to have as many in-depth customer discussions as possible to detect this early (while you still have resources left), and to take corrective measures. Set parameters on when you will make the hard decision.

What If My Technology Solves Only Part of the Customer Pain Point?

It is very unlikely that the customer is going to assemble pieces of a puzzle to fulfill a need. You must ensure that your product is complete and can actually solve a business problem. Of course, it is not necessary that you provide *all* the pieces of the puzzle. If you feel that other companies are better equipped to provide those technology pieces, then you should seriously consider partnering scenarios. Sometimes, the zeal to provide the complete solution yourself ends up diluting the value proposition of your technology.

Adoption of an unfamiliar product can be accelerated when you make it easy for your customers to integrate the new technology into their lives. This means providing complementary services and creating a superior customer experience: It's the creation of the total solution. In fact, Core technology usually is less than 50% of the total solution. That is why companies must consider all aspects of a customer's needs and give equal consideration to service elements and other customer-experience elements.

Because no product or company exists in a vacuum, a total solution will have implications on your product, partners, and business model. New technology companies must create a sustainable market infrastructure or ecosystem for continued business success. This entails building technology partnerships to deliver a total solution and marketing partnerships to leverage established players with reach and wherewithal. Your business model should then ensure that you create value for all the players in the ecosystem. This will enable you to create three key ingredients for success: scale, credibility, and access.

Positioning the Company

Positioning is the result of the analysis you have done so far. Understanding the target customer segments, their needs or pain points, competitive solutions, and your differentiation allows you to define the positioning of the company. You will know that you have attained the elusive goal of correctly positioning your company when you can clearly answer the following questions:

- **Who.** Who is my target customer segment?
- **What.** What pain points does my solution address?
- **Which.** In which category does my solution belong? Where does it stand in the value chain?
- **How.** How do I solve the pain point? What is the business benefit of my solution? Who are the main competitors, and how am I differentiated?

What Are the Criteria for Good Positioning?

Asking yourself the following three simple questions will provide you with the answer to this question:

- Does my offering resolve the primary needs of the target segment? Does it make a compelling argument for solving it?
- Can I provide evidence or demonstrate that my offering's promise is true? Customers will not believe in a plain statement.
- Am I the only supplier of this solution? A simple test here would be to replace your name in the statement with that of your primary competitors and see if it still makes sense. If it does, you are in trouble!

What Is a Brand? How Essential Is It to Develop a Brand for Technology Products and Services?

Branding, which is often confused with advertising, is closely related to positioning, but occurs more at the corporate level. The larger the company and the more products it has in its portfolio, the more important it becomes to link them with a common branding theme. Simply put, a brand has two components:

- **A promise.** A brand signifies a promise of delivery. The promise could be as simple as quenching thirst to something more esoteric like keeping you young. Sometimes, the promise can be abstracted to the level of values like honesty, integrity, and so on. The higher the level of abstraction, the more sustainable the brand—but the art of maintaining and communicating the essence of the brand becomes more and more difficult.
- **Consumer perception on whether the brand's promise is fulfilled.** This is the trickier part—ensuring that the customers believe in the promise of the brand (that is, making sure their experience is in line with the promise).

Although the basic tenets are the same, branding is very different between consumer goods and business goods or services. Even within business, technology has its own nuances. For start-ups in particular, it is important to know that every customer experience and every interaction in the ecosystem builds the brand. It is also imperative to realize that branding is not about telling the world who you are, but is about knowing what you stand for and sticking to it.

Essentially, technology brands—especially for companies offering products and services to other businesses—are all about evidence. The brand is created through consistent delivery on the promise. This evidence is then leveraged through a set of market participants to create an ecosystem that sustains and propagates the brand. (See the section "Marketing Communications" later in this chapter for more information.) As an entrepreneur, your focus should primarily be in creating the evidence that can be referenced, including case studies with marquee customers. For now, don't worry about mass propagation of your brand.

If you're not sold on this idea, consider Intel. For years, Intel was a B2B company. It never advertised its brand. For most of its customers, however, Intel, as a brand, always meant "dependable, reliable, and at the edge of technology." This was created through evidence—that is, years and years of delivering on Moore's Law. In fact, the "Intel Inside" advertising campaign was started at a time when Intel already had 80% of the market share. In the case of Intel, then, the creation of brand happened much before the mass communication of the brand.

Making Sure You Are Right

Apart from sales themselves, there are a number of signals—both internal and external— that can indicate whether you have created a strong company positioning.

Evidence of Weak Positioning

Internal	*External*
Tendency to copy competition versus innovate	Alliances difficult to secure
Sales force complains about high prices, inconsistent sales messages	Weak relationships with influencers and distribution
	Product/company not included in surveys, roundups

Evidence of Strong Positioning

Internal	*External*
Employee groups on same wavelength, can articulate positioning	Company and products/services highly visible
Company appears proactive, not reactive	Infrastructure acknowledges products/services are clearly differentiated
	Customers understand value proposition

Product Marketing

Your first priority is to get your product to market quickly—even if the technology you are developing has lots of functionality and you have ideas for a lot more. If you wait for all these features to be ready, you may run out of money before you get your product to market. One of the most critical things you have to do is to figure out the minimum set of features to get the first few customers and reference accounts, and set the stage for future growth. This is the responsibility of product marketing. At this early stage, however, you may not have product marketing or product managers to focus on this critical task. Therefore, the task of releasing the first product may fall on the shoulders of the founding team.

Product marketing is a very important function within a company. It is the link between R&D and customers. Product marketing responsibilities include

- Understanding customer requirements
- Prioritizing these requirements
- Converting a prioritized list of requirements into a product-requirements document

- Negotiating with R&D to come up with a list of features for the product release
- Reviewing the features as early releases of the product become available
- Managing the alpha and beta testing
- Product launch and communication with the market and sales channels
- Continuing to manage the product development and launch process for follow-on versions of the products

Product managers or product-marketing managers can be considered to be the business managers of their product. They define the positioning and come up with the strategy and messages for communicating with the outside world, which, in turn, drives the communication, advertising, and collateral strategy. They train the sales force, systems engineers, and channel partners. They are also responsible for keeping tabs on the competition.

Clearly, product-marketing managers must have a diverse range of skills. They must be technical enough to earn the respect of R&D, and in addition require in-depth technical knowledge in the product area—ideally both from a developer and user perspective. They must be very good communicators, who can tell the difference between product features and benefits.

What Is the Difference Between Product Management and Product Marketing?

Some large companies break the product-marketing function into product marketing and product management. Product managers tend to be more technically oriented and work with R&D to define the product, while product-marketing managers work on the outbound communications. Usually, however, it is better to have one person own both product-management and product-marketing functions because it is difficult to specialize in communications if you're not close to both the customers and the technology. This is especially true for small companies and start-ups. So when we use the term *product marketing*, we're including both product marketing and product management; we're using the term *product manager* to refer to an individual in this field.

tip Many companies make the mistake of hiring a technically astute but inexperienced person as a product manager. It's imperative that you hire a professional, experienced marketing manager early in your company's life. A good marketing professional can make all the difference between success and failure for your company!

What Are the Main Tasks of Product Marketing?

The function of marketing in an organization can be best described as the four "P"s, a concept outlined by Philip Kotler in *Principles of Marketing*:

- **Product.** The technology and everything that goes with it, including user documentation, training, support, and integration with other products—in short, everything needed to get the most benefits from your product as efficiently and as quickly as possible.
- **Price.** How much you should charge for your offering.
- **Promotion.** All communications with the outside world, including marketing communications, public relations, advertising, and so on.
- **Place.** The various sales and distribution channels through which the product is sold to customers.

Product

Although the original idea for the technology may have been developed by one of the founders, it is up to product marketing to mold it into a real product that customers will buy. A key role for product marketing is defining the product and developing a *market-requirements document* (MRD), also called the *product requirements document* (PRD). This document describes customers' needs and the product features necessary to address those. Product marketing uses this document to negotiate the final list of features in the upcoming product with development.

When you start out, you may be considering many features for your product. In order to get the product to market quickly, however, and to get a few early reference accounts, you must establish a minimum set of features that will address customers' needs. To do so, you'll need to go to customers to figure out what their needs are. Often, however, customers don't really know *what* they want. Your task is to uncover their most pressing problems and deduce the list of capabilities and features that you will need in the first version of your product. In the event this process results in a large number of requirements, you'll need to narrow the list to a minimum so that you can release your product in the shortest possible timeframe to make your product useful to the widest possible range of early customers.

You will never be able to respond to every request listed in the MRD. So how do you decide which ones to address and which ones to push out to the next release? You must prioritize by addressing those issues that give you the most bang for the buck:

- Which features do you need for competitive parity?
- Which features are unique and help you differentiate from the market?
- Which features solve the biggest problems for the largest number of customers?
- Which features have you promised to your largest customers?

What Do You Mean by Complete Product?

Just because you have completed the development of your product, it does not mean that the product is ready for customers. In order to create the *complete product*, you must make sure that the product is packaged appropriately. In addition, you must put user documentation and training in place so customers can start using your product effectively, and you have to set up a customer-support operation and call center in order to help customers when they have questions. Finally, you must price the product appropriately.

Product marketing works to set up the support, training, and documentation infrastructure in order to be ready for the product launch. Product marketing also works with sales channels and management to set the price structure for the product.

Price

How much should you charge? That is the proverbial $64,000 question. The price must be high enough for you to deliver a reasonable profit margin, but low enough to deliver an attractive return on investment for your customers. Although the cost of the product is an important factor, price should not be based only on cost. The cost of competing or substitute products/solutions also play a role in determining the price of your offering.

A low price can help build early market share, but if your competition can easily match your price, then a price war may ensue—which you, as a small company, may not be in a position to win. Except in the case of commodity markets, a low price does not provide a sustainable competitive advantage. On the other hand, a relatively high price can create a high perception of quality and value; as the saying goes, "You get what you pay for."

Pricing and packaging go hand in hand. You must decide whether to offer your product as a single offering or as a base product with several optional components. There are several advantages to breaking up the product into components; besides, in most cases, not all customers want all the features. By creating a base product with a common set of features, you can have a low entry price in the market. The optional components you offer will allow your customers to customize their solution to their specific needs as well as help you increase revenue opportunities. Such packaging also helps you draw attention to some exciting, unique, and valuable features of your product.

So what price should you charge? It is really up to you. Pricing is a subjective, inexact art. Even if you come up with a price after exhaustive market analysis, you may have to monitor market reaction and adjust your pricing strategy accordingly.

What Are Usage-Based Pricing and Term Licensing?

Until recently, a software product was offered with a perpetual license—that is, when customers paid for a product, they got to use in perpetuity. They also got updates and support for an annual fee—usually in the range of 15–20% of the price of the product. For consumer- and other lower-priced software products, support and product updates were priced separately. For example, if you buy Microsoft Office, you must purchase the next version when it comes out if you want to upgrade your system. The price for the upgrade is usually 20–40% of the price of the product.

Term licensing and usage-based licensing are new developments in software pricing. Instead of offering a perpetual license, software vendors are starting to offer monthly license-fee structures based on usage. For instance, you might have a license fee for a time period of months or years based on the number of users and/or CPUs and/or servers on your system. Such term licenses and usage-based pricing will include support and updates as well. These new license structures provide maximum flexibility for customers as well as predictable revenues for vendors.

Promotion

The product-marketing issues discussed previously are internally focused. Now that you have your complete product ready, however, it is time to discuss communications issues. Although marketing communications is discussed in detail later in this chapter, it is product-marketing organization's responsibility to come up with the messages that drive communications plans.

What Do You Mean by "The Messages"?

In order to create and execute an effective communications strategy, product marketing must create the "messages" about a product. *Messages* include information about the two or three key features and benefits of your product, described in a few simple and easy-to-understand sentences. Defining the messages for your product can be difficult and time-consuming because most people describe their product in terms of the underlying technology or technical features. You need to develop messages that are about the *benefits* of your product.

Messages should be simple and easy to understand, and should be used repeatedly and consistently throughout all product literature, presentations, and outbound communications. When communicating with people outside the company, everyone in the organization must consistently use the messages.

note You'll learn more about marketing messages later in this chapter, in the section "Marketing Communications."

How Do I Launch My Company and Products?

A number of milestones must be achieved before launching your company and products to the external world. The pre-launch process involves a number of activities. Following are some issues to consider and activities to complete as part of your launch process.

- **Timing.** "Not too early, not too late" is the motto here. If you launch too early without building credible evidence, then your long-term prospects suffer. If you launch too late, you are delaying your ability to scale and thus may be postponing critical revenue generation. You should launch when you have sufficient evidence both at the product and customer level, and when you believe that a wider dispersion of information will help the company scale.
- **Beta/reference customers.** Having a few (4–5) successful beta customers serves as excellent—indeed, probably the most important—evidence. Make sure that these customers are in your target market segment and are respected in the industry.
- **Ecosystem.** Although the launch will help you build your ecosystem, having a few marquee relationships—partners, system integrators, consultants, channels—before the launch helps in boosting the evidence.
- **Positioning.** Ensure that all employees, investors, and partners have the same understanding of the company's business, target market, and values. Inconsistent communication is more dangerous than no communication.
- **Presentation.** Develop one overall corporate presentation and multiple presentations targeted at different constituents of the market infrastructure, including potential investors, industry analysts, potential customers, technology enthusiasts, and so on. Tailor the message to meet their information needs.

- **Demonstration.** Create a portable demonstration of your product or service. Have different versions of the demo depending on your audience and how much time you are likely to get with it.
- **Materials.** Organize all material that you will need during the analyst and the press tours, including presentation copy, white papers, datasheets, customer contacts, analyst contacts, screen shots/photos, and drafts of press releases.

The actual launch will consist of an analyst tour, a press tour, the announcement, and follow-up. The importance of follow-up cannot be overstated. All questions that arise during the tours must be addressed with the relevant people within the promised timeframe. Remember that you are building long-term relationships here!

Place

One of the major responsibilities of product marketing is to train the sales force and/or channel partners. First, you must describe the target customer to the sales force. What kind of companies should sales go after? Which organization should sales seek out? What are the job titles to look for? Second, you must develop and provide a compelling sales presentation and, if applicable, a product demonstration. Third, you must describe the competition and competitive differentiators. Finally you have to help the sales force anticipate customer objections and show them how to overcome these objections.

If you have done your market segmentation correctly, you won't have any problem describing the target customer to your sales force. It is not enough to say that IT departments of global 2000 companies are your customers. You must be more specific. A good example of customer description is, "All vice presidents and directors of IT operations in banking, financial services, insurance, and manufacturing companies with revenues greater than $100 million in North America."

The sales presentation must be short, compelling, and hard-hitting. Fortunately, developing a sales presentation will be straightforward if you have done your homework by defining the messages and developing a list of features and benefits. A good sales presentation should describe the problem, explain how your solution addresses the problem, and describe features and benefits of your product. It should position your company and products properly and offer persuasive and compelling reasons why your prospect should buy the product. The presentation should take no more than 20–30 minutes and should be followed by a short supporting demonstration. You may be thinking, "My product has so many features that I cannot do justice to all of its capabilities by limiting the demo to 15–20 minutes." Keep in mind that the objective of the demonstration is *not* to show off its capabilities, but to make a sale. Making your product demonstration short, hard-hitting, and focused on key benefits will make the difference between getting the business and walking out empty-handed.

You also need to train the sales force to address objections. When a salesperson makes a presentation to a prospect, he or she will be faced with questions and objections. Customer objections may be about high prices, specific features or lack of features, competitive positioning, your company issues, and so on. Some of these objections may have been planted by your competition. By anticipating these questions and objections, coming up with answers and strategies, and training your sales force to handle them, you can help move the sales process along quickly.

Product marketing is also responsible for analyzing the competition. You must understand your competitors' products and strategies, and develop strategies of your own to compete effectively. It is not enough to simply be better, faster, or cheaper than the competition. You must be very creative in crafting your competitive strategy. You have to figure out how your products are different from those of your competition and how these differences provide you with a unique selling proposition (USP). There is a saying in marketing: "It is better to be different than better." Think about it!

Marketing Communications

Marketing communications is a platform to define the right messages, to identify the appropriate audience to receive the messages, and finally to deliver the messages to the relevant audience. All the activities involved in getting a company's desired marketing messages to its targets, regardless of the media used, constitute marketing communications.

Often, young companies have great difficulty defining messages in a clear, succinct, and simple language. They also fall victim to delivering wrong messages to wrong audiences! For example, The following is an example of a good message when talking to a potential customer, but a bad message when talking to a potential technology partner: "Our solutions can enable application development in hours as opposed to weeks, and thereby improve time to deployment by 50%." Similarly, the following is a good message when talking to a technology partner, but a bad message when talking to a customer: "By leveraging Semantic Web technology, we can quickly develop modular applications and thereby reduce the overall cost of deployment. Further, our technology is RDF-standards compliant and can interoperate with XML standards." These two examples clearly indicate the importance of not only the contents of the message (whether they are benefits specific or technology specific), but also the relevancy of the message to the audience!

The purpose of this section is to unravel the mystery behind the art of clear message definition and delivery. Remember that if you can't communicate clearly what your company does, then no customer or partner will ever hear your voice!

What Is an Elevator Pitch?

A good acid test on whether you have the right messages is your *elevator pitch.* Imagine that you are getting into an elevator for a short ride to the top of a building. Someone gets into the elevator with you, and asks you about your company and/or products. You need to be able to answer the question quickly—before the elevator reaches your listener's floor—in such a way that the listener leaves the elevator with a clear understanding of your company and products. If you can come up with an effective elevator pitch, you have your message.

How Do I Define the Contents of the Message?

Messaging is more than mere wordsmithing. A general rule of thumb is that messages should be catchy, simple, concise, and easy to understand. Further, they should be structured and logical, as they will be used repeatedly and consistently throughout all company literature, presentations, and outbound communications. Most importantly, a message should clearly address customer needs and benefits. It should be easily mapped and identified to a few key services/products/initiatives of the company. Further, messages should reflect a clear line of evidence.

Wrong Message

> *"Today, enterprises face an enormous cost in seamlessly integrating their partners' and strategic customers' infrastructure. XYZ's Web-services solutions are designed to precisely address that problem."*

Although this message is simple and concise, and clearly addresses the customer's pain point, it has three problems. First, it does not talk about customer benefit. Second, it is not clear on the company's product line or the initiative that the customer should know more about. Third, it is not believable, because it does not reflect any customer evidence. Evidence is what makes a claim believable!

Right Message

> *"Today, enterprises face an enormous cost in integrating their partners' and customers' infrastructure. By leveraging XYZ's new Everest Series solutions based on Web-services architecture, enterprises can expect to achieve 80% cost savings. XYZ's customers, by deploying the solution, saw more than 80% cost savings."*

This message clearly addresses the pitfalls mentioned previously and thus qualifies to be a right message.

What Are Customer Benefits? How Are They Different from Product Features?

Although messages must describe key customer benefits, many people find it difficult to articulate the value proposition in terms of benefit statements. They intuitively assume that the benefits are obvious if the product features are described. The fact that some early customers can intrinsically translate the features you describe into benefits only adds to this problem. Most mainstream customers, not being familiar with the technology, will not be able to translate features into benefits. Put simply: No benefits, no sales.

How can you identify a benefit when you see it? A *benefit* is the answer to the customer's question—what does it do for me? For example, these are benefits:

- Increases revenues by 15%.
- Reduces costs by 30%.
- Faster resolution of problems by 20%.
- Minimizes user errors by 90%.
- Reduces the number of service calls from 10 to 2 per week.
- Reduces the number of defects by 40%.
- Increases inventory turns from 6 to 8 per year.
- Lowers waste in the manufacturing process by 25%.

tip Quantifying the benefits with metrics is extremely effective. That is, saying "Lowers costs by 30%" is better than saying "Lowers costs."

The following, however, are *not* benefits:

- Java based multi-tier architecture using XML and J2EE.
- Monitors the performance of all users.
- Based on four-way symmetric multi-processors running at 32GHz.
- Provides real-time alerts.
- Compiles 20 million lines of code an hour.

Being able to clearly articulate the true benefits of your products is critical to your success. If your customers do not understand the benefits of your product, it is unlikely they will buy your product.

How Many Different Types of Messages Do I Develop?

A message must be developed to fulfill the informational needs of the target audience. At the highest level is an *umbrella message*, which sets the common theme or vision for all your audiences. Beyond that, broadly speaking, there are three types of messages:

- **Corporate message.** This primarily articulates the overall corporate strengths, including the key target market, size and growth, quality of the ecosystem (including executive management), key partners, and key customers. The primary purpose is to give an overall introduction of the company and to establish credibility at a business level. Typically, executive management uses the corporate message to describe the company's position.
- **Product message.** This message goes into the actual benefits that the product delivers and how it is differentiated. It also establishes the target customer segment and the competitive strength of the product (at the business level), as well as sending a clear message about the pain point that it solves. The product message is used by marketing and sales to communicate the product's benefits to customers.
- **Technology message.** This message provides the offering's key technical characteristics and highlights the technical differentiation. The technology message is used by the engineering community to describe either the core technology or the product architecture.

Each of these messages targets a different audience, and thus contains very different content and information. It is very important, however, to have the alignment across different levels. Otherwise, different sections of the company will tend to articulate the company's position in a different way, thereby confusing the market place. For example, the following messages are not aligned:

> Corporate message: "XYZ intends to be a leading player in the infrastructure-management space."
> Product message: "XYZ intends to be a leading player in the storage-management space."

Who Is the Likely Audience for the Message? Should the Audience Categories Be Targeted in Any Particular Order?

There are four main categories of audience, forming what could be called a *market infrastructure* for messaging:

- Company employees and investors
- Strategic customers, partners, and thought leaders
- External arbitrators (press, technical analysts, financial analysts, and so on)
- Potential customers

One of the key purposes of messaging is to influence the audience in favor of your company or your products. In traditional consumer markets, mass-media campaigns, through advertising, are usually a common means of reaching and influencing the target audience. In the fast-paced technology markets, however, a target audience is influenced more by clear evidence through customer success stories in some form. This is usually true because a technology product requires a complex purchasing decision, and such a decision can be influenced only by evidence that the product delivers what it claims to deliver.

The key question, then, is whether the company should broadcast its messages containing the necessary evidence to all categories of audience simultaneously, or target audiences in a specific order for maximum benefit. Fortunately, in high technology, the maximum benefit is usually achieved if the company first focuses on gaining the confidence of strategic customers, key partners, and thought leaders. Winning the hearts of one or two customers, partners, and thought leaders early on can go a long way in establishing strong credibility for your company and your products. For one, external arbitrators typically look evidence from these key strategic stakeholders before they will talk or write about the company and its products—and it is these external arbitrators who finally influence the company's potential customers through press articles, technology discussions, or financial reports. Following this sequence of logic indicates that there is a clear path of reference and influence that is built into the market infrastructure.

Who Should I Turn to for Help in Executing the Market-Communications Strategy?

Executing the strategy requires assistance from an experienced PR or market communications firm. These firms can help you refine your messages and help you reach your key target audience. It is pertinent to note that you need to take ownership of defining the contents of the message before these firms are brought in. Often these firms can only help in refining the contents and in delivering the message and not necessarily in creating them from scratch. In essence, these firms should be used more as a "sounding board" and as a "channel" to get the message out! It is also important to note these firms, through their own relationships/partnerships, help in deciding the most appropriate media to be used, ensuring cost-effectiveness in message delivery.

Sales

Now that you have articulated your value proposition, identified your target segment, and developed your marketing pitch, it is time to move on to the final challenge: finding the first four or five customers who will provide the foundation for your company's growth and eventual success. Finding customers who will part with money to buy your product or services is the ultimate validation of your efforts so far. Indeed, in the ultimate analysis, the only thing that matters is whether there are customers who put value on what you have to offer. Everything else that you do is irrelevant if you cannot persuade customers to see value in your offerings. For this reason, it is critical that you clearly understand the sales process and track it very closely.

Who Is Responsible for Sales?

Some entrepreneurs have the notion that they have done the difficult part—conceiving the product idea, raising money, building the product and the team—and that all they need is a crack salesperson whose job it is to deliver the revenue. This scenario may work out for a lucky few, but the reality in most cases is that the entrepreneur (with help from key members of the founding team, of course) owns the bulk of the selling process to the first few customers. You might hire a competent sales professional, but the nature of technology sales is such that the first few sales are made on the strength of the passion, conviction, and vision that only the founding team is likely to possess in the initial stages.

note As a founder/CEO, it is also very critical that you participate in all early sales discussions and negotiations. You are likely to be the person in your company who is most passionate about and intimately aware of the company and its products, and thus will do a better job during the missionary times. Participating in sales early on also allows you to detect and fix major issues with product roadmap or positioning.

Recruiting the Sales Force

When starting out, do not look to hire a VP of sales who could manage a team of 20 sales professionals. Look for someone who has a track record of selling new technology for small companies in your target market. Sales professionals from big established companies sometimes find it hard to transition to selling for small companies, especially if they have not sold new, unproven products before. The first sales professional you hire may not be VP material, but that doesn't matter at this stage. What matters most is the salesperson's proven track record, or the person's potential for securing the first few customers for a young start-up.

The salesperson certainly needs to be a go-getter, ideally with a good network in your space. Being a team player is also critical for the first few sales, because the salesperson will have to work with product, engineering, and the entire implementation team to solve the customer's problem and manage a smooth implementation. References from the first few clients are very important, and these references will depend not only on the sale, but on the implementation. If the whole process isn't smooth—facilitated by the salesperson—the references may not come.

At the initial stage—until you have secured your first few customers—all you need is one sales team (consisting of one salesperson and a technical-sales specialist). The technical-sales specialist is variously known as *systems engineer*, *field engineer*, or in some industries, *application engineer*. Essentially, this person has a thorough understanding of your product and its differentiation, and can explain how it uniquely meets the requirements of the customer. Sometimes, in the early stages of a company, a member of the founding team functions as a field technical specialist, providing technical backup to the sales person.

How do you know when to expand the sales force? Salespeople will rarely complain that they have too many accounts to handle. You can usually tell, however, by looking at the pipeline that the sales team is pursuing. If there is steady progress being made on the list of existing accounts being pursued by the sales team, but few (or no) new accounts are being pursued, it is a fairly good indication that the sales team is confident it will take its existing accounts to a logical conclusion (make the sale), but does not want to distract itself with new accounts. This is a good signal that it's time to expand your sales team.

note Sometimes, the constraints of geography dictate that you have more than one sales team from the get-go. It is important to ensure that the sales teams, no matter where they are, get adequate technical and marketing support from headquarters.

How to Manage the Sales Process

After you have sales teams on the ground, managing them for maximum impact becomes crucial to your success. Sales professionals are highly paid; their travel and telecommunications expenses are very high; and they can keep a large number of other resources in the company occupied supporting their process. In other words, it is very expensive to have a sales force. It is, therefore, critical that you manage this resource tightly to ensure proper return on investment. In particular, you'll want to consider the following:

- Sales cycle
- Forecast and funnel management
- Evaluation and trial
- Negotiating the first few deals
- Internal sales meetings

Sales Cycle

The underlying assumption is that every account goes through a cycle that is made up of distinct phases. Briefly, these phases are as follows:

- Suspect
- Prospect
- Qualified prospect
- Evaluation and trial
- Negotiation

Although different organizations and sales practitioners use different words and phrases for these phases and may have a different way of describing the sales cycle, one assumption common to all such frameworks is that the sales process can be broken down into different phases. This understanding of the sales cycle is crucial to building the management tools that ensure proper return on investment in the sales force.

To illustrate, suppose you have identified the financial-service industry as one of your target market segments, and you have decided to place a sales team in San Francisco. All the banks and brokerages in the area form the *potential universe* of your customers. When you have identified a contact person in each of the financial institutions, you have a *suspect list*. Upon initial contact, some of the people on this list respond to your voicemail/e-mail messages and agree to a face-to-face meeting; now you have a list of *prospects*. After an exchange of information, you decide that some of these prospects indeed meet most or all of the criteria you had identified earlier: They have an agreed-upon need for solving the problem that your product purports to solve; they have a budget; and they have a timeframe in mind for fulfilling the need. Now you have list of *qualified prospects*.

Upgrading a Prospect to a Qualified Prospect

Some questions to ask before upgrading a prospect to a qualified prospect are

- Does the prospect have the need/pain identified?
- Does the prospect care to solve this need right now, or are other priorities making this need less important?
- Does the prospect have the financial means to purchase your solution?
- Will this be a quick win or a long sales cycle? (A long sales cycle is okay, but it won't help you find your first few quick wins to build up a customer list.)

A subset of the list of qualified prospects should move on to the next stage, which may involve greater involvement of the potential customer in understanding your product and how it may fit in the customer's environment. This informed understanding might lead to an *evaluation and trial*. Successful completion of evaluation and trial should lead to discussions about pricing, support, your viability as a company, and your roadmap for future enhancements as well as management-level meetings. This stage should lead to the next stage, *actual negotiations* about terms and conditions, pricing, support, and so on. At the end of it all, you have a signed purchase order and a customer committed to paying you for your product. Time to uncork the champagne!

tip It is important to recognize at least two key groups of people in the customer organization: decision maker and influencer. A *decision maker* is someone who makes decisions, delegates responsibility to manage projects, and owns the budget; an *influencer* is someone who will not be involved in the final decision-making process, but has the ears of the decision maker. Starting your sales cycle at the level of the decision maker, while addressing the informational needs of the influencer, is the key to reducing the duration of the sales cycle. Most commonly, this means that you must have a high-level executive sponsor.

Forecast and Funnel Management

Understanding the dynamic of how many suspects lead to one prospect, how many prospects lead to one qualified prospect, and so on is important in making decisions about the size and effectiveness of the sales force. This dynamic is called a *sales funnel*; it has a wide top with a large number of suspects, and narrows steadily down to yield a few purchase orders at the end of the funnel.

Working with your sales and marketing team, you should define each stage of the sales cycle in the context of your company and demand that the sales team present the sales funnel in these terms to you every week. Doing so yields a number of benefits:

- It gives a common vocabulary across sales, marketing, and other departments to assess the progress that the company is making in different accounts.
- It is a tool for assessing the resources needed to move the company to the next stage of the sales cycle. For example, evaluation and trial could be very resource intensive in terms of technical support. If a large number of accounts are moving to that stage, the company must plan for availability of adequate technical resources.
- It gives you an objective way of assessing progress being made by each member of the sales team by account. If one salesperson has several accounts that do not move from one stage to another for weeks, while other salespeople keep making progress, you have an early indicator of a potential mismatch. If, however, this pattern is being repeated across a number of

salespeople, it could indicate the presence of some other problem. (In that case, you would be well advised to revisit earlier parts of this chapter for diagnosis.) Either way, the funnel-management system functions an early warning system.

Some important elements to remember are

- The ratio of prospects/cold calls to completed sales is very low (though the ratio does improve if the prospects are well qualified). That means a salesperson must call on many prospects to build a pipeline, assuming that only a low percentage of these prospects will close. (The ratio varies depending on the product, industry, and cost, but it could be as low as one sale for every 30–50 calls.)
- The first few sales will take longer, so allow more time for the sales cycle.
- These sales will require a lot of meetings. Make sure that these meetings occur in person whenever a decision maker is involved.

Evaluation and Trial

It is important to manage the evaluation-and-trial stage of the sales cycle well, because committing scarce technical resources is expensive, which means you need to commit them only to those accounts for which the probability of success is very high.

It is also important to manage the expectations of the potential customer and limit the scope of evaluation. Get a commitment to do specific things in a fixed timeframe, and agree upon specific evaluation criteria with a clear indication of what constitutes a successful evaluation. Be aware of "scope creep." Make sure both parties understand what is to be evaluated, in what timeframe, and who will put what kind of resources into this evaluation. Also, it should be clarified in the beginning what specific action the customer will take if the evaluation is successful.

Negotiating the First Few Deals

Assuming successful completion of evaluation, the time has come to negotiate the deal. Be prepared to give generous—even outrageous—discounts, but secure in writing the things the customer will do for you in return. For example, the customer might agree to provide a quote for your press releases, advertisements, and Web site, as well as be a customer reference and speak on your behalf at industry conferences. At this stage of the game, validation and endorsement by customers count far more than getting the list price for your products.

Before companies buy anything from a start-up, however, they want to know that it is a viable company, with good financial backing. Also, they want to know that they will be okay if your company doesn't make it. That means that even with your first sale, you will need references. At this point, these references will most likely come from your investors or members of your board of directors. (Of course, the best reference is profitability!)

Internal Sales Meetings

During the early stages of your company (and, arguably, forever), your entire focus should be to secure customers and to keep them happy. Set up meetings at least once a week where sales, marketing, and engineering get together to discuss the sales funnel, customer evaluations, and customer-satisfaction issues. The focus of the meeting is to discuss customer-specific issues, not top-level issues. Stick with the nitty-gritty details of specific customer problems. The benefit is a common understanding of the issues facing the company.

Compensation and Sales Incentives

In general, compensation consists of three components:

- Base salary
- Incentive payments (also called commission payments)
- Stock options

Your goal is to structure compensation in such a way that the interests of the sales person and that of the company are aligned. For example, if you want the salesperson to sell $1,000,000 of your products in his or her first year, you could structure the compensation in one of two ways:

- Base salary of $150K and commission payment of $50K on achievement of quota
- Base salary of $75K and commission payment of $100K on achievement of quota

Compared to the first scenario, which does not motivate the salesperson to work hard, the second scenario aligns the interests of the salesperson and the company a lot better. Typically, a good compensation plan rewards the salesperson at a higher rate for higher levels of accomplishment. For example, in the salesperson in the second scenario were to achieve $1.2 million in sales, the commission payment should not increase linearly to $120K, but to some higher number.

index

TiE

B

C

D

F

G

H

I

J-K

L

M

N

O

P

Q-R

S

T

U

V

W-Y